THE COMPLETE
GUIDE TO CAKE DESIGN
AND DECORATING

THE COMPLETE
GUIDE TO CAKE DESIGN
AND DECORATING

Edited by
Suzy Powling

MALLARD
PRESS

FACTS AND FIGURES

Oven temperatures

The cooking times in the recipes in this book may vary slightly depending on the individual oven. Pans should be placed in the center of an oven unless stated otherwise. Preheat the oven to the specified temperature in all cases. The table below gives recommended equivalents.

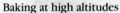

	°F		°F
Very cool	225	Moderately hot	375
	250		400
Cool	275	Hot	425
	300		450
Moderate	325	Very hot	475
	350		

Baking at high altitudes

All the recipes in this book were tested at or around sea level. If you live at an altitude over 2,000 feet, you will need to make certain basic changes when you prepare these cakes. In general, you will need less leavening (provided by baking powder, baking soda and self-rising flour) because of the reduced air pressure at higher elevations. To ensure that the carbon dioxide released by the leavening agent does not escape, it helps to substitute all-purpose flour for cake flour: all-purpose flour will provide a stronger structure for the cake. If self-rising flour is called for, use that which is made especially for high altitudes.

If beaten egg whites are used to give volume to a cake, take them straight from the refrigerator and try not to overbeat them.

It will also help to add a little more liquid to a batter, and to increase the oven temperature by 25°.

Shorten the rising time for yeast doughs.

When making sugar syrups, note that the candy thermometer temperatures given on page 49 are for sea level. To adjust for higher altitudes, lower the temperature 1° for each 500 feet of altitude.

CONTENTS

INTRODUCTION

For many of the important occasions in life, a beautifully decorated cake forms the centerpiece of the event, whether it be a wedding, christening or birthday party or a celebration like Christmas. The creation of a suitably elegant cake can be achieved successfully at home with impressively professional results.

The Complete Guide to Cake Design and Decorating aims to cover the range of techniques – from the simple to the specialized – involved in producing wonderful cakes for every possible occasion, and to point the way toward creative cake design after mastering these techniques. As well as giving basic recipes for all the batters for cakes suitable for decorating, the first section describes how to make the frostings and fillings most commonly used, how to apply them with skill and how to master the decorative techniques appropriate to each. Of these, piped designs are most important, and the varied effects that can be achieved are clearly illustrated, together with run-outs. Decorations made from marzipan and molding paste, whether cut out or molded, are another feature which can be used to ornament cakes for all sorts of occasions, from a grand wedding to

a children's party. There are instructions on sugaring and crystallizing fruits and flowers, and a look at the decorative possibilities of chocolate.

The recipes for individual cakes in Part 2 demonstrate the ways in which basic skills can be used to different effect, and in many instances variations are suggested to show how ideas can be developed. The recipes are given in a sequence that reflects a progression from relatively straightforward traditional cakes to complex celebration cakes and novelty designs. Chapter 4 shows the alternative forms of stunning decorations used in classic European cakes. The final chapters on cheese-cakes and small cakes and pastries give some dazzling ideas for desserts and miniature designs.

Time and patience are both important to the cake decorator, as well as a steady hand – though this can be acquired with practice. For the beginner, practice is the most important factor. It is wise to try out some of the simpler designs first, gradually working up to those which are more complicated as your skills increase. As your skills improve, so your confidence will grow, along with the pleasure you give and receive.

INTRODUCTION
PART 1

This first section lays the foundations of the course, beginning with a survey of the equipment needed for cake-making (decorating equipment is discussed on page 54) and the ingredients you will need to have in your pantry. The ability to make a good basic cake is of key importance in cake decorating. The recipes include batters for the different types of cake suitable for decorating; in part 2 individual recipes also include other ideas to extend your repertoire.

For European cakes and cheesecakes, a special pastry is often used. These pastries are described here, as well as the different kinds of meringue, a very useful item in the decorator's repertoire. Many cakes need a layer of marzipan to separate the cake from the icing. The base icing is carefully applied on top of the marzipan to give a background for the piped designs and other decorative features. With any frosting, and especially with the more complicated designs, it is very important to read through the whole recipe first. Most decorated cakes take several days to complete and many of the decorations need to be made in advance to give them time to dry.

An important factor in cake decorating is planning a design that fits the occasion. Some complex designs have a template to work from, most of these are on pages 52 and 62, or with the individual recipe. Cakes made from unusual shapes are discussed on page 53.

This book would not be complete without a section on chocolate, invaluable in decorating and delicious in the batter. Sugared fruits and flowers, included here, can add a special touch. Part 1 ends with suggestions of how simple bought decorations can create effective designs.

BASICS

This section describes the basic ingredients and equipment you will need, and shows how to prepare and line different shapes of pan for baking.

If you enjoy cooking, your kitchen will already be equipped with certain basic items, but for cake-making an additional range of specialized equipment is necessary. On pages 12–13 is a list of essential items. As you become more adventurous and as your range extends you will want to acquire more aids to creative cake-making. These are available from a number of specialist kitchenware stores and suppliers. Invest in good equipment which, if cared for, will last for years. Over time a good cook gets to know his or her equipment and gets increasingly better results with it.

Preparing pans correctly for baking is very important if the cake is to be unmolded cleanly without sticking to the sides. Instructions are given on page 14.

Like everything else you cook, a cake should be made from the best ingredients for a good result, especially if it is a formal cake for a special occasion. Absolute freshness is vital for eggs and cream; butter too must be fresh but can be kept in the freezer. Listed opposite are the basic ingredients which you will require. They do not all have an indefinite shelf life, but if you make cakes frequently there is little risk of the ingredients deteriorating in quality because they have been stored too long. Be ruthless with flavorings that have lost their potency. Throw them away and buy fresh. Spices, like dried herbs, lose strength very quickly if exposed to light. Add some simple decorative extras such as candied cherries and angelica, silver candy balls and crystallized fruits to your pantry and you will always have on hand the makings of a splendid cake.

INGREDIENTS

Almond extract is an extract of bitter almonds, and is so powerful that only 2–3 drops are needed to flavor a cake. It is an essential ingredient of marzipan. Use a pure extract without synthetic additives.

Butter is used in cakes and frostings. Unsalted butter is to be preferred for cake batters, though this is not essential. It is certainly the best choice for buttercream and enriched butter frostings. Store, covered or wrapped, in the refrigerator, away from strong-smelling foods, but allow to soften at room temperature for 1–2 hours before use.

Chocolate has many useful qualities, not only in cake batters (and desserts) where it gives added texture, but in fillings and frostings. The varieties of chocolate include unsweetened or baking chocolate, which is the pure form of the chocolate liquor extracted from cacao beans; semisweet or bittersweet chocolate, for which sugar and extra cocoa butter are added to the chocolate liquor; sweet or German chocolate, which is the sweetest; and milk chocolate. Use the chocolate specified in a recipe: do not substitute one for another.

Adding cocoa powder is the most economical way to achieve a good chocolate flavor in cakes. It must be blended evenly into the batter, either by sifting it with the other dry ingredients or by blending it with a little boiling water to make a paste which can be combined with the mixture.

Cocoa powder will keep for up to 1 year in a cool dry place. Chocolate should be stored in a cool dry place.

If you keep chocolate in the refrigerator in hot weather, it will lose some of its gloss. Wrap it well as it easily absorbs odors.

The so-called bloom that sometimes appears on chocolate happens when cocoa butter and sugar crystals rise to the surface after exposure to variations in temperature. It has no effect on flavor and disappears on melting.

Cream must be kept cool, clean and covered. For covering and filling cakes and for piped decorations heavy or whipping cream may be used. Everything must be really cold before whipping – the bowl, the beater and the cream itself. Whip quickly until a matt surface appears then slowly to avoid overwhipping and making it buttery (a tablespoon of cold milk added to the bowl helps to prevent this). Once fresh cream has been added to a cake it must be used the same day.

Eggs must be stored cool, in a refrigerator, away from strong-smelling foods and with the rounded ends uppermost. Before use, allow eggs to reach room temperature. When beating egg whites, make sure the bowl and beater are scrupulously clean and grease-free for the best results. Separate the yolks from the whites very carefully – a suspicion of egg yolk and the whites will not bulk out. Powdered albumen (egg white) can be used in frosting and solves the difficulty of using up leftover egg yolks. To make up, mix 1 teaspoon powdered albumen with 4 tablespoons of cold water per 4 cups confectioners' sugar, or follow the packet instructions. Strain before use.

Flour of many kinds is available, but for making cakes you will need all-purpose flour, the lighter, finer cake flour, and self-rising flour, (both all-purpose and cake), to which leavening and salt have been added.

Whole wheat flours are heavier, but, if you wish, a small quantity of white flour can be replaced by whole wheat flour for a healthier family cake. Cornstarch is used to lighten some batters, and to dust the rolling pin and your hands when working with fondant molding paste. Potato flour, the European equivalent of cornstarch, is used in some cheesecakes.

Flour does not have an indefinite shelf life. Once the package is opened, store the remainder in an airtight tin in a cool dry place. Use within 2 months of purchase.

Fruit and peel for fruit cakes includes dark and golden raisins and currants, dried peel (from the citron, a relative of the orange) and candied cherries. Dried fruit bought loose will need washing (see page 12), but packaged fruit from a reputable supplier should already be well cleaned. It is still worth checking to ensure that no stalks have slipped through. Peel can be bought ready-chopped, but often it needs to be cut more finely. Before use, candied cherries should be rinsed to remove the syrup and halved or chopped according to the recipe. Use all dried fruits within 3 months of purchase.

Glycerin is a harmless, sweet, colorless viscous liquid which may be added to royal icing to prevent it from setting too hard. It is available from specialist cake decorating suppliers.

Leavening agents, to make cakes lighter, work by expanding the air bubbles in the flour as it is heated. Baking powder is most commonly used, a mixture of cream of tartar and baking soda, but baking soda may be used alone in certain recipes. Always follow precisely the instructions about the quantity

of a leavening agent to be used – too much can result in a cake that rises well at first and then collapses, giving a heavy texture.

Liquid glucose is a sticky, colorless substance to make fondant molding paste (page 44). It is available from specialist cake decorating suppliers. Light corn syrup, a glucose derived from cornstarch, may be substituted.

Molasses is a byproduct of sugar production, the residual boiled liquid after sugar is extracted from sugar cane or beets. Light molasses comes from the first boiling; dark molasses from the second boiling; and blackstrap molasses, the thickest and darkest, from the third boiling. The flavor is stronger than sugar, and using molasses in a recipe will deepen the color, for example in a Rich Fruit Cake (pages 24–5).

Spices are indispensable in the kitchen. The most commonly used are cinnamon, in the form of sticks or powder; ginger, either ground or preserved (Jamaican ginger is the best) and nutmeg (ground, or bought whole and ground in a special grater whenever required). Apple pie spice is a useful item, but must be used soon after purchase – as with all spices bought in ground form, the flavor quickly fades.

Vanilla extract is used as a flavoring agent for cake batters, creams and frostings. Choose one made from pure vanilla, with no synthetic ingredients. Vanilla pods are the dried pods of the vanilla plant. To make vanilla sugar, cut a pod in half and store it in a jar of sugar. After 2–3 days the sugar will be deliciously scented (but leave the pod in the jar).

Washing Dried Fruit

Most packaged dried fruit is pre-washed. Dried fruit bought loose may require rinsing in cold water and thoroughly drying before use. Excess moisture can be removed with paper towels or clean dish towels and the fruit should then be spread out on baking sheets covered with paper towels or clean dish towels and left in a fairly warm (not hot) place to dry. This will take up to 24 hours and fruit should be moved around once or twice during this time. Never use wet fruit in cakes, as it will sink immediately.

EQUIPMENT

Basic equipment is listed below, while decorating equipment is discussed on pages 54–5.

a selection of mixing bowls (china or glass)
liquid measuring cup(s)
a set of measuring spoons
a set of dry measuring cups
nylon sieves
large metal spoon
wooden spoons
rubber spatulas
pastry brush
kitchen shears
large and small long metal spatula or a round-bladed knife
skewers
string
rolling pin
wax paper, non-stick parchment paper and aluminum foil

A selection of cake pans is necessary and these should be made of a good firm metal. If you can, try to collect a set of pans that graduate in size at 1 inch intervals – always measuring across the base of the pan. Pans that are round, square, hexagonal, horseshoe-shaped or heart-shaped or in other unusual shapes are all available in graduated sizes. If you need an unusual shape, write to one of the specialist suppliers. If they cannot help, bake the cake in a large pan and cut to the required shape using a template (see page 53 for details of shapes). Pans can sometimes be borrowed or rented.

Loose-bottomed or spring-form pans are useful for removing cakes such as butter cakes and whisked sponges or cheesecakes which are easily damaged. Cake pans can be non-stick or otherwise but do ensure that the corners of square pans really are square. If not it is difficult to get a true square edge to the cake unless you build it up with marzipan before adding the frosting.

If you don't have a cake pan of the size called for in a recipe, you can, in many cases, substitute a pan of another size, although you will need to monitor the cooking time carefully. In general, deep cakes that the recipe directs be baked in a loaf or tube pan can instead be baked in a shallow pan (layer, square or sheet) as long as the pans are of the same capacity. The reverse – substituting a deep pan for a shallow pan – is not successful.

Always keep your cake pans in a special cupboard when not in use to prevent them getting knocked and misshapen. It is also a good idea to keep a few wooden spoons aside just for cake-making and frosting. They are better than metal spoons but in general use can become tainted with strong-smelling food and have stains which could be transmitted to the frosting with horrific results! Always use nylon rather than metal sieves in cake-making, to avoid any danger of flour or confectioners' sugar becoming tainted when sifted. A rubber rather than a wooden spatula is best for scraping cake batter from the side of a mixing bowl.

A selection of cakepans and boards

Cake Boards

Round and square cake boards ranging from 7 to 16 inches are readily available from department stores. Other shapes available from specialist suppliers and some stores include the heart and the hexagon. Cake boards are usually finished in silver, but gold boards are also available. These cake boards are ideal for special occasions, but a wooden bread or meat board covered with ordinary aluminum foil is quite adequate for a child's party cake or a cake for an informal tea-party.

Electrical Items

While most cakes can be mixed successfully with nothing more sophisticated than a wooden spoon, and simply frosted with the aid of a spatula, there are occasions when electrical equipment is a boon. A food mixer or processor is very useful for making certain pastries, for example, and is particularly useful for the Quick Mix Cake on page 16. At the very least, a well equipped kitchen should include a hand-held electric beater. In the absence of a food processor, a blender will make short work of crushing praline or nuts.

We have not given microwave instructions in this course as we feel that conventional cooking gives the best results for the cake recipes here. However, a microwave can be very useful for melting butter or chocolate, softening marzipan, plumping dried fruit and even making glazes. Consult your manufacturer's handbook for more information.

LINING CAKE PANS

If using special non-stick pans, follow the manufacturer's instructions. With all other pans it is necessary either to grease and flour, or grease and line with wax paper and grease again. Use oil, shortening or melted margarine for greasing.

If you wish to use non-stick parchment paper, there is no need to grease the paper. The cake pan, whether plain or with a non-stick coating, must be scrupulously cleaned before it is lined.

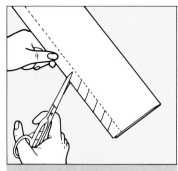

Round pan, base
Making slanting cuts along the unfolded bottom edge of the wax paper strip.

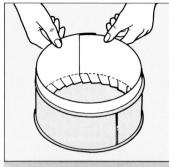

Round pan, side
Placing the strip into the pan to fit the sides. Cut edges spread over bottom.

Base-Lining a Round or Square Pan

This method prevents the bottom of the cake from falling out or sticking and is used for butter and sponge cakes and lightly fruited cakes, but not for the rich cakes.

1. Cut a single piece of wax paper to fit the bottom of the cake pan.

2. First grease the inside of the pan completely, then position the paper in the bottom and grease.

To Double-Line a Deep Round Pan

Rectangular pan, base
Cutting from the corners of the wax paper to the corners of the pan.

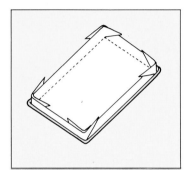

Rectangular pan, sides
Fitting the paper into the greased pan so corners overlap to make angles.

For rich mixtures which require long cooking you should use a double thickness of wax paper and line both the sides and bottom of the pan. With the richer fruit cakes tie two or three thicknesses of brown paper or newspaper around the outside of the pan as an added protection against overcooking the outside of the cake.

For less rich mixtures follow the instructions below, using only single thickness wax paper.

1. Cut one or two strips of doubled wax paper long enough to reach around the outside of the pan with enough to overlap, and wide enough to come 1 inch above the rim of the pan. Fold the bottom edge up about ¾ inch and crease it firmly. Open out and make slanting cuts into the folded strip at ¾ inch intervals.

2. Place the pan on a double thickness of wax paper and draw around the base, then cut it out a little inside the line.

3. Grease the inside of the pan, place one paper circle in the bottom and grease just around the edge of the paper.

4. Place the long strips in the pan, pressing them against the sides with the cut edges spread over the bottom. Grease all over the side paper.

5. Finally position the second circle in the bottom and grease again.

To Double-Line a Deep Square or Rectangular Pan

Follow the instructions for the deep round pan but make folds into the corners of the long strips.

To Line a Shallow Rectangular Pan

It is always wise to line and grease pans for easy removal of jelly rolls and similar cakes.

1. Cut a piece of wax paper about 3 inches larger than the pan (and larger still if the sides of the pan are deeper than 1 inch).

2. Place the pan on the paper and make a cut from the corners of the paper to the corners of the pan.

3. Grease inside the pan, put in the paper so that it fits neatly, overlapping the paper at the corners to give sharp angles, and grease again.

To Line a Loaf Pan

Use the same method as for lining a shallow rectangular pan but cut the paper at least 6 inches larger than the top of the pan. Grease the pan, position the paper, fitting the corners neatly, and grease again.

CAKE BATTERS & MERINGUES

These classic recipes cover the basic sponge and fruit cakes you will need to make the recipes in Part 2. Flavor variations are also included.

None of these cakes are made by the simple "rubbing-in" method used for coarser textured cakes. Achieving a really light cake is the hallmark of an experienced cake maker and the lightest of all is the butter cake, the texture of which is achieved by thoroughly creaming butter with sugar in the first stage, as is also done for Rich Fruit Cake. This preliminary creaming process, after which the butter and sugar mixture is very pale and fluffy, is extremely important. If it is incomplete, the mixture will not accept the rest of the ingredients as it should. The Whisked Sponge Cake does not require the same amount of effort, but it is still important to incorporate as much air as possible into the eggs-and-sugar mixture at the initial stage. Thorough blending is required for the Quick Mix Cake, but by combining the ingredients simultaneously the preparation is reduced, leaving you time for decorations.

The keeping qualities of the basic plain cakes vary. The whisked sponge is best eaten on the day it is cooked, or frozen for up to 2 months; the Genoese sponge should be eaten within 3 days or frozen for up to 1 month; the quick mix cake keeps well for 1 week; and the pound and butter cakes will keep for 7–10 days. These last three can also be frozen, the quick mix and butter cakes for 1–2 months, the pound cake for 6 months. If you do not intend freezing them, store in an airtight container in a cool, dry atmosphere.

Quick Mix Cake

This is a very quick and easy cake to prepare and bake to use for many occasions. However, as it is made without proper creaming, it does not keep as well as a normal butter cake, so it should be baked, frosted and used within a week for the best results. Consequently it is not advisable to use this mixture for an elaborately frosted and decorated cake using royal icing for a special occasion. In this instance, for non-fruit cake eaters, a pound cake should be used, as it will stay fresh for much longer.

The Quick Mix Cake can be baked in a variety of shapes and sizes. If you want to bake in something a different shape from those in the chart, simply fill your chosen baking container with water and see which size of pan on the chart holds the same amount of liquid – this will tell you the amount of batter you will require. The baking may have to be watched a little carefully; if the container is shallower allow a little less time and if it is deeper allow a little longer before testing. Remember always to use a good quality soft margarine for this cake and don't forget to add baking powder.

Preparation time: about 5 minutes
Cooking time: see chart
Oven: 325°F

1. Put the margarine, sugar, eggs, sifted flour and baking powder and vanilla extract into a bowl.

2. Mix together with a wooden spoon or hand-held electric beater, then beat hard for 1–2 minutes until smooth and glossy.

3. Turn into a greased and floured (or single-lined and greased) pan and level the top. Bake in a preheated oven for the time suggested in the chart or until well risen, just firm to the touch and the sides of the cake are just beginning to shrink from the sides of the pan.

Step 1
Put all the ingredients together into a bowl.

Step 2
Mix together well, then beat hard until smooth and glossy.

4. Cool for about 30 seconds in the pan, then loosen the sides of the cake from the pan and unmold onto a wire rack. Invert the cake onto another wire rack, unless baked in a ring mold or other mold. This prevents ugly marks from the wire rack which can show through a thin frosting. Leave to cool.

5. The cake is now ready to fill and/or frost.

Step 4
Unmold cake onto a wire rack. Invert onto another rack so top does not mark.

QUICK MIX CAKE INGREDIENTS						
CAKE SIZES	2 7-inch layer cake pans	18 cup cake cases	8-inch layer cake pan, 8-inch ring mold, deep 7-inch square pan	1-quart pudding basin or steaming mold	about 26 cup cake cases	2 8-inch layer cake pans
soft margarine, chilled	½ cup	½ cup	½ cup	½ cup	¾ cup	¾ cup
sugar	½ cup	½ cup	½ cup	½ cup	¾ cup	¾ cup
eggs (extra large)	2	2	2	2	3	3
self-rising cake flour	1 cup	1 cup	1 cup	1 cup	1½ cups	1½ cups
baking powder	1 teaspoon	1 teaspoon	1 teaspoon	1 teaspoon	1½ teaspoons	1½ teaspoons
vanilla extract	4 drops	4 drops	4 drops	4 drops	6 drops	6 drops
approx. cooking time	25–30 minutes	15–20 minutes	35–40 minutes	about 50 minutes	15–20 minutes	30–35 minutes

*add ¼ cup cornstarch sifted with the flour

Fatless Sponge Cake

Variations

Chocolate Omit the vanilla extract and add 1 tablespoon sifted cocoa powder for the 2-egg mixture; 1½ tablespoons for the 3-egg mixture; 2 tablespoons for the 4-egg mixture; and 2½ tablespoons for the 5-egg mixture.

Coffee Omit the vanilla extract and add 2 teaspoons instant coffee powder (not granules) or 1 tablespoon coffee essence for the 2-egg mixture; 1 tablespoon coffee powder or 1½ tablespoons coffee essence for the 3-egg mixture; 4 teaspoons coffee powder or 2 tablespoons coffee essence for the 4-egg mixture; and 5 teaspoons coffee powder or 2½ tablespoons coffee essence for the 5-egg mixture.

Orange or Lemon Omit the vanilla extract and add 2 teaspoons finely grated orange or lemon zest for the 2-egg mixture; 1 tablespoon for the 3-egg mixture; 4 teaspoons for

the 4-egg mixture; and 5 teaspoons for the 5-egg mixture.

Spiced Add 1 teaspoon apple pie spice, ground cinnamon or ground ginger for the 2-egg mixture; 1½ teaspoons for the 3-egg mixture; 2 teaspoons for the 4-egg mixture; and 2½ teaspoons for the 5-egg mixture.

Nut Add ⅓ cup finely chopped or grated walnuts, hazelnuts, pecans, unsalted peanuts or toasted almonds to the 2-egg mixture; ½ cup to the 3-egg mixture; ⅔ cup to the 4-egg mixture; and ¾ cup to the 5-egg mixture.

Fudgy Replace from half to all the granulated sugar with sifted light brown sugar for all the sizes of cake.

This very light sponge cake makes the ideal base for a rich topping such as cheesecake or whipped cream and fruit. It can be made 1–2 days in advance if kept in an airtight tin, or may be frozen for 2–3 months.

1 tablespoon flour mixed with 1 tablespoon sugar, for dusting
⅔ cup sugar
5 eggs, separated
1 tablespoon grated lemon zest
1 cup cake flour, well sifted

Preparation time: 20 minutes
Cooking time: 30 minutes
Oven: 350°F

1. Grease a deep 9½- or 10½-inch round cake pan and line the bottom with non-stick parchment paper. Grease again and dust with the flour and sugar mixture. Shake off any excess.

2. Set aside 2 tablespoons of the sugar. Beat the egg yolks with

the remaining sugar until they are thick, pale and creamy. Mix in the lemon zest.

3. Beat the egg whites until they hold firm snowy peaks, then beat in the reserved sugar.

4. With a large metal spoon mix 2 tablespoons of the beaten egg white into the egg and sugar mixture. Fold in the remaining egg white in batches, alternating with dredgings of sifted flour. Do not beat the mixture, but let it retain as much air as possible.

5. Turn the batter into the prepared pan. Lightly smooth the surface. Rap the pan once on the worktop to disperse any air bubbles, and bake immediately in a preheated oven for 30 minutes.

6. When the cake is well risen and browned remove from the oven and leave to stand on a wire rack for 10 minutes. Unmold from the pan and leave to cool completely.

QUICK MIX CAKE INGREDIENTS						
deep 9-inch round cake pan	2 1½-pint oval ovenproof glass dishes	11- × 7- × 1½-inch baking pan, 8-inch round, square or petal-shaped cake pan	1-quart pudding basin or steaming mold	11½- × 8½- × 1½-inch baking pan	9-inch round, square or petal-shaped cake pan	12- × 10- × 2-inch baking pan
¾ cup	¾ cup	¾ cup	¾ cup	1 cup	1 cup	1¼ cups
¾ cup	¾ cup	¾ cup	¾ cup	1 cup	1 cup	1¼ cups
3	3	3	3	4	4	5
1½ cups	1½ cups	1½ cups	1½ cups	2 cups	2 cups	2½ cups
1½ teaspoons	1½ teaspoons	1½ teaspoons	1½ teaspoons	2 teaspoons	2 teaspoons	2½ teaspoons
6 drops	6 drops	6 drops	6 drops	8 drops	8 drops	10 drops
about 45 minutes	40–45 minutes	35–40 minutes	about 1 hour	about 40 minutes	about 1 hour	50–60 minutes

The cakes in this book which are based on the Quick Mix batter are: Easter Egg Cake, page 120; Easter Basket, page 122; Numeral Birthday Cakes (alternative, Pound), pages 138–9; Pirate's Treasure Chest, page 140; Basket of Chocolates (alternative, Pound) page 140; Hickory Dickory Dock Cake, page 144; Executive Case, page 145; Humpty Dumpty, page 148; Rocket Cake, page 156; Peppermint Racer, page 157; Willie Wasp, page 158; Japonaise Cake, page 165 and Sponge Cake Dice, page 210.

Butter Cake

This mixture produces one of the lightest textured cakes, perfect simply filled with good preserves and dusted with confectioners' sugar. The quantities in this light mixture are fairly critical, so cannot be given for different sized pans as in the other recipes. However, to make a larger cake, use 1 cup of sugar and butter or margarine, 1⅔ cups flour, 4 eggs and just over 1 tablespoon of water. Bake in a deep 8-inch round cake pan, allowing about 1 hour to cook (a square pan of the same size will take a little less time). The same quantity can be baked in a deep 9-inch round pan and will need 45–50 minutes' cooking time.

¾ cup sugar
1½ sticks butter or soft
   margarine
3 eggs (extra large)
1½ cups self-rising cake flour
1 tablespoon cold water
a few drops of vanilla extract

Preparation time: about 30 minutes
Cooking time: 20–25 minutes
Oven: 375°F

1. Grease two 8-inch round layer cake pans and either dust with flour or base-line with wax paper and grease again. Alternatively grease and flour or base-line a rectangular pan measuring 11 × 7 × 1½ inches.

2. Cream the sugar and butter or margarine together until light, fluffy and very pale in color.

3. Beat in the eggs, one at a time, following each with a spoonful of the flour.

4. Sift the remaining flour and fold it into the mixture alternately with the water. Finally add the vanilla extract.

5. Divide the batter between the cake pans, or fill the larger pan, and level the tops. Bake in a preheated oven for 20–25 minutes or until well risen and firm to the touch. The larger cake may take a few minutes longer. Unmold onto a wire rack and leave to cool.

Variations

Chocolate Replace ¼ cup of the flour with sifted cocoa powder and add ½ teaspoon baking powder with the flour.

Coffee Replace the water with coffee essence or dissolve 2 teaspoons instant coffee powder (or granules) in 1 tablespoon boiling water, cool and use in place of the water.

Lemon or Orange Omit the vanilla extract and add the very finely grated zest of 1 lemon or 1 orange. The water may be replaced with fruit juice.

Fudge Replace the granulated sugar with sifted light brown sugar.

Cakes in this book which are based on the Butter Cake batter are: the Mother's Day cakes, pages 104–5; Lion Cake, pages 150–1 and Layered Orange-Coffee Cake, page 180.

From the top: Pound cake, layered butter cake.

POUND CAKE INGREDIENTS						
CAKE SIZES	6-inch round or square cake pan	7-inch round cake pan	deep 7-inch round cake pan, 9- × 5- × 3-inch loaf pan	7-inch square cake pan	8-inch round or petal-shaped cake pan	deep 8-inch round or petal-shaped cake pan
butter	1 stick	1 stick	1½ sticks	1½ sticks	1½ sticks	2 sticks
sugar	½ cup	½ cup	¾ cup	¾ cup	¾ cup	1 cup
self-rising cake flour	1 cup	1 cup	1½ cups	1½ cups	1½ cups	2 cups
cake flour	½ cup	½ cup	¾ cup	¾ cup	¾ cup	1 cup
eggs	2	2	3	3	3	4
grated lemon zest	½–1 lemon	½–1 lemon	1 lemon	1 lemon	1 lemon	1½ lemons
approx. cooking time	1 hour	50 minutes	1¼ hours	1 hour and 5–10 minutes	1 hour	1 hour and 15–20 minutes

Pound Cake

Pound cake can be covered with marzipan and royal icing or fondant molding paste or other frosting. It may also be brushed with apricot glaze and simply covered in fondant molding paste. The traditional flavoring of lemon zest and juice may be replaced with orange for an Orange Pound or altered as in the variations below.

Preparation time: about 15–20 minutes.
Cooking time: see chart
Oven: 325°F

1. Grease and single-line the chosen pan (page 14).

2. Cream the butter and sugar together until light, fluffy and very pale.

3. Sift the flours together. Beat in the eggs, one at a time, following each with a spoonful of the flours.

4. Fold the rest of the flours into the creamed mixture followed by the grated lemon zest and juice.

5. Turn into the prepared pan and level the top.

6. Bake in a preheated oven for the time suggested or until well risen, firm to the touch and golden brown.

7. Cool in the pan for 5–10 minutes, then unmold onto a wire rack and leave until cold. Do not peel off the lining paper but wrap as it is in foil or store in an airtight container until required. If you plan to frost the cake, leave it for at least 24 hours to allow it to settle. Pound cakes may be frozen for up to 6 months. Thaw still in the wrappings at room temperature.

Variations

Ginger Omit the lemon zest and add 1 teaspoon ground ginger to the 2-egg mixture plus 2 pieces finely chopped stem ginger, if liked. Add 1½ teaspoons ground ginger to the 3-egg mixture; and 2 teaspoons to the 4-egg mixture with more chopped stem ginger as desired.

Coffee Walnut Omit the lemon zest and replace the lemon juice with coffee essence. Add ⅓ cup finely chopped walnuts to the 2-egg mixture; ½ cup walnuts to the 3-egg mixture; and ⅔ cup walnuts to the 4-egg mixture.

POUND CAKE INGREDIENTS

8-inch square cake pan	9-inch round cake pan	11- × 7- × 1½-inch baking pan cake pan	deep 9-inch round or petal-shaped	9-inch square cake pan	10-inch round or petal-shaped cake pan	12- × 10- × 2-inch baking pan
2 sticks	2 sticks	2 sticks	2½ sticks	2½ sticks	2½ sticks	2½ sticks
1 cup	1 cup	1 cup	1¼ cups	1¼ cups	1¼ cups	1¼ cups
2 cups	2 cups	2 cups	2½ cups	2½ cups	2½ cups	2½ cups
1 cup	1 cup	1 cup	1¼ cups	1¼ cups	1¼ cups	1¼ cups
4	4	4	5	5	5	5
1½ lemons	1½ lemons	1½ lemons	2 lemons	2 lemons	2 lemons	2 lemons
1 hour and 15–20 minutes	1 hour and 10 minutes	1–1¼ hours	1 hour and 30–40 minutes	1 hour and 25–30 minutes	1 hour and 20 minutes	1 hour and 15–20 minutes

Cakes in this book which are based on the Pound cake batter are: Santa's Stocking, page 112; Numeral Birthday Cakes (alternative, Quick Mix), pages 138–9; Basket of Chocolates (alternative, Quick Mix), page 142 and Flower Cake, page 152.

Whisked Sponge Cake

The butter in this recipe is added for extra keeping quality but it can be omitted if preferred. Without the added fat the cake should be eaten within 48 hours, with fat it should keep for 48 hours longer, but it does not keep indefinitely in prime condition.

This cake will freeze for up to 2 months if wrapped securely in foil or put into a rigid container; take care as it can easily be damaged without good protection.

Preparation time: 10–15 minutes
Cooking time: see chart
Oven: see chart

1. Line the chosen pan with non-stick parchment paper or greased wax paper.

2. Put the eggs and sugar into a heatproof bowl set over a saucepan of hot but not boiling water. Beat until the mixture becomes very thick and pale in color and the beater leaves a heavy trail when lifted. Remove the bowl from the saucepan and continue beating until the mixture is cool. Alternatively the beating may be done with an electric mixer, in which case it isn't necessary to put the bowl over hot water.

3. Sift the flour and baking powder together, then sift again over the beaten mixture. Using a metal spoon, fold in the flour quickly and evenly, followed by the cooled but still runny butter (if used).

4. Turn into the prepared pan(s) and shake gently or spread out lightly with a spatula until even, making sure there is plenty of batter in the corners. Bake for the time suggested in the chart or until the cake springs back when gently pressed with the finger-tips and has begun to shrink a little from the sides of the pan.

5. Unmold onto a wire rack and remove the lining paper. Leave to cool.

6. If making a jelly roll, invert the cake onto a sheet of wax paper sprinkled liberally with sugar or onto a sheet of non-stick parchment paper without the sugar, unless specified. Quickly peel off the lining paper and trim the edges of the cake with a sharp knife. Fold the top short edge of the cake in about 1 inch, then roll up the cake loosely with the paper inside. (This process must be done immediately the cake is taken out of the oven for it will not roll up without cracking if it is allowed to cool any more than necessary.) Fold back the top of the paper, so that it does not stick to the cake as it cools and spoil the top surface.

7. Leave to cool for a few minutes to allow the cake to set, then carefully unroll and remove the paper.

8. Fill with jam, buttercream or fruit and whipped cream, and roll up again.

Whisked sponge cake with (top left) jelly roll variation.

WHISKED SPONGE CAKE INGREDIENTS						
CAKE SIZES	2 7-inch layer cake pans	8-inch layer cake pan, 7-inch square cake pan	11- × 7-inch jelly roll pan	18 sponge drops	8-inch round cake pan	2 8-inch layer cake pans
eggs (extra large)	2	2	2	2	3	3
sugar	¼ cup	¼ cup	¼ cup	¼ cup	6 tbsp	6 tbsp
cake flour	½ cup	½ cup	½ cup	½ cup	¾ cup	¾ cup
baking powder	½ teaspoon	½ teaspoon	½ teaspoon	½ teaspoon	½ teaspoon	½ teaspoon
melted butter (optional)	1 tablespoon	1 tablespoon	1 tablespoon	1 tablespoon	2 tablespoons	2 tablespoons
approx. cooking time	20–25 minutes	25–30 minutes	10–12 minutes	5–10 minutes	35–40 minutes	20–25 minutes
oven	350°F	350°F	375°F	375°F	350°F	350°F

The cakes in this book based on a Whisked Sponge batter are: Sugar Plum Fairy Castle, page 141 and Ballet Shoes, page 146.

Step 2
Beat the eggs and sugar over hot water until mixture is thick and creamy.

Step 4
The cake will shrink from the sides of the pan and feel "springy" to touch.

Step 6, jelly roll
Rolling the cake up with the wax paper inside. A dish towel is placed underneath.

Step 8, jelly roll
Spreading a buttercream filling over the unrolled cake before re-rolling.

11- × 7-1½ inch slab cake	12- × 9-inch jelly roll pan	13- × 9-inch jelly roll pan
3	3	4
6 tablespoons	6 tablespoons	7 tablespoons
¾ cup	¾ cup	¾ cup
½ teaspoon	½ teaspoon	½ teaspoon
2 tablespoons	2 tablespoons	2 tablespoons
30–35 minutes	12–15 minutes	15–20 minutes
350°F	400°F	375°F

Variations

Lemon or Orange Add the grated zest of ½ lemon or orange with the flour.

Chocolate Replace 2 tablespoons flour with sifted cocoa powder.

Coffee Add 2 teaspoons instant coffee powder (not granules) to the mixture with the flour.

Spiced Add ½ teaspoon ground cinnamon, apple pie spice or ground ginger sifted with the flour.

Walnut Add ¼–⅓ cup very finely chopped or ground walnuts, folded into the cake mixture with the butter.

Genoese Sponge Cake

A Genoese (also known as a Torten) sponge cake is a type of whisked sponge to which butter is always added. This improves its keeping qualities, but the texture remains light and moist. This is a good cake for cutting into fingers or into different shapes for frosting and decorating (Genoese pastries).

3 tablespoons butter
2 eggs
5 tablespoons sugar
½ cup cake flour, sifted

Preparation time: 20 minutes
Cooking time: 35–40 minutes
Oven: 350°F

1. Brush a 7-inch square cake pan with melted butter. Line with greased wax paper and dust lightly with sifted flour.

2. Place the butter in a bowl set over a saucepan of hand-hot water and let it melt without becoming hot.

3. Place the eggs in a mixing bowl and beat for 1 minute. Add the sugar, set the bowl over a pan of hot, not boiling water and beat until the mixture is light and creamy and has doubled in volume. The beater should leave a trail when pulled across the surface. Remove the bowl from the heat and continue to beat until the mixture is cold. Alternatively, the beating may be done with an electric mixer, in which case it isn't necessary to put the bowl over hot water.

4. Pour in half the melted butter, leaving the sediment behind. Add half the flour and fold in carefully with a metal spoon. Fold in the remaining melted butter and flour in the same way.

5. Pour the mixture into the prepared pan and place in a preheated oven. Bake for 35–40 minutes or until the sponge is golden brown, firm to the touch and begins to shrink from the side of the pan.

6. Leave in the pan for 1 minute and then unmold the cake onto a folded dish towel to cool. (This light cake is easily marked by the lines on a wire rack.)

Step 4
Add the flour after the melted butter and fold into the egg and sugar mixture.

Step 6
To avoid marks, the cake should be unmolded onto a folded dish towel to cool.

Cakes in this book that are based on a Genoese sponge batter are: Pâques Cake, page 104; Praline Cake, page 178; Coffee-Chestnut Cake, page 182; Italiens, page 194 and Printaniers, page 194.

Healthy Sponge Cake

The carrots and apples in this version of a Quick-mix sponge give sweetness as well as a moist texture to the cake. With the addition of nuts and honey it is delicious, and not over-sweet. The mixture is very quick and easy to combine because vegetable oil is used rather than butter or margarine.

The cake will keep for up to 7 days in an airtight tin. While it can be substituted for any recipe based on the Quick-mix Sponge, it is versatile enough to take any of the classic icings or frostings.

Preparation time: about 10 minutes
Cooking time: see chart
Oven: 330°F

1. Put the apple, carrot, nuts, oil, sugar, honey and eggs in a bowl and mix well.

2. Sift together the flours, baking soda, salt and cinnamon. Stir into the carrot mixture until well blended.

3. Turn into a greased and base-lined pan and level the top. Bake in a preheated oven for the time given in the chart or until well risen, just firm to the touch and the sides of the cake are just beginning to shrink from the sides of the pan.

4. Cool for about 2 minutes in the pan then loosen the sides of the cake from the pan and unmold onto a wire rack. Leave to cool.

Healthy sponge cake

CAKE SIZES	2 7-inch layer cake pans	18 paper cup cake cases
apple, chopped	1 cup	1 cup
carrot, grated	1 cup	1 cup
nuts, chopped	½ cup	½ cup
vegetable oil	7 tablespoons	7 tablespoons
brown sugar	½ cup	½ cup
clear honey	1½ tablespoons	1½ tablespoons
eggs	1	1
egg yolk	1	1
cake flour	¾ cup	¾ cup
whole wheat flour	¾ cup	¾ cup
baking soda	¾ teaspoon	¾ teaspoon
salt	pinch	pinch
ground cinnamon	1½ teaspoons	1½ teaspoons
approx. cooking time	25–30 minutes	15–20 minutes

HEALTHY SPONGE CAKE INGREDIENTS

8-inch layer cake pan or ring mold, deep 7-inch square cake pan	1-quart pudding basin or steaming mold	2 8-inch layer cake pans	9-inch round cake pan	2 1½-pint oval ovenproof glass dishes	11- × 7- × 1½-inch baking pan, 8-inch round or square cake pan	12- × 10- × 2-inch baking pan
1 cup	1 cup	1½ cups	1½ cups	1½ cups	1½ cups	2 cups
1 cup	1 cup	1½ cups	1½ cups	1½ cups	1½ cups	2½ cups
½ cup	½ cup	¾ cup	¾ cup	¾ cup	¾ cup	1¼ cups
7 tablespoons	7 tablespoons	½ cup	½ cup	½ cup	½ cup	1 cup + 2 tablespoons
½ cup	½ cup	⅔ cup	⅔ cup	⅔ cup	⅔ cup	1⅓ cups
1½ tablespoons	1½ tablespoons	2 tablespoons	2 tablespoons	2 tablespoons	2 tablespoons	4 tablespoons
1	1	2	2	2	2	4
1	1	—	—	—	—	—
¾ cup	¾ cup	1 cup	1 cup	1 cup	1 cup	2 cups
¾ cup	¾ cup	1 cup	1 cup	1 cup	1 cup	1¾ cups
¾ teaspoon	1 teaspoon	1 teaspoon	1 teaspoon	1 teaspoon	1 teaspoon	2½ teaspoons
pinch	pinch	pinch	pinch	pinch	pinch	pinch
1½ teaspoons	1½ teaspoons	2 teaspoons	2 teaspoons	2 teaspoons	2 teaspoons	4 teaspoons
35–40 minutes	50 minutes	30–35 minutes	45 minutes	40–45 minutes	40 minutes	55 minutes

Rich Fruit Cake

This fruit cake improves with keeping and makes a delicious Christmas cake. When making the smaller cakes, especially the top tiers of a wedding cake, it is often a good idea to add a little gravy browning (about 1 teaspoon) to the mixture, so that it will be the same color as the larger cakes, which tend to go darker during the longer cooking time.

Preparation time: about 30 minutes
Cooking time: see chart
Oven: 300°F

1. Grease and double-line the chosen cake pan (page 14).

2. Mix together the currants and raisins in a large bowl.

3. Cut the candied cherries into quarters. Rinse them under warm water and dry thoroughly on paper towels or a clean cloth.

4. Add the cherries to the dried fruit mixture with the mixed peel, almonds and grated lemon zest. Mix well.

5. Sift the flour, ground cinnamon and apple pie spice together.

6. Cream the butter until soft, then add the sugar and continue creaming until light, fluffy and much paler in color. Do not overbeat or the cake will become coarse in texture and heavy.

7. Add the eggs to the creamed mixture one at a time, beating in thoroughly and following each with a spoonful of flour.

8. Fold in the remaining flour, followed by the dried fruit mixture.

9. Add the molasses, if liked.

10. Turn the batter into the prepared pan and level the top. Using the back of a spoon, make a slight hollow in the center of the batter, so that the top of the cake comes out flat when baked.

11. Fold sheets of brown paper into long narrow strips of about six thicknesses and tie around the outside of the pan for protection during cooking. Place in a preheated oven and bake for the time suggested in the chart. If the cake seems to be overbrowning, lay a sheet of parchment paper lightly over the top. With very large cakes it is sometimes better to turn the oven down to 275°F after about three-quarters of the cooking time has been completed.

12. To test if the cake is done, insert a skewer in the center: it should come out clean. Remove from the oven and leave to cool in the pan. Unmold onto a wire rack and remove the lining paper.

13. Prick the top of the cake all over with a skewer, then spoon several tablespoons of brandy or other spirit over the top. Wrap in wax paper and foil and store. If possible add more brandy at intervals of 2 weeks while the cake is maturing. This cake should be allowed to mature for 2–3 months but can be used after 2 weeks or so. It will keep for 6–8 months.

Step 6
After creaming the butter, add the sugar. Cream until just light and fluffy.

Step 8
Fold in the remaining flour after all the egg has been incorporated.

Step 10
Level the top of the batter and make a slight hollow in the center.

Step 11
Tying strips of brown paper around the outside of pan to protect during cooking.

RICH FRUIT CAKE INGREDIENTS

SQUARE	5-inch	6-inch	7-inch	8-inch	9-inch	10-inch	11-inch	12-inch
ROUND or PETAL-SHAPED	6-inch	7-inch	8-inch	9-inch	10-inch	11-inch	12-inch	
SLAB CAKE				11½- × 8½- × 1½-inch	12- × 10- × 2-inch			
currants	1 cup	1⅔ cups	2½ cups	3 cups	4½ cups	5⅔ cups	8 cups	9½ cups
golden raisins	½ cup	⅔ cup	¾ cup	1⅓ cups	1½ cups	2½ cups	3 cups	3½ cups
raisins	½ cup	⅔ cup	¾ cup	1⅓ cups	1½ cups	2½ cups	3 cups	3½ cups
candied cherries	⅓ cup	½ cup	⅔ cup	¾ cup	1 cup	1½ cups	2 cups	2½ cups
mixed candied peel, chopped	¼ cup	⅓ cup	⅓ cup	½ cup	⅔ cup	¾ cup	1 cup	1½ cups
blanched almonds, chopped	¼ cup	½ cup	½ cup	¾ cup	1 cup	1¼ cups	1¾ cups	2¼ cups
lemon zest, grated	¼ lemon	½ lemon	¾ lemon	1 lemon	1 lemon	1 lemon	1½ lemons	2 lemons
cake flour	1 cup	1½ cups	2 cups	3 cups	3½ cups	5¼ cups	6 cups	7¼ cups
ground cinnamon	½ teaspoon	½ teaspoon	¾ teaspoon	1 teaspoon	1½ teaspoons	2 teaspoons	2½ teaspoons	2¾ teaspoons
apple pie spice	¼ teaspoon	¼ teaspoon	½ teaspoon	¾ teaspoon	1 teaspoon	1¼ teaspoons	1½ teaspoons	1¾ teaspoons
butter	6 tbsp	10 tbsp	1½ sticks	2½ sticks	3 sticks	4½ sticks (1 lb 2 oz)	5 sticks + 2 tbsp (1 lb 5 oz)	7 sticks (1 lb 12 oz)
brown sugar	½ cup	1 cup	1¼ cups	2 cups	2½ cups	3½ cups	4¼ cups	5½ cups
eggs (extra large)	1½	2½	3	5	6	9	11	14
molasses (optional)	1 teaspoon	1 teaspoon	1 tablespoon	1 tablespoon	1 tablespoon	2 tablespoons	2 tablespoons	2 tablespoons
approximate cooking time	2 hours	2½ hours	2¾ hours	3¼ hours	3¾ hours	4¼–4½ hours	5¼–5½ hours	6–6½ hours
approximate cooked weight	1½ lb	2½ lb	3¼ lb	4½ lb	6 lb	9 lb	11 lb	14 lb
brandy, added after cooking	2 tablespoons	3 tablespoons	3 tablespoons	4 tablespoons	5 tablespoons	6 tablespoons	7 tablespoons	8 tablespoons

Cakes in this book based on a Rich Fruit Cake batter are: Hexagonal Wedding Cake, page 92; Rose Wedding Cake, page 94; Three-tier Wedding Cake, page 98; Christening Cakes, pages 100–1; Round Christmas Cake, page 108; Square Christmas Cake, page 109; Christmas Cake with Angels, page 114; Golden Wedding Cake, page 128; Good Luck Horseshoe, page 126; Confirmation Cake and Good Luck Cake, pages 124–5; Eighteenth or Twenty-first Birthday Cake, page 132; Sporting Birthday Cake, page 134 and Square Birthday Cake, page 130.

Light Fruit Cake

This is a well-flavored cake made more moist by the inclusion of grated apple, but it does not keep for longer than about 2 weeks. It is therefore better to use it only for a simply decorated cake. Like all fruit cakes, it can be covered with marzipan and with any of the icings.

The currants suggested in the recipe may be replaced with finely chopped, pitted dates or with a mixture of finely chopped, tenderized dried apricots and chopped, pitted prunes.

This fruit cake will keep well in the freezer for up to 3 months. Do not remove the lining paper from around the cake once it has cooled, but overwrap it securely in foil.

Preparation time: about 20 minutes
Cooking time: see chart
Oven: 350°F

1. Grease and double-line the chosen pan (page 14).

2. Sift the flour, baking soda, apple pie spice and ginger into a bowl.

3. In another bowl cream the butter or margarine with the sifted brown sugar until very light, fluffy and pale in color.

4. Beat in the eggs one at a time, following each with a spoonful of the flour mixture, then fold in the remaining flour.

5. Mix the raisins, currants, candied peel and fruit zest together and add to the mixture.

6. Peel, core and coarsely grate the apples, add to the mixture and stir through evenly.

7. Turn the mixture into the prepared pan, level the top and bake for the time suggested on the chart, in the center of the oven. The largest size of cake cooks better if the oven is turned down to 325°F after 1½ hours to prevent overbrowning.

8. To test if the cake is done, insert a skewer into the center. It should come out clean. Cool the cake in the pan for 5 minutes. Unmold onto a wire rack and leave until cold. When cold, wrap in foil or put into an airtight container for 24–48 hours before use.

Variations

An even more sumptuous fruit cake can be made by modifying the Rich Fruit Cake mixture.

Reduce the quantity of currants slightly, increasing the quantity of candied cherries accordingly; add the grated zest of half an orange and a good pinch of nutmeg to the mixture. Add sherry with the flour, using 2 teaspoons for the smallest size, graduating up to 5–6 tablespoons for a 12-inch cake.

Before wrapping the cooked, cooled cake in foil (it must be kept for 2 weeks before use) prick the top all over with a skewer and spoon 2–8 tablespoons sherry or brandy over the surface (depending on the size of the cake).

Both fruit cake recipes can be finished in Dundee-cake style with blanched whole almonds arranged on top of the unbaked cake to cover it completely. Another luxurious way of finishing a fruit cake which is not to be formally iced is to add candied fruits and nuts to the top with a coating of warmed and sieved apricot jam.

Use this decoration of colorful fruits on a light fruit cake, arranging them on a topping of glacé icing which is just beginning to pour over the sides of the cake. The contrast of dark cake, white icing and red, green and yellow fruits is very effective. If you increase the amount of grated orange or lemon zest in the mixture, use an orange or lemon-flavored and colored glacé icing and the appropriate crystallized fruits.

See Pâques Cake (page 119) and Cassata alla Siciliana (page 194) for examples of decorating with crystallized fruits.

Opposite page: Light fruit cake

LIGHT FRUIT CAKE INGREDIENTS				
CAKE SIZES	7-inch round 6-inch square	8-inch round 7-inch square	9-inch round 8-inch square	10-inch round 9-inch square
cake flour	1½ cups	2 cups	3 cups	4 cups
baking soda	⅓ teaspoon	½ teaspoon	¾ teaspoon	1 teaspoon
apple pie spice	⅓ teaspoon	½ teaspoon	¾ teaspoon	1 teaspoon
ground ginger	good pinch	¼ teaspoon	⅓ teaspoon	½ teaspoon
butter or margarine	1 stick	1½ sticks	2¼ sticks	3 sticks
light brown sugar	⅔ cup	1 cup	1½ cups	2 cups
eggs	2 (large)	2 (extra large)	3 (extra large)	4 (extra large)
raisins	1 cup	1⅓ cups	2 cups	2⅔ cups
currants	½ cup	⅔ cup	1 cup	1⅓ cups
golden raisins	½ cup	⅔ cup	1 cup	1⅓ cups
chopped mixed candied peel	¼ cup	⅓ cup	½ cup	⅔ cup
grated orange or lemon zest	1	1	1½–2	2
grated tart apple	1 cup	1½ cups	2 cups	3 cups
approx. cooking time	1–1¼ hours	1¼–1½ hours	about 1¾ hours	2–2¼ hours

MERINGUES

The ability to make good meringue is invaluable to the cake maker and decorator. Many European cakes are based on meringue – in layers or shells sandwiched with whipped cream and fruit, or as a decoration, perhaps dusted with cocoa. This section takes the mystery out of making meringues and gives recipes for all applications.

There are several types of meringue but the most commonly used is called Meringue Suisse. This is made by beating egg whites until they are very stiff, then beating in half the sugar gradually and folding in the rest. This is piped or spread for disks and other shapes as well as meringue shells. Meringue Cuite is easier to handle and holds its shape better. It is made by heating the egg whites and sugar over a pan of gently simmering water while the mixture is being beaten. The meringue is used mainly for basket and shell shapes. It will also "hold" chopped nuts or other tiny pieces of flavoring baked into it.

With all meringue making the bowl and beaters must be scrupulously clean and free from all traces of grease to obtain the best results and most bulk. Measure the sugar accurately. If you use too much sugar the result will be sticky, soggy meringues. The type of beater you use will also affect the result. A balloon whisk gives greater volume but takes longer than a rotary beater. An electric mixer saves time but gives the least volume. If you use a balloon whisk, put the egg whites in a wide bowl; a rotary beater works best in a narrow deep bowl.

The best sugar to use is superfine sugar, or a mixture of half superfine sugar and half confectioners' sugar, which gives very white, crisp meringues. For delicious pale brown meringues make Meringue Suisse and replace ¼ cup white sugar with light brown sugar, and sift it with the white sugar before adding it to the egg whites. Bake in the same way.

Meringue Suisse

4 egg whites (extra large)
1 cup superfine sugar

Preparation time: about 10 minutes
Cooking time: 2 hours (shells, stars, bars); 2½–3 hours (disks)
Oven: 225°F

1. Place the egg whites in a large grease-free bowl. Beat the whites using a rotary beater, balloon whisk or electric mixer, until the mixture is thick, white and stands in stiff peaks.

2. Beat in half to two-thirds of the sugar about a tablespoon at a time, making sure it is completely incorporated and the mixture is stiff again after each addition.

3. Using a metal spoon, fold in the remainder of the sugar, again a little at a time. The meringue is now ready to pipe or spread and should be used immediately; it will deflate if left before cooking.

Step 1
Beat the egg whites until they are thick, white and stand in stiff peaks.

Step 2
Stiffly beat in half to two-thirds of the sugar, a tablespoon at a time.

Step 3
Use a metal spoon to fold in the remaining sugar a little at a time.

Meringue Disks

Makes 2 circles + 6–8 individual meringues for decoration

1. Cover 2 baking sheets with non-stick parchment paper or greased wax paper and draw a circle of the required size on each: 8 or 9 inches are the usual sizes but disks may be made larger if you are baking for a party. Alternatively draw three circles each 1–1½ inches smaller than the last to give graduated sizes, beginning with the largest at 7–8 inches.

2. Fill a pastry bag fitted with a large plain tube ½–¾ inch in diameter or a large star tube, and, beginning in the middle of the circle, pipe a continuous spiral to fill the drawn circle. Repeat with the second circle.

3. Bake in a preheated oven, reversing the sheets in the oven after each hour. Cool on the paper, then peel off and store in an airtight container.

Meringue Shells, Stars and Bars

Makes 24–36, depending on size and shape

1. Line 2 baking sheets with non-stick parchment paper or greased wax paper.

2. Fit a pastry bag with a large star tube and fill with meringue.

3. On the paper pipe out shell shapes, stars or whirls or any other shapes to use to decorate the top of meringue disks or to form the sides for a meringue basket. For bars, use the same tube and pipe out straight lines of mixture about 4–5 inches long or squiggle the tube back and forth to give zigzag bars. Piping a continuous twisted line will give a meringue bar with a professional appearance.

4. Bake in a preheated oven, reversing the baking sheets in the oven after an hour to give even cooking on both sheets. When ready the meringues should be crisp and dry and should peel easily away from the paper. Leave on the paper to cool, then store between sheets of wax paper in an airtight container.

Meringue Cuite

Makes about 8 nests or 1 large basket

2 cups confectioners' sugar
4 egg whites
few drops vanilla extract

Preparation time: about 20 minutes
Cooking time: about 2 hours
Oven: 225°F

1. Sift the confectioners' sugar at least twice to ensure it is completely free of lumps.

2. Put the egg whites into a heatproof bowl and beat until frothy.

3. Add the confectioners' sugar and beat until blended. Stand the bowl over a saucepan of very gently simmering water and beat the mixture until it becomes thick, white and stands in peaks. Beat in the vanilla. The meringue cuite is now ready for piping into the shape you want.

4. For meringue nests, put the meringue into a pastry bag fitted with a ½-inch plain tube or a large star tube. Line 2 baking sheets with non-stick parchment paper and draw circles of 4–5 inches over them.

5. Use the meringue to fill these circles beginning in the center of each; then pipe a ring on top of the outside of the meringue circle to form the raised sides of the nest. Alternatively, instead of the outside ring, a series of dots or rosettes may be piped around the edge of the circle.

6. Bake in the oven for about 2 hours, reversing the baking sheets in the oven after 1 hour. Cool the meringue on the paper before peeling off. A large basket may be made in the same way beginning with a circle of about 9–10 inches and piping at least 2 rings on top of each other to form the sides.

Step 3
Whisking the mixture over a pan of simmering water to stiff white peak stage.

Meringue Based Cakes

Meringue disks can be sandwiched together with whipped cream and fruit or a combination of whipped cream and crème pâtissière. Any of the light, fruity cheesecake mixtures could also be used as an unusual filling: use half to sandwich the meringue layers and spread the remainder on top. Decorate with sugared or crystallized fruits.

To use meringue as the base for a cheesecake, make meringue cuite with ½ cup chopped nuts for a firmer result. Layers can be made in a rectangular shape if you prefer. The recipe opposite for meringue suisse will make 3 layers. Draw rectangles of 12 × 4 inches on lined baking sheets. Pipe in the meringue in a backwards and forwards pattern. Bake in a preheated oven for 2½–3 hours.

Recipes in this book based on meringue are Austrian Meringue Basket (page 166), Petits Vacherins (page 215), Yellow Chicks (page 210) and Chestnut Meringues (page 218).

Note: Baked meringues of all shapes and sizes will store satisfactorily for 7–10 days before use if kept in an airtight container.

PASTRY

Good pastry making is an important skill in the cake maker's repertoire. Many of the European-style cakes are based on different types of pastry.

In the area of cakes and cake decorating, boundaries are becoming blurred. Tradition has it that a special occasion calls for a fruit or sponge cake with a suitable, often elaborate icing. Different countries, however, have different traditions. In France, many wedding feasts include a huge *galette de pommes*, a flat apple tart in which thin apple slices are carefully arranged in circles over a filling of apple purée and glazed. *Croquembouche* appears at weddings in France and Italy – a pyramid of tiny choux puffs filled with liqueur-flavored cream and swathed in spun sugar.

The European influence has spread, introducing pastry-based confections as the centerpiece of a celebration, with layers of custard or cream and a message or name scripted in piped chocolate. Luxurious cakes such as these and cheesecakes are also frequently presented as company dinner desserts. For this category of cakes the ability to make good pastry of various kinds is an invaluable skill, and extends your range to include fruit tarts and cakes for tea.

The great quality of pastry-based cakes, tarts and cheesecakes is the contrast between the light, crisp, delicately flavored pastry and the filling it contains. A shell of pâte sucrée may hold an array of raspberries arranged on a layer of crème pâtissière or little choux puffs may be filled with whipped cream and covered in chocolate. To make the famous *mille feuilles* sheets of puff pastry are layered with cream and crème pâtissière, covered in glacé icing and sliced.

Basic pie pastry and its enriched variations, puff and choux pastry are described here. Strudel pastry is included on page 204.

Like cake-decorating, pastry-making is an art, and to be successful it is essential to master the basic techniques. All-purpose flour must be used for all the dessert pastries described here – self-rising flour results in a spongy texture. The fats used should be butter or hard margarine (hard fats are easier to rub in) with a proportion of lard in some cases to give a crisp texture when baked.

Keep everything cool. Make the pastry at a time when the kitchen is cool; chill any water that may be needed; the fats too should be cold when used. When rubbing the fat into the flour, always use only the fingertips as this is the coldest part of the hand. If you have warm hands, hold them under cold running water for a few moments to cool down before you start.

Rubbing or cutting in the fat can be done with two round-bladed knives or a pastry blender, used to cut the fat into small pieces in opposite directions, shaking the bowl from time to time to bring the larger lumps to the surface. Finish the rubbing in using the fingertips. A food processor will give similar results in seconds.

The amount of water added to the fat and flour to bind them together will vary each time, as some flours will absorb more water than others. Make sure that enough water is added, as too dry a mixture will make the pastry crumbly and impossible to handle, and too wet a mixture will result in a crust that is too tough to eat. Add the water a little at a time, stirring it quickly into the flour with a round-bladed knife. Ensure that at least two-thirds of the given liquid is added.

The pastry is moist enough when it will gather together to form a soft ball without much kneading. If the pastry is dry and crumbly, add a drop more water to bind it together. Turn the dough out of the bowl onto a lightly floured work surface and knead quickly until it is smooth, handling the pastry as little as possible. Wrap in plastic wrap and chill for 10–15 minutes before using – this allows the pastry to firm up and relax before being used, and makes rolling out easier.

Rolling Out

Roll out carefully using light even pressure with both hands on the rolling pin – light flowing movements are better than heavy abrupt actions. Always roll away from yourself. Keep the pastry in a round shape and lift and turn it often to make sure that it does not stick to the work surface and that it keeps its shape. Sprinkle with a little flour to prevent it sticking to the table or rolling pin, but do not turn the pastry over, as this will incorporate too much flour into the pastry. Before baking the pastry should be lightly chilled in its finished shape to prevent excessive shrinkage.

To Bake

It is essential to bake the pastry in a preheated oven at a fairly high temperature to ensure quick rising and "set" before it has a chance to shrink and collapse.

Proportions If a recipe calls for 2-cup quantity pastry, this means 2 cups flour and does not refer to the sum total of all the ingredients. Any pastry recipe can be doubled or halved, but always keep the proportions the same in each case. It is a good idea to master basic pie pastry before attempting any others.

Lining a tart pan

1. Choose a tart pan with a loose bottom, or a French flan ring used on a baking sheet. China tart and quiche dishes do not conduct the heat quickly enough.

2. Roll the pastry out thinly, about 1/8-inch thick, to a circle 1 1/2 inches larger than the diameter of the tart pan.

3. Lift the pastry on the rolling pin and lower it into the pan. Press it carefully into the bottom and sides, taking care not to stretch it at any time.

4. Trim the edges, using a rolling pin to roll the pastry level with the rim.

5. Prick the bottom with a fork to allow any steam to escape while cooking.

6. Chill the lined tart pan for at least 10 minutes.

Baking Blind

A tart shell case is baked blind when the filling is to be cooked for only a short time or not at all.

Oven: 400°F

1. Line the pastry shell with wax paper, aluminum foil, or a double layer of paper towels.

2. Weight it down with dried beans (kept specially for this purpose, they can be used indefinitely). You can also buy special ceramic beans. Take care to put in enough beans to compensate for the filling. Push them well to the edges to support and hold up the sides.

3. Bake the pastry shell in the center of a preheated oven for about 15 minutes.

4. Remove the beans and paper and bake for a further 10 minutes or until the pastry is dry and golden brown.

5. Allow to cool on a wire rack before carefully removing from the tart pan (or follow the recipe instructions).

Decorations for tarts

Pastry trimmings can be used to make decorations. Roll them out thinly and cut into small shapes with pastry cutters, or make leaf shapes or tassels.

To make leaves, cut the pastry into 1-inch strips and then diagonally across into diamond shapes. Mark the shapes with the back of a knife to represent veins on the leaves.

To make a tassel, cut a 1-inch strip, then make cuts along the length three-quarters of the way through at intervals of 1/4 inch and roll up neatly. Open up like a flower and place on the pastry topping.

Glazing Brush the decorated tart with glaze before baking to give it a really professional look. For savory pastry, a whole egg, beaten with a large pinch of salt, gives a rich golden color. For sweet pastry, brush with a little milk or beaten egg white and dust with granulated sugar before baking to give a frosted look. *To make a lattice pattern* for open tarts see the instructions given with Frangipan Tart on page 184. For a more decorative effect the strips of pastry can be carefully twisted before being laid in position, sealed and trimmed in the usual way.

PIE PASTRY

This is the standard pastry for tarts and pies. It is very easy to make and provided you follow the golden rules of handling the pastry no more than is necessary and avoiding adding too much water, it will reward you with excellent texture and taste. For a special occasion, decorate the crust with appropriate pastry shapes or letters, or add warm glacé icing, pouring it over the cooked crust while the pastry is warm. If you wish to increase the quantity, remember that there should be half the weight of fat to flour, a pinch of salt and a measured amount of water: for 1¼ cups flour, use 1½ tablespoons water, for 1⅔ cups flour, no more than 2½ tablespoons.

The combination of half butter or hard margarine and half lard gives the color and flavor of butter with the crisp texture characteristic of white fat. This basic pie pastry should be light and crisp with a delicately tinted color.

Basic Pie Pastry

Makes ¾-cup quantity: 1 8-inch pastry shell or 12 tartlet shells

¾ cup all-purpose flour
pinch of salt
2 tablespoons butter
2 tablespoons lard
1 tablespoon water

Preparation time: 10 minutes
Cooking time: 25 minutes for pastry shell; 15 minutes for tartlet shells
Oven: 400°F

1. Sift the flour and salt into a bowl. Add the fats and, using a round-ended knife or pastry blender, chop finely. Rub the fat into the flour with the fingertips.

2. When the mixture looks fine – like bread crumbs – shake the bowl to bring any remaining lumps of fat to the surface and rub them in.

3. Add a little cold water and mix, first using a round-ended knife and then the fingertips, to bind the pastry together to a ball of dough. Add a little more water if necessary, but a wet dough makes a tough pastry.

4. Knead the dough lightly on a floured board. The pastry can be used immediately or wrapped in plastic wrap and kept in a cool place for 15–30 minutes.

For perfect Pâte Brisée

Use ice water or the coldest possible. A touch of lemon juice will give a good flavor.

Use as little water as possible. Although damper pastry is easier to handle, because it is not so crumbly, it will be tough when cooked.

Handle the pastry as little as possible.

Always roll the pastry in one direction only – straight ahead of you. Turn the pastry around as you roll; do not change the direction of rolling.

Never overstretch the pastry – it will only shrink back as it cooks.

Pâte Brisée (Rich Pie Pastry)

Use this pastry for tarts with a moist filling. It has a firmer texture than basic pie pastry and is very elastic, making it easy to roll out without breaking. Allow it to rest for a few minutes after rolling to let it spring back before lining the pans. The traditional French way to make this pastry is directly on a board avoiding the use of a bowl.

Makes ¾-cup quantity: 1 8-inch pastry shell or 10 tartlet shells

¾ cup all-purpose flour
1 tablespoon sugar
pinch of salt
4 tablespoons butter, chilled and diced
1 egg yolk
2 teaspoons chilled water or egg white

Preparation time: 15 minutes
Cooking time: 25 minutes for a pastry shell; 15 minutes for tartlet shells
Oven: 400°F; then 350°F (for pastry shell)

1. Sift the flour, sugar and salt onto a board or into a bowl. Make a well in the center and add the butter, egg and water or egg white.

2. With the fingertips of one hand only work the butter, egg and water mixture until the butter is smooth and pliable.

3. With a long narrow spatula bring the flour in over the wet ingredients and cut it in very lightly.

4. As soon as the mixture is well coated use the heel of the hand to bring the pastry together, squeezing it firmly, letting go immediately and turning it over as it falls. Continue to work in this way until the pastry comes together, adding a little more water if it seems very dry. Knead very lightly until smooth.

5. Wrap in foil or plastic wrap and chill for at least 20 minutes. The pastry is then ready to use. Bake a pastry shell in a pre-heated moderately hot oven for 10 minutes and then reduce the temperature for 15 minutes. Bake tartlet shells in a pre-heated oven for 15 minutes

Pâte Sucrée (Sweet Pie Pastry)

This famous French pastry is crisp and thin when baked. It is used for the most delicate sweet tarts. Like Pâte Brisée, only the fingertips – of one hand – should be used in mixing, and it is made on a board. Because it is very soft when made, it must be wrapped and thoroughly chilled for at least an hour after preparation or it will be difficult to roll out. It must be rolled thinly; if this proves tricky, roll it between two sheets of non-stick parchment paper or plastic wrap. Alternatively, it may be pressed into the pans by hand, patching any little cracks with additional small pieces of pastry.

Makes ¾-cup quantity: 1 8-inch pastry shell or 10 tartlet shells

¾ cup all-purpose flour
pinch of salt
¼ cup sugar
4 tablespoons butter (at cool room temperature)
2 egg yolks
2 drops vanilla extract, or ½ teaspoon grated lemon zest (optional)

Preparation time: 15 minutes plus chilling
Cooking time: 25 minutes for a pastry shell; 15 minutes for tartlet shells
Oven: 400°F; then 350°F (for pastry shell)

1. Sift the flour and salt into a pile on a working surface or board and make a well in the center. Add the sugar, diced butter, egg yolks and vanilla extract or grated lemon zest, if using.

2. Using the fingertips of one hand "pinch and peck" the butter, sugar and yolks together until the mixture is smooth and pale. Try not to work in too much flour at this stage as it will toughen the finished pastry.

3. Clean your fingertips with a long narrow spatula and use it to draw the flour over the yolks. Use your fingertips and then the heel of the hand to bring the pastry together in a ball. Knead lightly until smooth.

4. Shape the ball of dough into a flattened round. Wrap in plastic wrap and chill for 1–2 hours before use. To use, roll out very thinly on a lightly floured surface.

5. Line a tart pan or tartlet pans. Bake a pastry shell in a pre-heated moderately hot oven for 10 minutes, then reduce the temperature for 15 minutes. Bake tartlet shells in a pre-heated moderately hot oven for 15 minutes only.

Step 1
Make a well in the center of the flour and salt and add the remaining ingredients.

Step 2
Work the butter, sugar and yolks together until the mixture is smooth and pale.

Step 3
When you have worked in the flour, form the pastry into a ball and knead lightly.

Step 4
Roll the chilled pastry out very thinly on a lightly floured surface.

Basic Puff Pastry

Puff pastry (pâte feuilletée) is the lightest and richest of all the pastries and rises in the most dramatic way. It is also the most difficult to make. Homemade puff pastry is unrivaled for taste and texture; however, ready-made puff pastry can be purchased which rises well too.

The secret of successful puff pastry lies in making the dough soft enough to be elastic, but not so wet that it becomes soggy and sticky. Care must be taken when rolling out the pastry to keep it even in shape, as poor layering gives an uneven rise. The pastry needs to be kept cool all the time, so use ice water to mix if the kitchen is warm and handle it as little as possible. Butter, rather than margarine, should be used, as the flavor is important to the taste of the pastry. Always keep the butter chilled in the refrigerator until it is needed.

It is best to make the pastry the day before it is required, which gives it time to relax and chill thoroughly before rolling out. If you wish, make the pastry as far as the fourth rolling on one day, and complete the rolling and folding and shaping on the next day. When chilling the pastry make fingermarks on the pastry to indicate the number of rollings given – it is easy to forget where you are when doing other things at the same time.

For a well-risen pastry, the oven must be correctly pre-heated and really hot when the cold pastry is put in so that the sudden heat makes it rise into light, flaky layers. The baking sheet need not be greased as the pastry contains so much fat; instead, dampen it with a little cold water. This turns to steam and helps the pastry to rise well. A breadmaking flour gives elasticity to the dough and also helps make the pastry rise well.

Basic Puff Pastry

Makes 1⅔-cup quantity: 8 patty shells (vol-au-vent cases)

1⅔ cups all-purpose flour
½ teaspoon salt
2 sticks butter
about ⅔ cup ice water with a
* squeeze of lemon juice*
* added*

Preparation time: about 50 minutes, plus chilling
Cooking time: See individual recipes
Oven: 425–450°F

1. Sift the flour and salt into a bowl. Take about 3 tablespoons of the butter and rub into the flour until the mixture is like fine bread crumbs.

2. Use the ice water to bind to a fairly soft dough, working it in with a knife. You may not need all the liquid. Knead lightly in the bowl until smooth. Wrap the dough in plastic wrap and chill for 15 minutes.

3. Place the butter between 2 sheets of plastic wrap or wax paper. Soften it by beating it with a rolling pin, and form it into an oblong measuring 8 × 4 inches.

4. On a lightly floured surface roll out the pastry to a square of about 9 inches and about ½ inch thick. Take the butter and place it on the pastry.

5. Fold the pastry over the butter, corner by corner, to form an enclosing envelope. Seal the edges of the pastry with the rolling pin.

6. Turn the pastry envelope if necessary so that the fold is on the right. "Rib" the pastry by pressing the rolling pin across the pastry at regular intervals. This helps to distribute the air evenly through the pastry and makes the butter easier to roll out.

7. Roll out the pastry into a long thin strip straight in front of you so that it is three times as long as it is wide, to measure approximately 4 × 12 inches.

8. Fold the bottom third of the strip upwards and the top third of the strip downwards over the rest of the pastry so it is quite even and square.

9. Seal the edges with the rolling pin and "rib" it as before. Put the pastry into a plastic bag and chill for 15–20 minutes.

10. Repeat the rollings and foldings (steps 7 and 8) four times more, giving the pastry a quarter turn each time so the fold is always on the right. Mark the dough each time with fingerprints to show how often it has been rolled. Wrap and chill for 30 minutes after every two rollings. If the pastry is still streaked with fat, roll and fold again.

11. Wrap the dough in plastic wrap and chill for 30 minutes before using.

CHOUX PASTRY

Often known as a paste, choux pastry differs from all other types of pastry: it is much softer in texture, and is piped or spooned onto dampened baking sheets rather than being rolled out. It has many uses, both sweet and savory. Success in making it begins with accurate measuring. Make certain that the butter has melted before the water starts to boil, and that the water is boiling when the flour is added. Do not open the oven door until at least three-quarters of the cooking time has elapsed.

Step 1
Place the butter into a saucepan with the measured water.

Step 3
Add the sifted flour and salt to the pan and mix in with a wooden spoon.

Step 4
Beat the mixture until it is smooth. When it forms a ball, remove pan from heat.

Choux Puffs

Makes 6–8

½ cup all-purpose flour
pinch of salt
4 tablespoons butter
⅔ cup water
2 eggs, beaten

Preparation time: about 15 minutes, plus cooling
Cooking time: see individual recipes
Oven: 425°F; then 375°F

1. Sift the flour and salt onto a piece of wax paper. Put the butter into a heavy-based saucepan with the water.

2. Heat gently until the butter melts then bring quickly to a boil.

3. Add the flour to the pan all at once and mix in with a wooden spoon or rubber spatula.

4. Beat until the mixture is smooth and forms a ball, leaving the sides of the pan clean. Do not over-beat.

FAULT FINDING GUIDE FOR PASTRY

FAULT	Causes & Solutions	FAULT	Causes & Solutions
RUBBED IN PASTRIES – Basic pie, pâte brisée (rich pie), pâte sucrée (sweet pie)		**PUFF PASTRY (continued)**	
Crumbly dough	Insufficient mixing. Knead lightly to form a ball. Not enough liquid. Add more, a few drops at a time.	Uneven rising	Poor folding – corners must be eased out and pastry folded neatly into 3 layers. Uneven rolling.
Sticky dough	Too much liquid. Add a little more flour. Flour not measured accurately. Pâte sucrée and pâte brisée not chilled before rolling.	Fat breaking through the dough	Fat too hard so that it breaks through when rolling. Insufficient chilling. Over-handling. Over-heavy rolling.
Cooked pastry hard and tough	Too much water worked in. Over-handled. Rolled out in too much flour. Flour sprinkled over pastry during rolling.	Fat running out during cooking	Fat broke through the dough while making (see above). Oven temperature too low.
Cooked pastry soft and crumbly	Too much fat used. Too little liquid added. Self-rising flour used for pâte brisée and pâte sucrée.	Pastry hard and tough	Too much water or too little water added to dough – it should be soft but not sticky.
Pastry shrunk	Stretched during lifting or shaping. Pâte brisée and pâte sucrée not allowed to relax before using. Pastry cooked in too cool oven.	Pastry shrinking	Insufficient resting. Pastry stretched during cutting, shaping or lifting.
Tart sides collapsed	Oven temperature too low. Insufficient baking beans used, or they were not piled up against sides of shell.	Damp and soggy inside	Insufficiently cooked. Patty shells not put back into the oven to dry after the insides have been removed.
Soft under-cooked pastry	Oven temperature too low. Oven not properly preheated. Baking sheet not used under a pie or tart pan. Too much liquid used in a pie. Top pastry crust not slit to allow the steam to escape.	**CHOUX PASTRY**	
		Mixture too soft	Wrong proportions of ingredients used – measure accurately. Water not boiling when flour added. Mixture not cooked until it leaves sides of pan. Too much egg added at once. Insufficient beating when each amount of egg is added.
PUFF PASTRY		Mixture not risen	Wrong proportions of ingredients used. Mixture too soft. Mixture not beaten enough. Oven too cool. Temperature lowered too soon. Oven doors opened during cooking. Not cooked long enough.
Sticky dough	Flour incorrectly measured. Too much water added. Add a little more flour before rolling out. Dough not chilled enough.	Sinking when removed from oven	Not cooked long enough – return to the oven quickly.
Pastry not risen	Fat not cool enough. Dough too tight; insufficient water added. Insufficient resting and chilling. Over-heavy rolling.	Soft and soggy inside	Bases not pricked to allow the steam to escape. Not returned to oven after pricking to dry.

Remove quickly from the heat and spread the paste out evenly over the bottom of the pan. Leave to cool for 10 minutes.

5. Beat the eggs vigorously into the paste, a little at a time, to give a smooth glossy pastry. A hand-held electric beater is best for this as it helps to incorporate the maximum amount of air required for a good rise. The pastry may not take the last spoonful of beaten egg.

6. The pastry must be able to be dropped from a spoon but remain stiff enough to pipe or spoon and hold its shape. The pastry is now ready for use.

FROSTINGS, ICINGS & FILLINGS

Perfect frosting is the key to successful decorating. Here are frostings ranging from buttercreams and crème pâtissière to royal icing and fondant molding paste.

Frostings can be divided into those that are simple to make and easy to apply, such as glacé icing and buttercream and its variations, and the more advanced types such as fondant molding paste and royal icing. Glacé icing is suitable for light sponge cakes and pastries. Buttercream can be used for all these as well as fancy cakes and tarts. Crème pâtissière is used for filling tarts and choux pastries. Fondant molding paste is suitable for covering fruit cakes, pound cakes and butter cakes, while royal icing is only used on rich fruit cakes or sometimes a pound cake as it is too heavy for sponges. Some frostings give an informal "roughed-up" finish to cakes. Frosted cakes should be decorated – with nuts, crushed caramel or sugared fruits – before the frosting sets. Many frostings involve making a syrup first. Syrup-making is included in this section as it has many uses in baking and sweet-making.

Apricot glaze is brushed over the surface of a cake to prevent crumbs being drawn into a covering of fondant molding paste or marzipan. It is also good for joining together different shaped pieces of cake before covering them with frosting.

Good almond paste or marzipan is a vital element in cake decorating. Homemade almond paste is superior in flavor to commercially prepared marzipan, which is made from the same ingredients but includes food additives and preservatives.

Glacé icing is the simplest to make but must be used rapidly as it dries quickly. It can only be used for covering cakes, and feather icing. Once it has been poured over the cake it must be left to set completely, as a sudden movement may crack the surface. It can be flavored and colored.

Simple buttercream consists basically of creamed butter and sugar with a little flavoring. It can be used as a filling, covering and for piping, although the results are not as refined as with royal icing. It can be smoothed with a long narrow spatula or whirled into patterns.

Classic buttercream is made from a sugar syrup base. It differs from simple buttercream in that, while the proportion of sugar is lower, more butter may be used and the mixture is enriched with egg yolks. The thicker texture makes it unsuitable for piping, but the flavor is more luxurious and it is good for filling and covering cakes. Crème au beurre mousseline is a slightly lighter variation.

Crème au beurre is a butter icing made lighter with the addition of a meringue mixture. This makes it perfect for filling sponge cakes or for meringue baskets or layers. It can be flavored. Not suitable for piping.

Crème pâtissière is a rich, delicious custard which has a velvety smooth texture and combines well with fresh fruit.

Frostings give an attractive finish to elaborate or simple cakes. In general, they are cooked. One of the most popular is 7-minute frosting, which sets quickly into stiff peaks but remains soft underneath.

Fondant molding paste is available ready made but is easily made at home. Soft and pliable, it can be used to cover cakes and to mold decorations. As a cake covering it gives a beautifully smooth, slightly polished finish and gently rounded edges. Once on a cake or molded into shape, it should be left for 2–3 days to dry. It can be colored and flavored, which makes it ideal for "novelty" cakes. If used on tiered cakes it is advisable to apply a coat of royal icing to the tops to take the weight of the other tiers without sinking.

Fondant icing is softer than fondant molding paste and is used for covering cakes only, not for molded decorations, as the consistency when ready to use is that of thick cream. It keeps for up to 2 months and can be colored and flavored.

Satin icing can be used like fondant molding paste to cover cakes, but the sugar is bound with butter melted with lemon juice, giving a slight flavor to the finished product.

Royal icing It gives an exceptionally smooth finish and can be sculpted into exact corners. The range of piped work possible with royal icing is limitless – it is an extremely versatile medium. Too heavy for light-textured sponges, it is the most appropriate icing for rich fruit cakes, and can also be used on a pound cake, if you wish to make a formal cake but prefer a lighter texture.

MARZIPAN OR ALMOND PASTE

Almond paste is generally homemade and marzipan purchased. Both are used for covering all cakes to be coated with royal icing and for most cakes to be covered in fondant molding paste, especially if a fruit cake; for decorative tops to cakes; or for molding all sorts of shapes, such as flowers, leaves and animals.

Make up in quantities of not more than 2 pounds at a time, otherwise it becomes unmanageable. You can make up small quantities using ½ cup ground almonds, etc. However, if you need small amounts for coloring, it is often best to use a commercial marzipan. The remainder, if it is securely wrapped in plastic wrap, will keep for up to a month or so.

To make a creamy-white marzipan, the natural color of almonds, use 2 lightly beaten egg whites instead of the egg or egg yolks for mixing.

Marzipan does not freeze.

Adding Color To color marzipan, simply add several drops of the chosen food coloring or colorings, then knead and squeeze the marzipan until the color is evenly distributed throughout with no streaking. Powder or paste colorings can be used in the same way, adding sufficient until the required color is obtained. If the marzipan becomes a bit soft, knead in a little sifted confectioners' sugar as well.

Makes 1 lb

½ cup granulated sugar
1 cup confectioners' sugar, sifted
2 cups ground almonds
1 teaspoon lemon juice
few drops almond extract
1 egg or 2 egg yolks, beaten

Preparation time: about 10 minutes

1. Combine the sugars and ground almonds and make a well in the center.

2. Add the lemon juice, almond extract and sufficient egg or egg yolks to mix to a firm but manageable dough.

3. Turn onto a lightly sugared surface and knead until smooth. Take care not to overknead or the paste may begin to turn oily. (There is no remedy for this and it then becomes difficult to use.) It can be wrapped securely in plastic wrap or aluminum foil and stored for up to 2 days before use.

Commercial marzipan is available ready to roll in the traditional yellow or "white" which is in fact the natural color. They are both good and easy to use and the natural one is ideal for adding colors to for molding as it gives truer colors than the yellow version.

Make sure you buy fresh marzipan, either by checking the date on the package or by pressing it with your finger. If it is so hard that you cannot make a slight indentation, you should not buy it.

MARZIPAN (approximate quantities)								
Square Cake size		6-inch	7-inch	8-inch	9-inch	10-inch	11-inch	12-inch
Round Cake size	6-inch	7-inch	8-inch	9-inch	10-inch	11-inch	12-inch	
Marzipan	¾ lb	1 lb	1¼ lb	1¾ lb	2 lb	2¼ lb	2½ lb	3 lb

Apricot Glaze

As well as forming a layer between the surface of a cake and its covering of fondant molding paste or marzipan, apricot and other jam glazes can also be brushed over fruits in tarts.

The cooled, sieved glaze can be stored in an airtight container in the refrigerator for up to a week, but it must be boiled and cooled again before applying it to the cake. The smallest quantity you can make up is 2 tablespoons of jam and 1 teaspoon of water.

Makes about 5 tablespoons

½ cup apricot jam or preserves
2 tablespoons water

Preparation time: about 5 minutes
Cooking time: about 5 minutes

1. Put the jam into a small saucepan with the water and heat gently, stirring until the jam has completely melted.

2. Rub through a sieve and return the purée to a clean saucepan.

3. Bring back to a boil and simmer for 1 minute or until it is the required consistency. Allow to cool before use.

Applying apricot glaze to the top of a fruit cake. Marzipan has been used to level the top of the cake.

Covering a Cake in Marzipan

The same method is used for both round and square cakes and any other shape you wish to cover. For fancy shapes, such as petal or oval, simply use the cake pan as a pattern for cutting out the top section of marzipan.

To calculate quantities for different shapes, calculate roughly what the finished size of the baked cake will be and allow about 4 ounces more than the amount given in the chart for a similar-sized round or square cake.

1. Place almost half of the marzipan on a working surface dredged with confectioners' sugar, or between two sheets of plastic wrap. Roll out evenly until 1 inch larger than the top of the cake.

2. Brush the top of the cake with apricot glaze (see picture, left) and if the surface is uneven or very curved, build up the edges or fill in any holes with scraps of marzipan. If the cake is very uneven, roll it out as smoothly as possible, or cut off the bumps and turn the cake upside down and cover the base with marzipan instead.

3. Invert the cake onto the marzipan and carefully turn the cake the right way up. Alternatively lift the marzipan shape on to the top of the cake, keeping it even. Trim off any excess and smooth the edges with a small narrow spatula.

4. Stand the cake marzipan side up on a cake board and brush the sides with apricot glaze.

5. Cut two pieces of string, one the exact height of the cake and the other the complete circumference. Roll out the remaining marzipan and using the string as a guide, cut a strip to the height and circumference of the cake. Two shorter lengths can be cut if this is easier.

Step 3
Invert the cake onto the rolled-out marzipan.

Step 3 continued
With the cake right way up, trim off any excess marzipan and smooth the edges.

Step 6
Unroll the measured marzipan strip around the side of the cake.

Step 7
Smooth the joins at the end of the strip and where it meets the marzipan on top.

6. Loosely roll the marzipan strip(s) into a coil. Place one end on the side of the cake and unroll carefully, molding the marzipan as you go and making sure the base of the marzipan touches the board.

7. Using a small narrow spatula, smooth the join at the ends of the strip and where the strip meets the marzipan on top of the cake. If the marzipan seems unduly moist, rub it all over with confectioners' sugar, and brush off the surplus.

8. Store the cake, uncovered, in a warm and dry, but not too hot, place for at least 24 hours before applying any icing. For tiered wedding cakes and those which you want to keep for a while after icing, allow up to a

week; otherwise the oils from the marzipan will seep through into the royal icing and leave unsightly marks.

Note

Some people prefer to add the sides of marzipan to the cake before the top; it doesn't really matter which way you do it as long as it is kept neat and even and you fill in any holes or dents before you start.

For notes on making decorative items from marzipan, see pages 66 (holly and mistletoe leaves and berries), 64–5 (fruits) and 63 (rose buds, flowers and leaves).

ROYAL ICING

Royal icing can be made in any quantity as long as you allow 1 egg white to each 2 cups confectioners' sugar. However, it is better to make up not more than an 8-cup quantity of icing at a time because the icing keeps better if made in small quantities. It is difficult to make up very small quantities, although it is possible to use ½ egg white and 1 cup sugar.

The icing can be stored in an airtight container in a cool place for about 2 days. However, it must be stirred very thoroughly before use, and if necessary a little extra sifted confectioners' sugar added to correct the consistency. The icing often seems to soften if left to stand for more than a few hours.

While using the icing, cover the bowl with a damp cloth to prevent a skin forming. Egg albumen powder, available from specialist cake decorating suppliers, can be made up according to the instructions on the package and used in place of fresh egg whites.

Glycerin can be added to help soften the icing and make cutting easier. It should be omitted from the icing for the first 2 coats on the top surface of the bottom tier of a wedding cake and the first coat on the top surface of the middle tier, as a hard surface is needed to take the weight of other tiers. It should be used carefully as too much glycerin will make a very soft icing.

CONSISTENCY CHART FOR ROYAL ICING

Royal icing can be made to varying consistencies suitable for different purposes. In each case, beat for 1 minute before adding the required water or confectioners' sugar.

Consistency	Method	Appearance
1 For coating; flooding for run-out.	Add 4 tablespoons water to the rest of the ingredients.	A soft consistency which should form a blob thick enough to cover the back of a spoon. It should not be runny.
2 For lines, trellis, scroll, lacework, writing, outlines for run-outs, scallops, beading, bells, doves.	Add 3 tablespoons water to the rest of the ingredients.	To test for correct consistency, use the back of a spoon to pull up some of the mixture; it should form a small peak. Add more sugar if the mixture is not stiff enough.
3 For borderwork, shells, rosettes, leaves, edging, frills and basketwork.	Add 3 tablespoons water to the rest of the ingredients. Add more sugar to achieve the required stiffness.	The mixture should form a peak which stands erect, slightly curling over at the top.
4 For flowers and snow; also for securing decorations to the cake.	Add 2 tablespoons water to the rest of the ingredients.	The mixture should form a stiff erect peak. If the mixture is too soft the petals of the flowers will spread out and blend into one another.

Makes 6-cup quantity

3 egg whites
approx. 6 cups confectioners'
*   sugar, sifted*
1 tablespoon strained lemon
*   juice*
1– 1 ½ teaspoons glycerine
*   (optional)*

Preparation time: about 15 minutes, plus standing

1. Put the egg whites into a clean, grease-free bowl and beat until frothy. Using a wooden spoon, gradually beat in half the sifted sugar. (A hand-held electric beater can be used but it will incorporate a lot of air and the resulting bubbles will be difficult to disperse.)

2. Add the lemon juice, glycerin and half the remaining sugar. Beat well until smooth and very white.

3. Gradually beat in enough of the remaining sugar to give a consistency which will just stand in soft peaks.

4. Put the icing into an airtight container or cover the bowl with a damp cloth and leave to stand for an hour or so, if possible, to allow most of the air bubbles to come to the surface and burst.

5. The icing is now ready for coating a cake; or it can be thickened a little with extra sifted sugar for piping stars, flowers, etc.; or thinned down for flooding run-outs, etc., by adding a little lightly beaten egg white or lemon juice. See above for guide to consistency. Several cakes in chapters 2 and 3 include decorative elements, such as flowers, fans, birds and butterflies, made from the basic white or tinted royal icing.

ROYAL ICING

Approximate quantities of confectioners' sugar for two thin coats of royal icing on round and square cakes. Calculate for other shapes from these amounts allowing a little extra.

Square		6-inch	7-inch	8-inch	9-inch	10-inch	11-inch	12-inch
Round	6-inch	7-inch	8-inch	9-inch	10-inch	11-inch	12-inch	
Confectioners' sugar	4 cups	5 cups	6 cups	8 cups	9 cups	10 cups	12 cups	14 cups

Covering a Cake in Royal Icing

Some people prefer to ice the top of the cake first, then the sides; others do it the other way around. It doesn't really matter, as long as you add several thin coats rather than one thick coat, since this gives the smoothest surface for flat-icing. It is wise to apply the icing to one surface at a time rather than all in one go, allowing each application time to dry before continuing, or you may spoil the surface already put on the cake.

After each coat to the top or sides, it is important to pare or cut off any lumps or bumps in the icing, using a finely serrated-edge knife.

An ordinary royal iced cake requires two coats on the top and sides. Sometimes an extra coat on the top is necessary, if it is not as smooth as you would like. A wedding cake, however, requires three coats all over, with an extra coat on the top for the lower tiers, to help them hold the weight of the other cakes.

To Flat Ice the Top

1. With a dab of icing, attach the cake to a cake board, which is 1–2 inches larger than the cake. Put a quantity of icing in the center of the cake and smooth out with a long narrow spatula, using a paddling movement. This helps to remove air bubbles and distribute the icing evenly. Remove the surplus icing from the edges.

2. Take an icing ruler or long narrow spatula and draw across the cake toward you, carefully and evenly, keeping the ruler or spatula at an angle of about 30°. Take care not to press too heavily or unevenly.

3. Remove surplus icing by running a narrow spatula around the top edge of the cake, holding it at right angles to the cake.

4. If not sufficiently smooth, cover with a little more icing and draw the ruler or spatula across the cake again, repeating until smooth. Leave to dry.

Step 2
Draw an icing ruler across the top of the cake toward you at an angle of about 30°.

Step 3
Straighten the edges with a narrow spatula held at right angles to the cake.

To Flat Ice the Sides

Place the cake on an icing turntable if possible, or use an upturned plate.

For a Square Cake

The best way of achieving good even corners is to ice two opposite sides first, leave to dry, then ice the other two.

1. Spread some icing on one side, then draw the comb or narrow spatula toward you, keeping the cake still to give an even finish.

2. Cut off the icing down the corner in a straight line; cut the surplus off the top and base of the cake. Repeat with the opposite side and leave to dry.

Step 1
Icing the second side. Smooth the icing, drawing the comb toward you.

Step 2
Using a narrow spatula, cut surplus icing off the top.

3. Repeat the process with the two remaining sides, keeping the corners neat and tidy. Leave to dry.

For a Round Cake

1. Spread a thin but covering layer of icing all around the sides of the cake. Again use a paddling action to push out as much air as possible, keeping the icing fairly smooth.

2. Hold an icing comb or scraper or a narrow spatula at an angle of about 45° to the cake. Starting at the back of the cake, with your free hand slowly rotate the cake, and at the same time move the comb slowly and evenly around the sides of the

cake. Remove the comb at an angle and fairly quickly, so the join is hardly noticeable.

3. Lift any excess icing from the top of the cake using the spatula, again rotating the cake. If not sufficiently smooth, wipe the spatula and repeat. Leave to dry.

To Flat Ice Irregular Shapes

Ice a cake according to the basic shape it most closely resembles. Those similar to a round cake, e.g. heart, oval, and petal are smoothed off all at once after adding a smooth and even coating of icing all around the sides. An oval is very similar to a round; with a petal take care to dip evenly into the "dents."

Other shapes tend to be multi-sided such as octagonal or hexagonal. These are iced in the same way as a square cake, adding the icing to every other side and, when dry, filling in those not already iced.

FAULT FINDING GUIDE ROYAL ICING		
Fault	**Causes**	**Solutions**
While mixing Lumpy consistency; icing is not very white, possibly with a yellowish tint; mixture is too soft and misshapen	Confectioners' sugar stored in damp place or container; sugar not sifted sufficiently; not enough egg white; not enough beating; too much heat in the atmosphere; too much fluid.	Buy good quality confectioners' sugar; store in a plastic bag in a dry place; always sift well; use the largest grade egg or 2 egg whites from small eggs; beat a little longer; add a drop of water; add more sugar to stiffen.
While coating a cake Air bubbles	These always appear whether beating by hand or with a mixer. There are more when you use a mixer but since it is the easiest, quickest method of beating be prepared for them.	Leave the icing to stand overnight. Before using, stir slowly with a spoon to help disperse the bubbles. Use a pin to disperse any bubbles on the surface of the cake, pricking the bubble at its side.
When first coat has set Rough edges, lines or streaks on the icing	An accumulation of loose particles of confectioners' sugar. Insufficient beating in the early stages.	Cover with a thin layer of flooding icing.
Uneven surface	The icing has set before all air bubbles were dispersed. Insufficient beating, or final stir was not given.	Using a wide clean paintbrush, dab over the icing with a little water. This wets the crust and seeps into the air pockets. When this is dry, apply another coat of icing.
Drip markings down the sides of the cake	Not removing excess icing from the cake.	If the icing is still wet, remove the excess with a rubber spatula. If it has partly set, use a narrow spatula, dipped in warm water and immediately pressed straight onto the drip mark. The heat and moisture should melt the icing slightly so the drip mark disappears.
When the icing is on the cake Almond paste is visible so cake has a yellowish tint; icing looks dirty	Not enough layers of icing applied.	Add one or two more layers.
Icing has not set hard	Moist atmosphere caused by too much steam.	Move the cake to a dry place.
Uneven surface to the icing	Not applying the coats of icing evenly.	Apply a final layer and vibrate the turntable to allow it to flow into the uneven areas.

Adding Second and Third Coats of Icing

1. Repeat the method for the top and sides when applying each subsequent coat but make sure each layer is dry before adding the next or you may disturb the previous layers. Drying will usually take from 3 to 6 hours, but can vary according to the room atmosphere.

2. Leave the cake to dry, uncovered, for 24 hours after completing the icing. The cake is now base-iced ready for the decoration.

Rough Icing

As an alternative to a smooth finish, royal icing can be pulled up into peaks with a round-bladed knife to give a snow-peaked effect. The Christmas cakes on pages 110, 113, and 117 demonstrate how attractive this finish can be. Royal icing can also be used on novelty cakes to represent water, if the icing is tinted a pale blue. The contrast between a smooth sided cake and its rough-iced top (or vice versa) can be very decorative.

Icing the Cake Board

Sometimes it is a good idea to ice the cake board too, either before adding a decoration to it, or simply to cover up the expanse of silver board which some people find unsightly. To do this, first completely base ice the cake on its board and leave to dry. Then stand the cake on its board on an icing turntable and coat the board with a thin layer of icing (it may spread more easily if thinned slightly with a little egg white or lemon juice). Either run a narrow spatula around the edge while revolving the cake or hold an icing comb at an angle to the icing while rotating. Remove surplus icing from the edge of the board with the spatula. With a square cake use the same method but take care with the corners.

The board may also be decorated in other ways. Flowers or other decorations on the cake may be used to decorate the board, too. Piping to match that on the top edge or around the base can be added to the board. If the cake has any lacework decoration on it, the board can be covered with lacework icing to match.

GLACÉ ICING

This is the quickest of icings to make and is useful for icing all kinds of butter, sponge and other cakes, as well as small cakes and cookies. It cannot be used for piping stars or anything fancy. The icing will remain liquid for a short time if the bowl is placed in another large bowl containing hot water; otherwise, unless used quickly, it will set in the bowl.

Cakes covered in glacé icing must not be moved until the icing has set completely or it will crack. The cake must be put on to a board which is firm enough not to bend, before the icing is added for it can't be moved after adding the icing.

Glacé icing can be colored and flavored in any way you like to blend with any type of colored decoration and flavor of cake.

Make up a small quantity in the same way as a large one; if it becomes too runny simply add more confectioners' sugar.

Glacé icing must be used at once, as it does not keep. Once on the cake it will keep as long as the cake, i.e. up to 2 weeks. It is not generally used on rich fruit cakes which last much longer.

Makes sufficient to ice the top of an 8-inch round cake. Use double quantities to ice the top and sides.

2 cups confectioners' sugar
2–4 tablespoons hot water or
  fruit juice
food coloring and/or flavoring
  (optional)

Preparation time: about 5 minutes

1. Sift the confectioners' sugar into a bowl.

2. Gradually beat in sufficient water or juice to give a smooth icing, thick enough to coat the back of a spoon easily. Extra water or sugar can be added to achieve the correct consistency.

3. Add a few drops of food coloring or flavoring, if used. Use at once or place over a bowl or pan of hot water for a short period.

4. Alternatively all the ingredients can be put into a saucepan and heated gently, stirring continuously, until well mixed and smooth; take care not to overheat or the icing will crystallize. Use very quickly.

5. If a crust begins to form on the icing before it is added to the cake, rub it through a sieve before use.

Variations

Lemon or Orange Use strained fruit juice instead of the water. A few drops of food coloring can also be used.

Coffee Use a little coffee essence or very strong black coffee in place of part or all of the water.

Chocolate Sift 1–2 tablespoons cocoa powder with the sugar and continue as recipe. A few drops of vanilla extract may also be added.

Mocha Sift 2 teaspoons cocoa powder and 1 or 2 teaspoons instant coffee powder with the sugar and continue as recipe. Alternatively, you could sift the cocoa with the sugar and add 1–2 teaspoons coffee essence with the water.

To Coat the Top of a Cake with Glacé Icing

1. Make sure the cake is completely ready before you begin.

2. Make the glacé icing, add color if desired, then, when it is thick enough to coat the back of a wooden spoon, pour it over the middle of the cake. Using a round-bladed knife spread it out quickly and evenly over the top almost to the edge. If the icing drops over the edge, quickly remove it with a knife or narrow spatula or leave it until it has set, when it can be cut off with a sharp knife. Do not disturb the icing as it sets, or it will crack.

3. Alternatively tie a piece of non-stick parchment paper all around the sides of the cake to come about 1-inch above the top of the cake. Pour on the icing, spreading it out almost to the edge. It will then run out by itself and be held in place by the paper. Prick any air bubbles that may appear and leave to set. When set, very carefully ease off the paper.

4. Either add decorations to the glacé icing as it begins to set, or wait until it is quite set.

To Coat a Whole Cake in Glacé Icing

1. It is a good idea to stand the cake on a thin cake card the exact size of the cake, as this keeps the cake rigid when it is moved and should prevent the icing from cracking. Stand the cake on a wire rack over a plate or tray.

2. Pour almost all of the icing over the middle of the cake and spread it out evenly, allowing it to run down the sides. Use a narrow spatula dipped in hot water to help spread the icing over the sides; fill in any gaps with the icing left in the bowl.

3. Leave to set, then trim off drips. Remove the cake carefully.

Decorating with Glacé Icing

Glacé icing lends itself to an attractive design known as feather icing, used in the Strawberry Feather Bar on page 82. To achieve this design, make up the amount of glacé icing required for the cake plus an extra ½ cup confectioners' sugar. Remove about 2 tablespoons of icing and color it a fairly bright color. Put the colored icing into a parchment

paper decorating cone (see page 56) without cutting the tip off or adding a tube. Use the white icing to coat the top of the cake then immediately cut the tip off the colored icing cone and pipe straight lines across the top of the cake at ½–¾ inch intervals. Immediately draw a skewer or the point of a knife across the lines at right angles about 1 inch apart.

Quickly turn the cake around and draw the skewer across again in between the first lines but in the opposite direction to complete the feathered effect.

A variation on this idea is the spider's web design. To make this, pipe the colored icing in a continuous circle, starting in the center of the cake and working toward the outside edge. Quickly draw a pointed knife

from the center to the edge, marking the cake into quarters. Then draw from edge to center between the lines to complete the pattern. This pattern is particularly effective if the cake is iced in coffee-flavored icing and the lines are drawn in chocolate-flavored icing.

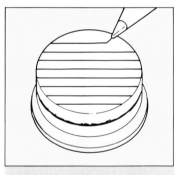

1. Using colored icing, pipe evenly spaced straight lines across the top of the cake.

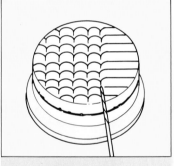

2. Draw a skewer across the lines at right angles about 1 inch apart.

3. Turn the cake around.

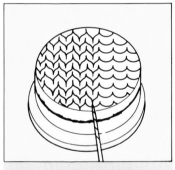

4. Draw the skewer across again between the first "feathers" but in the opposite direction.

FONDANT MOLDING PASTE OR COVERING

This icing is simple to use once you get used to its consistency and you can achieve a professional result more quickly than with royal icing. It is also easy to make, since extra sifted sugar can be added until it is sufficiently malleable. Use it for covering cakes either after adding a layer of marzipan to the cake, when it needs to be brushed lightly with egg white to make the icing adhere, or add it directly to a sponge or pound cake after brushing the cake with apricot glaze.

It should be rolled out on a surface sprinkled with a mixture of sifted confectioners' sugar and cornstarch and, for ease of movement, it can be rolled out on a sheet of plastic wrap sprinkled with the sugar mixture. To smooth it, simply rub in a circular movement (take care if you have long nails or are wearing rings) with the fingertips, which have been dipped in confectioners' sugar and cornstarch. The paste can be colored by adding liquid or powder or paste food colorings; and flavorings can be added, too. Apart from cake covering, it is also good for molding all types of animals, flowers and other shapes. It can be painted with liquid food coloring for extra effect.

Fondant molding paste can be used almost interchangeably with royal icing but take care when covering tiered wedding cakes for sometimes the paste does not set hard enough to take the weight of heavy top tiers. Make sure it is given extra time for drying out (see step 7 of recipe) and it may help to add 1–2 coats of royal icing to the tops of the cake before adding the molding paste.

Liquid glucose or glucose syrup is available from most specialist cake decorating suppliers. A number of these are listed at the end of this book.

It is difficult to make up quantities of more than 2 pounds because of the kneading required. It blends most easily when made in 1–1½ pound quantities. Smaller quantities can be used but the egg white and liquid glucose quantities must be measured very accurately. If only small quantities are required, use a purchased fondant paste, which will keep for up to a couple of months if wrapped securely in plastic wrap. It is obtainable in supermarkets as well as from specialist cake decorating suppliers.

Makes 1 lb

4 cups confectioners' sugar
1 egg white
¼ cup liquid glucose or glucose syrup
food coloring and/or flavoring (optional)

Preparation time: about 10–15 minutes

1. Sift the confectioners' sugar into a mixing bowl to remove all lumps and make a well in the center.

2. Add the egg white and liquid glucose. Beat with a wooden spoon or spatula, gradually pulling in the confectioners' sugar from the sides of the bowl, to give a stiff mixture.

3. Knead the icing thoroughly, mixing in any remaining sugar in the bowl to give a smooth and manageable paste. To see if it is ready, press your thumb into the icing. If the indentation is perfect, the icing is ready. Add a little more confectioners' sugar if the paste sticks to your thumb.

4. Add coloring and flavoring as desired and extra sifted confectioners' sugar, if necessary, to obtain the correct consistency – i.e. suitable for rolling, which you will soon be able to judge with practice.

5. The icing can be stored in a tightly sealed plastic bag or a plastic container in a cool place for 2–3 days.

Covering a Cake in Fondant Molding Paste

If the cake is covered with marzipan, first brush the marzipan lightly all over with egg white.

If the cake is without marzipan, brush it first with apricot glaze (page 38).

1. Either roll out the icing on a sheet of plastic wrap dredged with a mixture of confectioners' sugar and cornstarch or directly on a working surface dredged with the same mixture. Make sure the rolling pin is also dredged with the sugar mixture. Alternatively roll it out between 2 sheets of plastic wrap. Roll it until it is the width of the top of the cake plus the sides, plus about 1 inch extra; this usually means about 5–6 inches larger than the top of the cake.

2. Support the icing on a rolling pin, pull off the plastic wrap, if using, and place the icing centrally over the top of the cake.

3. Press the icing onto the sides of the cake working it from the center of the cake out to the edge, then down the sides, using your fingers (dipped in a mixture of confectioners' sugar and cornstarch) and using a circular movement to give an even covering.

4. Trim off the excess icing from around the base of the cake using a sharp knife. Smooth out around the base and trim again if necessary. Any wrinkles or marks can be removed by rubbing over in a circular movement with the fingers.

5. For square cakes, if you want straight-edged, rather than rounded-edged corners, you can cut out a piece of icing from each corner, then mold it carefully to conceal the join. However, the joy of this icing is the "soft" edges it gives to corners, which look so good.

6. For any other shaped cake, mold the icing in the same way, but if for a difficult shape, such as a horseshoe, it will be necessary to cut the icing in one or two places to achieve a good even covering.

7. Leave for at least 24 hours to dry and preferably 2–3 days before adding the decoration.

To make molded decorations from fondant molding paste see page 63 for roses and other flowers and page 130 for frills.

Placing the rolled-out paste on top of the cake.

Pressing the paste onto the sides of the cake.

Trimming off excess paste with a sharp knife.

FAULT FINDING GUIDE FOR FONDANT MOLDING PASTE

Fault	Cause	Solution
While mixing the paste The ingredients will not mix together.	Missing ingredients; not enough fluid to stick everything together.	Add missing ingredients; add water then knead and squeeze the icing mixture until it forms a soft but firm ball. Use the thumb test (see page 44).
The mixture is a soft sticky mass which will not form a ball.	Too much fluid has been added.	Remove half the quantity of icing and keep it in a separate bowl covered with a lid so it is not exposed to the air. Add sifted confectioners' sugar to the remaining half, little by little, until you achieve the desired consistency.
After rolling out The fondant cracks or breaks off. It has a scale-like appearance or a dull matt finish.	Not enough fluid has been added.	Add fluid until the mixture is workable. Use the thumb test (see page 44).
The fondant isn't elastic enough; it cracks around the corners and edges as it is placed on the cake.		Work a long spatula gently over the corners until the cracks are sealed. Finish by using your cupped hand to polish and smooth over the corners.
Small air bubbles appear; the fondant is difficult to handle and sticky to the touch.	The consistency is too wet.	Place the fondant back in the bowl and add more sifted confectioners' sugar until the consistency is soft but firm.
The fondant has a wet look.	The atmosphere is causing the icing to sweat.	Leave it and the atmosphere will soon dry it out.
When paste is on the cake The icing is too dry so it is unworkable.		If possible, discard that fondant and use fresh. If this is not possible, take the fondant off the cake in one or two pieces. Remove any yellowish stains (caused by almond paste) and place the icing in a bowl. Dampen your fingers with water and knead the icing until it is workable.
After polishing with cornstarch The icing looks dull.	The surface is too dry and has been polished with too much cornstarch.	Dampen your hands with a clean cloth. Stroke the top of the cake lightly with a circular movement, polishing it until it is smooth. Dampen your hands again and treat the sides in the same way.

FONDANT MOLDING PASTE (approximate quantities)

Square Cake size		6-inch	7-inch	8-inch	9-inch	10-inch	11-inch	12-inch
Round Cake size	6-inch	7-inch	8-inch	9-inch	10-inch	11-inch	12-inch	
Molding paste	¾ lb	1 lb	1½ lb	1¾ lb	2 lb	2¼ lb	2½ lb	3 lb

OTHER FROSTINGS, ICINGS AND FILLINGS

Not to be confused with molding paste, this is a soft icing made from a concentrate and diluted to the consistency of thick cream.

Fondant Icing

To ice an 8-inch round cake

⅔ cup water
2¼ cups granulated sugar
1 tablespoon liquid glucose
a few drops of flavoring or food coloring (optional)

Preparation time: 15 minutes plus cooling

1. Gently heat the water and sugar in a heavy-based pan until the sugar has dissolved. Bring to a boil slowly and add the glucose. Boil until the sugar registers 238°F on a candy thermometer (the soft ball stage).

2. When the bubbles subside, pour one third of the syrup into one bowl and the remainder into another bowl. Leave to cool until a skin forms.

3. Working with the smaller quantity first, beat with a wooden spoon until it is thick and white. It will change from a liquid to a paste and finally to a solid white mass. Knead with the fingers until smooth. Shape into golf-ball sized pieces.

4. Repeat with the larger quantity of fondant icing. If stored in an airtight jar, this icing will keep for up to 2 months.

5. To use, place 3 or 4 pieces of fondant in the top of a double boiler. Warm gently, stirring, until the fondant is smooth and the consistency of thick cream. Add flavoring or coloring if using. If the icing is too thick, add a little water.

Satin Icing

This is a true molding icing with a lemony flavor.

To ice a 9-inch round cake

4 tablespoons butter
4 tablespoons lemon juice
6 cups confectioners' sugar, sifted
a few drops of food coloring

Preparation time: 20 minutes

1. Place the butter and lemon juice in a small saucepan over a gentle heat and stir with a wooden spoon until the butter has melted.

2. Add 2 cups of the confectioners' sugar and heat gently, stirring, until dissolved. When the mixture begins to simmer at the sides of the pan, increase the heat slightly and cook for 2 minutes until it boils gently; do not overboil at this stage or the icing will be too hard.

3. Remove the pan from the heat and add 2 cups more confectioners' sugar. Beat thoroughly with a wooden spoon, then turn the icing into a mixing bowl.

4. Gradually mix in enough of the remaining confectioners' sugar to give a soft dough. Turn the dough onto a surface dusted with confectioners' sugar and knead until it is smooth. Add color, if using.

5. Wrap the ball of icing in plastic wrap and store in the refrigerator for up to 6 weeks. To use, roll out and use as fondant molding paste.

Simple Buttercream

This standard and favorite frosting can be colored and flavored in a wide variety of ways to complement the type of cake being filled and/or frosted; it is also ideal for adding pretty but simple decorations with or without a pastry bag and tube, on cakes covered in buttercream or fondant molding paste. It can be applied straight onto a cake or over a layer of marzipan. If the cake to be covered in buttercream appears to be crumbly, it is best to brush it with apricot glaze first to prevent the crumbs from getting mixed into the frosting. It is simple to make up half quantities of the buttercream. It will also freeze once made.

To frost the top and sides of a 7-inch layer cake; or to fill the cake and frost the top.

1 stick unsalted butter or ½ cup soft margarine
1½–2 cups confectioners' sugar, sifted
a few drops of vanilla extract or other flavoring (optional)
food colorings (optional)
1–2 tablespoons milk, half-and-half, evaporated milk or fruit juice

Preparation time: about 10 minutes

1. Cream the butter or margarine until very soft.

2. Beat in the sugar a little at a time, adding flavoring to taste and coloring, if liked, and sufficient milk or other liquid to give a fairly firm but spreading consistency.

3. Store in an airtight container in the refrigerator for up to a week, if wished. Allow to return to room temperature before use.

4. If using for piping lattice or writing the buttercream may need the addition of a little more milk to make it flow easily without breaking. For piping with a star tube the consistency can be firmer.

Variations

Coffee Omit the vanilla and replace 1 tablespoon of the milk with coffee essence or very strong black coffee; or beat in 2–3 teaspoons coffee powder with the sugar.

Chocolate Add 1–1½ squares melted semisweet chocolate; or dissolve 1–2 tablespoons sifted cocoa powder in a little hot water to give a thin paste, cool and beat into the buttercream in place of some of the milk.

Orange or Lemon Omit the vanilla, replace the milk with orange or lemon juice and add the finely grated zest of 1 orange or lemon and a little orange or yellow liquid food coloring.

Mocha Dissolve 1–2 teaspoons cocoa powder in 1 tablespoon coffee essence or very strong black coffee and add in place of some or all the milk.

Almond Replace the vanilla with almond extract and beat in about 2 tablespoons very finely chopped toasted almonds if

liked. A few drops of green food coloring may be added to give a pale almond green colored buttercream.

Apricot Omit the vanilla and milk and beat in 3 tablespoons sieved apricot jam, a pinch of grated lemon zest, a squeeze of lemon juice and a touch of orange liquid food coloring.

Minted Replace the vanilla extract with peppermint extract – but in moderation – add a few drops green food coloring and/or 3–4 crushed minted chocolate matchsticks.

Liqueur Omit the vanilla and replace the milk with brandy, whiskey, rum, sherry or other liqueur. A few drops of an appropriate food coloring can be added.

Classic Buttercream

Rich and creamy, this makes a good covering or filling but is not suitable for piping.

Makes sufficient to fill and frost the top of a 7- to 8-inch layer cake

6 tablespoons sugar
4 tablespoons water
2 egg yolks
1–1½ sticks unsalted butter

Preparation time: about 20 minutes

1. Put the sugar into a small heavy-based saucepan with the water and mix gently over a low heat until the sugar has completely dissolved. Put a candy thermometer into the pan and boil until it reaches the thread stage, 230°F. If you do not have a thermometer, dip the back of a teaspoon in the syrup and pull the syrup sharply away with the back of another spoon. If no thread forms, boil for a little longer and test again.

2. Put the egg yolks into a bowl and beat well – a hand-held electric beater is ideal for this job. Gradually pour the syrup in a thin stream onto the eggs while beating the mixture continuously.

3. Continue beating the mixture until it is cold and thick.

4. Put the butter into another bowl and beat until soft and creamy, then beat in the egg-yolk mixture a little at a time, until smooth and of a spreading consistency. Use at once, or add flavorings as for buttercream.

Variations

Crème au beurre mousseline is made in the same way as Classic Buttercream, except that the quantity of water is doubled and the diced butter added bit by bit to the egg and syrup mixture. The result is a little lighter. It can be flavored with 1–2 tablespoons liqueur or fruit

juice or a few drops of vanilla extract. To flavor with chocolate, melt 2 squares semisweet chocolate in a bowl set over a bowl of hot water. When the chocolate is liquid and smooth, beat it into the crème au beurre mousseline. Leave in a cool place to set.

Crème au Beurre

To frost and fill an 8-inch layer cake

2 egg whites
1 cup confectioners' sugar, sifted
1 stick unsalted butter
a few drops of flavoring or food coloring (optional)

Preparation time: 15–20 minutes

1. Place the egg whites and sugar in a mixing bowl set over a pan of simmering water and beat until the mixture holds its shape. Cool slightly.

2. Place the butter in a mixing bowl and cream until soft. Beat in the meringue mixture a little at a time. Flavor or color as desired. The crème is ready to

use or can be stored in an airtight container in the refrigerator for 2–3 weeks.

Variations

Chocolate Melt 2 squares semisweet chocolate in a bowl set over a pan of hot water. Cool and beat in with the meringue mixture.

Coffee Add 1 tablespoon coffee essence with the meringue mixture.

Praline Add 3 tablespoons crushed praline (see page 49) with the meringue mixture.

Crème Pâtissière

Makes about 2 cups

1¼ cups milk
¼ cup sugar
2½ tablespoons all-purpose flour
2 tablespoons cornstarch
1 egg + 1 egg yolk
a few drops of vanilla extract
1–2 tablespoons butter

Preparation time: about 10–15 minutes, plus cooling

1. Heat the milk gently in a saucepan but do not let it boil.

2. Put the sugar, flour, cornstarch, egg and egg yolk into a bowl and whisk or beat until very smooth and creamy. Beat in a little of the hot milk.

3. Add the egg mixture to the rest of the milk in the pan and beat until smooth, then cook gently, stirring continuously, until the mixture thickens and comes just to a boil.

4. Add the vanilla extract and butter and cook gently over a low heat for a minute or so, still continuing to stir.

5. Remove from the heat and turn into a bowl. Cover tightly with plastic wrap, or put a piece of wet parchment paper onto the surface of the custard to prevent a skin forming. The custard can be stored in the refrigerator for up to 48 hours before use, preferably in an airtight plastic container.

7-Minute Frosting

Suitable for most cakes, this frosting has a crisp outer crust with a soft inside. To guarantee success a candy thermometer must be used, and it is vital to beat until the frosting really does stand in peaks or it may slide off the cake.

To frost and fill an 8- to 9-inch cake

2¼ cups granulated sugar
⅔ cup water
pinch of cream of tartar
2 egg whites
a few drops of food coloring (optional)

Preparation time: 25 minutes

1. Put the sugar and water into a large heavy-based saucepan and heat gently until the sugar has dissolved. Add the cream of tartar.

2. Insert a candy thermometer. Bring syrup to a boil. Boil to a temperature of 238°F.

3. Meanwhile, beat the egg whites until they are very stiff.

4. Pour the sugar syrup in a thin stream onto the beaten egg whites, beating briskly all the time. Continue to beat until the frosting is thick enough to stand in peaks with the tips just bending over. Add food coloring while beating, if using.

5. Quickly spread the frosting over the cake, pulling it into peaks all over. Leave to set.

Caramel Frosting

To frost and fill an 8-inch round cake

1¼ cups light brown sugar
1 egg white
2 tablespoons hot water
pinch of cream of tartar

Preparation time: 5–7 minutes

1. Put all the ingredients in a bowl set over a pan of hot water and whisk for 5–7 minutes until the mixture is thick. Use immediately, forming into swirls on the cake with a long narrow spatula.

Variation

Mock Frosting Replace the brown sugar with granulated sugar. This can be used as a substitute for 7-minute frosting if you do not have a candy thermometer.

Fudge Frosting

To frost and fill an 8-inch cake

6 tablespoons butter
3 tablespoons milk
3 tablespoons light brown sugar
1 tablespoon molasses
3 cups confectioners' sugar, sifted

Preparation time: 15 minutes

1. Put the butter, milk, brown sugar and molasses in a heatproof bowl over a saucepan of hot but not boiling water. Stir occasionally until the butter and sugar have melted, then remove the bowl from the saucepan.

2. Stir in the confectioners' sugar, then beat with a wooden spoon until the frosting is smooth.

3. Pour quickly over a cake for a smooth coating, or leave to cool, then spread over the cake and swirl with a small narrow spatula. Leave the frosting to set, then decorate as desired.

Praline

SUGAR SYRUPS

This delicious ingredient – basically caramelized almonds – is quickly made and can be stored for 6 weeks in a screw-top jar. It is used in desserts and sauces as well as a flavoring for frostings and fillings. Usually made with almonds, it can be made with any hard nut such as hazelnuts, walnuts or pistachio nuts. Use whole or chopped nuts, skinned or unskinned, toasted or plain, but if making praline powder the nuts should be skinned.

¾ cup unblanched almonds
½ cup sugar
4 tablespoons water

Preparation time: 10 minutes
Cooking time: 20 minutes

1. Wash the almonds in cold water to remove the powder which clings to the skins.

2. Place the sugar and water in a small heavy saucepan over a gentle heat and stir with a wooden spoon until the sugar has dissolved. Remove the spoon and do not stir again (see notes on sugar boiling on page 49).

3. Add the almonds to the syrup, bring to a boil and boil rapidly until it reaches the caramel stage (see right), on the candy thermometer and turns a rich brown color.

4. Pour the nuts and caramel onto an oiled baking sheet resting on a pot stand or board to protect the working surface from the heat. Leave to cool.

5. When cold, crush the praline in a pestle and mortar or with a rolling pin. If very fine praline is needed grind it in a blender.

Sugar syrups are used extensively for making some frostings and toppings like praline and caramel. In cake-making and decoration it is important to be familiar with the different stages of sugar boiling.

When sugar is boiled, its character changes. First it becomes syrupy, then as the temperature rises, it gets thicker and sets to a soft consistency. The boiled sugar continues to change until it becomes a rich brown caramel which is hard and crisp when set. These changes happen at certain temperatures; because of this it is possible to get good results even without a candy thermometer, although it is a useful piece of equipment. Choose one which is clearly marked. A large handle at the top makes it easy to move and a clip on the side ensures it stands upright in the pan and makes it easier to take an accurate reading.

Utensils

Pan Use a clean pan with a heavy base – thin ones will distort with the extreme heat. Aluminum and stainless steel are excellent, or you may be lucky enough to own a copper sugar boiling pan, which, because it will not be tinned, must only be used for boiling sugar. Enamel pans are not suitable and non-stick pans will be scratched by the sugar grains. To clean the pan after use, let it cool, fill with warm water and cover with a lid. Boil until all the sugar has dissolved.
Spoons Always use wooden spoons or spatulas. Metal spoons will scratch the pans, and if the handle becomes hot, will cause unpleasant burns. Plastic spoons will melt.
Heat diffuser This can be useful on a gas burner when long slow cooking is needed.

Ingredients

Sugar Unless otherwise stated, use granulated sugar.
Butter This will give a good flavor to the finished recipe.
Glucose This is used in some sweet-making recipes to prevent crystals forming in the syrup. Sometimes a very small amount of cream of tartar can be used for the same purpose.

For Successful Sugar Boiling

1. Prepare all utensils before starting to boil the sugar.

2. Keep a small pan of water boiling on the stove and keep the thermometer and spoons in this when not in use.

3. Allow the sugar to dissolve slowly, stirring occasionally.

4. Make certain that all the sugar has dissolved before the syrup comes to a boil.

5. Never stir a boiling syrup unless a recipe states otherwise.

6. Wash any sugar crystals from the side of the pan with a clean pastry brush dipped into water.

7. Remove any scum which forms on the top of the syrup with a metal spoon.

8. Cook over a moderate heat unless told to cook gently.

9. Have patience. Sugar may take a long time to rise from one temperature to another and will then rise very rapidly. When the correct temperature is reached, remove the pan from heat.

10. Unless the syrup or caramel is to be used at once, arrest further cooking by plunging the base of the saucepan in a large bowl of cold water.

STAGES OF SUGAR BOILING

The temperature at which sugar reaches each stage can be affected by the atmosphere, and even different bags of sugar can react differently. Altitude affects sugar boiling too; temperatures here are for sea level. For accuracy the full range of temperatures is stated.

Thread (230–234°F). The sugar looks syrupy. Using a small spoon remove a little of the syrup and allow it to fall from the spoon onto a dish. The syrup should form a fine thin thread when the correct stage has been reached. Used in crème au beurre mousseline.

Soft Ball (234–240°F). Drop a small amount of the syrup into cold water then mold into a soft ball with the fingers. Used for fudge.

Hard and Firm Ball (244–266°F). Drop a little syrup into cold water then mold with the fingers into a ball which is firm but pliable. Used for caramels and marshmallows.

Soft Crack (270–290°F). Drop a little syrup into cold water: it should set hard, but will bend slightly and stick to the teeth when bitten. Used for toffees.

Hard Crack (300–310°F). The syrup dropped into cold water will form brittle threads which snap easily. Used for hard toffee.

Caramel (310–338°F). The syrup becomes a light golden brown. As the temperature rises it gets darker in color. If it becomes too dark, the flavor is bitter. When it is almost black it can be used as gravy browning. Used for praline.

DECORATIVE TECHNIQUES

Decoration can be modest or elaborate. Whatever style you choose, you can demonstrate your own individual and creative flair.

This chapter takes you through the basics of cake designing and the repertoire of techniques available. The most important of these is piping with royal paste, a delicate and satisfying skill which takes practice to perfect but which has breathtaking results. Making models and novelty shapes with fondant molding paste is almost equally important for celebration and novelty cakes. The most modest glacé-iced cake can be elevated to elegance with a decoration of sugared fruits, and the versatility of chocolate in cake decoration is unrivaled.

As a beginner, you will find purchased decorations a great help, but as your confidence grows, you will probably find yourself buying less and making more, especially when you discover how easy it is to do quite complicated designs after mastering the techniques outlined in this chapter.

It is worth spending some time planning the design of a cake, particularly if it is to be used for a specific purpose. The most important factor in any design is suitability. Finding the right cake for a particular occasion may not be difficult if that occasion is a little girl's birthday or a family Christmas party, but even then you have the choice of a traditional design or one that is more imaginative. In this book there are ideas for both, and if there is a cake you find attractive, try adapting it.

CAKE TEMPLATES

Soon after you become interested in decorating cakes, you will want to put patterns on top of the cakes. For this it is necessary to have a guide or template, which is placed on top of the base-iced cake to help achieve an exactly symmetrical design. A template can only be used on a hard icing, such as royal icing or fondant molding paste, as softer frostings are marked by the templates.

It is also possible to buy metal or plastic symmetrical rings and cake markers, which help to make curves and scroll shapes on cakes.

Templates are first drawn on thick paper or thin cardboard with the help of rulers, compasses or anything else which will assist in drawing the design or shape you require. Begin with a square or a circle the same size or about 1 inch smaller in width than the cake, depending on the size of the cake. The template must be exact and symmetrical in all ways, because if it is only a little irregular, the whole design of the cake will be spoiled. Once you have made the template it can be kept and used repeatedly. To make it easy to remove the template from the cake it is wise to cut a "V" in the center, which can be bent up rather like a handle.

The template should be positioned centrally on the cake. If it is being used for an outline, you then pipe just around the outside using a pastry bag and writing tube. If it is for some other type of piping, then the design must be pricked out so it remains on top of the cake; simply use a long sharp pin and prick straight through the cardboard or paper to the icing, so that a design is left clearly visible.

A template can also be made for the sides of the cake and is essential if curves or scallops are incorporated into the design.

Don't forget that with tiered cakes you need to make similar templates in graduated sizes to fit each tier.

When piping out the design keep as close as possible to the template, or pipe exactly over the pin-pricked design keeping the curves even. Where sharp corners are required, break the icing at the corner and start again. Trim off with a pin if the icing is not absolutely even. Do not lift off the template until the piped outline is completely dry, otherwise you are likely to disturb the piping.

Other designs can be worked freehand, but if it is to be even in any way, then a template is a necessity.

1. Cutting out a template for the Square Birthday Cake on pages 130–1.

2. Lay the template on top of the cake and prick out the design around it.

To Make a Template for a Round Cake

1. Cut a circle of paper the size of the top of the cake or up to 1 inch smaller.

2. For an 8-point design, fold the circle in half then into quarters and again into eighths, creasing the folds firmly.

3. For a 6-point design, fold the circle first in half then carefully into three making sure each piece is exactly even (it is most accurate if you use a compass).

4. Check the design and how it needs to be drawn onto the folded paper, then draw it. Cut out carefully and open out the template, to check whether it is correct. If preferred, the template can be drawn on wax paper first to make sure it is right, before transferring to thick paper or cardboard.

Designs suitable for round cakes

Scallop Fold a circle of paper into eight points and draw a scallop.

Hilary Use a circle of paper and fold into eighths (fold into quarters and then once again). Draw a deep curve to come about halfway across the paper; then draw a second shallow curve to go right up to the edge.

Curved Both concave and convex curves are suitable. Use a circle of paper, fold into eighths and draw a curve across the end.

Heart Use a circle of paper and fold into eighths. Fold in half again to find the center of the heart and mark a point ¾–1½ inches down the fold. Draw the heart shape from this point around to the other edge.

Petal Use a circle of paper and fold into eighths, then fold again just to mark the center of each section at the edge. Draw and cut out a deep petal shape coming to the mark.

Laura Use a circle of paper and fold into eighths. Cut out a scroll or scallop, beginning about 1 inch down the fold and ending about 1 inch along from the corner on the curved edge.

Fleur Use a circle of paper and fold into sixths. Cut out a concave curve. For a **Hexagon** cut a straight edge across the top.

Eighteenth Birthday Cake Use a circle of paper and fold into sixths. See page 132 for full instructions.

Three Tier Wedding Cake Use three circles of paper for the cakes and one for the board. See page 98 for full instructions.

Round Christmas Cake Use a circle of paper and fold into sixths. See page 108 for full instructions.

To Make a Template for a Square Cake

1. Cut a square of wax or other paper the size of the top of the cake or up to 1 inch smaller.

2. For a 4-point design, fold the square in half diagonally to give a triangle, then in half again to give a smaller triangle.

3. For an 8-point design, fold in half a third time to give a still smaller triangle.

Designs Suitable for Square Cakes

The scallop, Hilary and Laura designs can be used on square cakes as well as on round cakes by using a square shaped paper template.

Pointed Petal Fold a square of paper into quarters and then into eighths. Keep the fold to the left and make a mark 2–4 inches (depending on the size of the cake) down the right-hand side. Draw a deep curved arc to the point of the fold.

Eliza Use a square of paper and fold into quarters. Keep the folded edges downward and cut

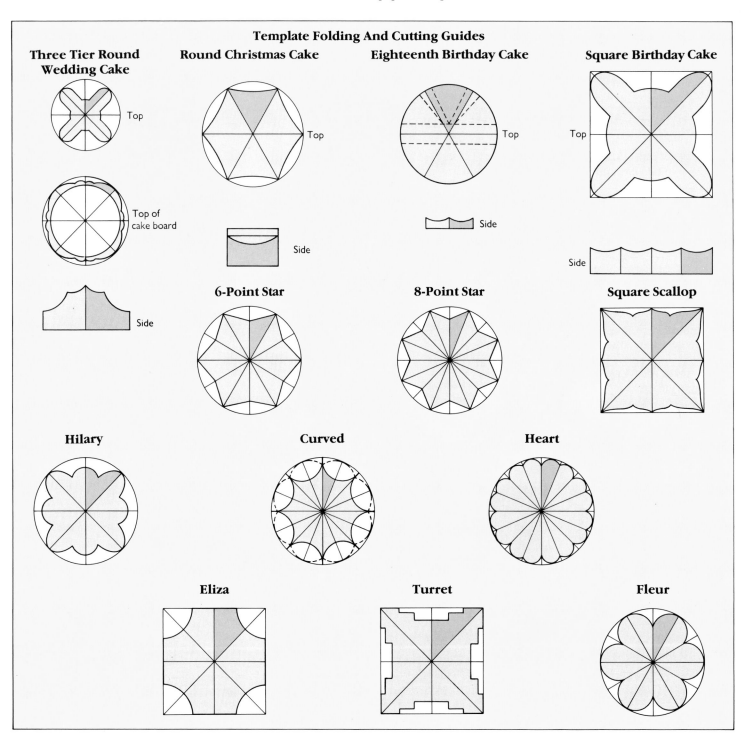

Template Folding And Cutting Guides

Three Tier Round Wedding Cake — Top, Top of cake board, Side

Round Christmas Cake — Top, Side

Eighteenth Birthday Cake — Top, Side

Square Birthday Cake — Top, Side

6-Point Star

8-Point Star

Square Scallop

Hilary

Curved

Heart

Eliza

Turret

Fleur

out a semicircle from the top corner.

Turret Fold a square into eighths. Beginning at the outer open edge draw two downward steps toward the opposite edge. The sizes of the steps can be varied for different designs, or make just one step.

Square Birthday Cake Use a square of paper and fold into a triangle; fold the triangle in half, then in half once again. See page 130 for full instructions.

To Make a Template for the Sides of a Cake

1. For a round cake, measure the circumference of the cake with a piece of string, then use to cut a strip of paper the length of the sides and the depth of the cake. If a 4- or 8-point design, fold the paper into quarters or eighths, then draw the design onto the section, and cut right through the rest to give a design to reach around the whole cake. If a 6-point design, fold into sixths and cut as

before. If preferred, the shape can be transferred to thick paper (but not cardboard), so that it is firm enough to be held around the sides of the cake while the design is pricked out or is outlined in icing. If it is a difficult pattern to follow, for instance with lots of curves, it is simpler if the cake is tilted slightly while you ice.

2. For a square cake, it is necessary only to cut a piece of paper the size of one side of the cake (provided they are all symmetrical). Halve this and draw the design, then cut out, unfold and use as for a round cake, holding the template against each side in turn.

Making Special Shaped Cakes

Cakes made in shapes different from the traditional round or square give opportunities for some different decoration styles as well. It is not necessary to have specially designed cake pans, either; round or square cakes can be adapted without difficulty to numerous shapes.

To Make a Horseshoe-Shaped Cake

Begin with a round cake and, using a paper pattern, first cut out a central circle 3–3½ inches in diameter. Cut out an even wedge-shaped piece from the ring to complete the horseshoe.

A horseshoe-shaped cake in this book is the Good Luck Cake on page 110.

To Make a Petal-Shaped Cake

A petal cake can be cut from a slightly larger 9-inch round cake. First draw a template using a pair of compasses to get it exactly even; then place on the cake and, using a sharp knife, cut out the scallops taking it right down to the base. Trim up until perfectly even. This cake will need a thicker than usual layer of apricot glaze to keep the crumbs of cake in place.

To Make an Oval-Shaped Cake

Select an oval glass dish whose length matches the diameter of the round cake you have made. Using this as a pattern, place on top of the cake and cut all around it with a sharp knife, keeping the sides straight. Alternatively, draw an oval shape the size you require on a piece of cardboard and cut around this.

To Make a Heart-Shaped Cake

Begin with a round cake. Cut a heart-shaped paper pattern. The "V" should be about 1½ inches deep on an 8-inch round cake and gradually deeper on larger cakes. The piece taken out should then be cut in half, reversed and put at the other end of the cake to make a point. You will need to trim off a small triangular piece to make a good fit. Attach to the cake with apricot glaze or buttercream.

Heart-shaped cakes in the book are the Basket of Chocolates on pages 142–3, and the Valentine's Day cakes on pages 102–3.

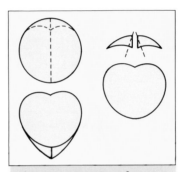

Cutting instructions for making a heart-shaped cake.

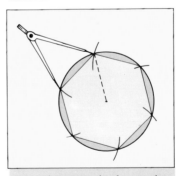

For a hexagonal cake, mark six points with a compass.

To Make a Hexagonal-Shaped Cake

Begin with a round cake. Take a compass and measure the length from the center of the cake to the edge. Make a mark on the edge. Using the same measurement, position the compass point at the mark on the edge and make another mark with the other end, also on the edge. Continue in this way to mark off six equal sections at the edge. Join the marks with straight lines and cut the cake straight downwards along the lines to make the hexagonal shape.

A two-tier Hexagonal Wedding Cake is included in this book on pages 92.

To Make an Octagonal-Shaped Cake

An eight-sided cake may be cut quite simply from a square cake. Bake a square cake slightly larger than required, then carefully cut off each corner as evenly as possible to give eight sides all the same length.

All types of shaped cake pans are usually available to buy or rent from specialist cake decorating suppliers (see page 224) and some larger kitchenware stores.

EQUIPMENT

To decorate cakes with a professional finish it is important to have the correct equipment. The beginner can get started with a few essentials. The more ambitious your projects, the more you will enjoy building up a collection of specialized items that will enable you to achieve a wide range of spectacular effects in your designs.

It is essential to have the items necessary for cake icing and decorating gathered together before you start. Icing does not take kindly to being left while you dash out to buy a forgotten tube or icing comb. Some things are everyday kitchen items but others are more specialized and may have to be obtained from kitchenware stores or cake decorating suppliers. Store the equipment carefully so that it does not get damaged. A chip out of an icing ruler will always leave a dent in the icing when used. A bent tube will always result in uneven lines.

It is advisable always to buy the best quality equipment available; it will last well and should not rust, bend out of shape or chip in awkward places.

If possible keep some equipment especially for making icing. For instance, wooden spoons and plastic bowls pick up flavors from strongly flavored foods and get stained too. Wooden spoons are better than metal for making and beating royal icing and preferable to using a mixer, because although it makes the task easier, a mixer produces far too many air bubbles. These are difficult to disperse and can ruin the flat surface of a cake if they are not carefully removed.

Stainless steel and plastic icing rulers are available in various lengths. They should be

firm enough to keep straight but slightly flexible to help keep the icing smooth as the ruler is drawn across the cake. Practice will soon teach you how much pressure to use when doing this. You can also get serrated plastic rulers which can be used on both royal icing and buttercream to obtain a serrated effect.

The iced sides of a cake can be smoothed with a long narrow spatula but a plastic icing comb or scraper makes the job much easier. They produce perfectly smooth sides and sharp corners, or, in the case of a serrated-edged comb,

interesting wavy designs. It is easiest to use an icing comb if you have an icing turntable to swivel the cake at a regulated pace as the comb or scraper is pulled around the sides. For the beginner, an upturned plate or a simple turntable will suffice, but as you advance it is wise to invest in a really good one. Whether plastic or metal it should be heavy enough to take any size of cake and should swivel easily and smoothly at the touch of a finger. Choose a high- or low-standing one as you prefer.

CAKE DECORATING EQUIPMENT

The following items are needed to supplement those listed on page 12.

icing ruler
icing comb or scraper
wooden toothpicks
small bowls or containers with
    airtight seals
selection of basic decorating
    tubes including fine, medium
    and thick writing, small
    medium and large star,
    rosette, ribbon, small petal
    and leaf
pastry bags (see right)
tweezers
kitchen shears
selection of liquid food
    colorings
As you become more skillful,
    you may want to add the
    following:
icing turntable
icing nail
metal or plastic templates
pair of compasses and/or cake
    markers
fine paintbrushes

For cutting shapes out of fondant molding paste, you can use a cookie cutter, a pastry cutter, a piping tube, even lids and tops, as long as they are scrupulously clean. Printing shapes onto fondant icing can be almost as effective as piping on decorations with royal icing.

A selection of decorating equipment

PASTRY BAGS

Four different types of pastry bag are available, either hand-made or bought from department stores. The most useful are parchment paper decorating cones. They are the simplest to use for all types of icings, and any size tube can be used. They are ideal for piping small quantities of icing and it is a good idea to make several at a time. Do not overfill the cone; instead open it carefully and refill it when necessary, taking care not to split it or let it unfold. The filled cone can be kept in a plastic bag for a few hours, while completing another decoration. Because you can make several at a time it is useful if you need to use different colored icing on the same cake.

Plastic heat-sealed pastry bags are washable and re-usable. Because they prevent moisture seeping through they do not get sticky on contact with your hands. A coupling may be required for attaching tubes to the bag. They are difficult for the novice to use, as it is easy to overfill the bags, making them stiff to use and inclined to burst at the seams. Nylon bags may also need a coupling and can cause the hands to sweat. They are long-lasting and hygienic. Canvas pastry bags are very well made and can be boiled after use. They usually need a coupling to attach the tubes.

Preparing the Pastry Bags

If using a paper decorating cone (see page 56), cut about ½ inch off the tip and insert the tube. Half to two-thirds fill the cone with icing, using a small spatula or teaspoon to push it well down into the cone, then fold over the top carefully, continuing to push the icing down to the tip. Do the same with a nylon pastry bag after fitting the special screw coupling and

tube, but do not put in too much icing or the bag will be difficult to manipulate. The easiest way to fill a nylon bag is to place the tube between the finger and thumb of your left hand and fold the rest of the bag over your hand so it is inside out; in this way as you spoon in the icing with the right hand it can be pressed down to the tip by the left hand and the outside of the bag stays free of icing.

Holding the Pastry Bag

You will soon know how you prefer to hold the pastry bag to make it work best for you, but here is the easiest way. For paper decorating cones, open your hand and place the bag across your palm with tip toward the ends of your fingers. Place the thumb on the folded end of the cone (to keep in the icing), then fold over the other four fingers to hold the cone tightly. Use the other hand to steady it and apply a steady pressure to the cone until the icing begins to come out of the tube. With a nylon pastry bag, place the thumb and forefinger around the icing in the bag and twist the bag tightly two or three times to prevent the icing coming out or moving up the bag. Then hold the bag tightly over the twist, again with the thumb and forefinger, with the rest of the fingers folded over the bag. Apply pressure with the other hand.

Alternatively, for fine work and lattice hold the bag in both hands with the thumbs over the end, and the rest of both hands supporting the weight underneath.

Consistency of Icings

It is most important to use icing of the correct consistency for the job in hand. Royal icing varies with the type of icing to be done (see page 39). For dots, shells, rosettes, etc., it should be stiff enough to stand in well formed but not hard peaks, but for writing or trellis it must be slacker or the icing will break. However, it must not be too soft or it will not hold its shape. Glacé icing for piping lines, straightforward writing, etc., needs to be stiffer than that used to coat a cake: add extra sifted confectioners' sugar. Buttercream should be stiff enough to pull into softish peaks, but not too firm or it will not pipe evenly. This can be used to work designs of shells, stars, etc., on a cake.

Trial Run

With all decorating, practice makes perfect. Once piped, royal icing becomes hard and cannot be used again, so if you are a complete beginner try practicing with a nylon pastry bag filled with reconstituted instant mashed potato, using the varying shapes of large tubes. The potato can be scooped up many times and re-used until you get the "feel" of handling a pastry bag. Even when you are using royal icing, if you are not quite sure or are trying out a new design, practice an edging, border or writing on something other than the cake. An upturned cake pan is ideal and the icing will soak off easily in warm water.

Decorations other than those actually piped onto the cake should be made at least 24 hours in advance. Base-iced cakes are also best left uncovered at room temperature for 24 hours before beginning the decorations.

Making a Parchment Paper Decorating Cone

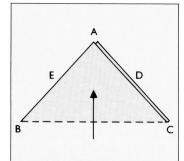

1. Cut a piece of non-stick parchment paper to a 10-inch square and fold in half to form a triangle.

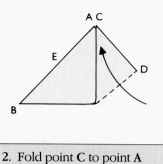

2. Fold point **C** to point **A** on a flat surface and crease firmly.

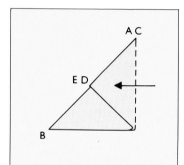

3. Fold point **D** over to point **E** and crease firmly.

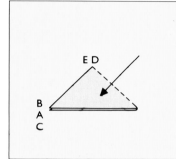

4. Fold point **AC** down to point **B** and crease firmly. Hold the bag at point **ED** and open it up to make a cone.

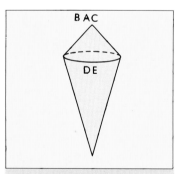

5. Secure the join with tape. Fold the top point down firmly inside the cone.

6. Cut off the tip so that the tube will fit neatly inside the cone with about one third of the tube showing.

COLORING FROSTINGS AND ICINGS

It is now possible to buy just about any color and shade of liquid food coloring, or powder or paste, to tint frosting or icing any color you may wish. However, if you can only obtain the more basic colors, it is useful to know how to mix them to make other colors.

You get a truer color when you are adding colorings to a white frosting or icing, such as royal or glacé, than you do when coloring buttercreams, because they are cream-colored to start with.

It is not possible to be precise about the amount of food coloring to add to achieve a specific color but do remember to add colors very sparingly; it is very easy to add more, but impossible to remove the color once added. Dip the tip of a toothpick into the coloring, then add this to the frosting or icing. Continue to add color in this way, beating after each addition until the correct color is obtained. It may take longer but is a really safe way of doing it. The color of royal icing darkens slightly on drying. All these colors can be used with marzipan.

MAKING AND MIXING COLORS

Color required	Mixture	Use for
Pink	Pink coloring or a touch of red.	Christening and birthday cakes.
Peach	Peach food coloring, which may need a touch of pink to prevent it looking too orange; or mix it with pink and yellow and possibly a touch of orange.	Marzipan fruits. Frosting, icing and decoration.
Flesh tone	Bright red with a little yellow.	For molded decorations.
Cream	A touch of golden yellow (not primrose) with a touch of pink and/or orange.	Wedding cake piped decorations and flowers.
Red	A paste or powder coloring is needed to produce clear red.	Christmas cake decorations, Ruby Wedding Anniversary Cake.
Mauve/Purple	Use a mauve color if available, but add a touch of true blue if it is too pink. Make your own mauve/purple color with pink and blue but be careful that it does not go too gray.	Piping, and molded decorations.
Dark green	Add 2 drops of green to 1 of blue.	For marzipan leaves.
Light green	Add 1 drop green to royal icing for a delicate shade.	Run-outs and piping.
Apple green	Bright green shade.	For marzipan fruits.
Golden yellow	1 drop bright orange.	For marzipan fruits.
Orange	Use bright yellow with a little red.	For marzipan fruits.
Brown	Red and green makes a mid-brown; add a touch of blue for a darker tone, a touch of yellow for a sandy tone.	For molded decorations, e.g. teddy bears.
Black	Black with a touch of blue is very deep.	For details on novelty cakes.

DECORATING TUBES

Decorating tubes are also known as tips and nozzles. There is a large range available, in both plain and screw-on types, covering all styles. They are sold by number which can be confusing, because – with the exception of writing tubes which are uniformly graded from 00 (very fine) to 4 (thick) – not all manufacturers use the same number for the same shaped tube. The numbers given here are used by at least two manufacturers, and the name will identify the style in question. Even so, always check on a particular manufacturer's chart before buying. Screw-on tubes are specially for use with icing syringes or nylon pastry bags. Although screw collar tubes can also be used in paper decorating cones, plain tubes are best because they fit neatly into the cone.

Make sure when you select tubes that they are perfectly shaped, with no dents or badly fitting seams. For example, misshapen points of rosettes will give unevenly piped stars and writing tubes which are slightly oval instead of perfectly round will affect the resulting design.

Larger tubes, sometimes called "large," "vegetable" or "meringue" tubes are available in metal or plastic. They are used for piping whipped cream, mashed potato, meringues, éclairs and so on. They come in a range of sizes, plain, rope and star-shaped, and are often used on elaborate layer cakes or something needing a heavy decoration.

USING THE TUBES

Plain Tubes

Place the tube in the pastry bag (fine, medium or thick writing) and fill with icing. Before you begin make sure the tip of the tube is wiped clean.

Straight lines Place the tip of the tube where the line is to begin. Press the icing out slowly and as it emerges lift the tube about 1 inch above the surface. Move your hand in the direction of the line to be piped using the other hand to guide the bag and keeping the icing flowing evenly. About ½ inch from where the line should finish, stop squeezing and bring the tip of the tube gently back to the surface. Break off the icing. By holding the icing above the surface it helps even shaky hands keep straight lines – with a little practice! Some people prefer to pipe lines toward them while others like to work from left to right or vice versa – it doesn't matter which. If you finish with a blob of icing at the end of a line, remove it carefully with a small sharp knife.

Dots Hold the tube upright and just touching the surface. Squeeze the bag gently, at the same time lifting the tube to allow the icing to flow out. Stop squeezing when you have the size of dot you want and remove the tube quickly with a slightly shaking action, to avoid leaving a tail. If a tail does remain, remove it with a hat pin. Dots can be made in all sizes and with any of the writing tubes. Two-tier dots can be formed by dipping the tube downward into the icing halfway through, giving the dot a large base and small top.

Lattice This attractive way of using straight lines can be worked in many ways. First pipe a series of parallel straight lines in one direction, keeping them evenly spaced over the area of the cake to be covered. Leave to dry. Turn the cake and pipe a second layer of parallel lines over the first set but at right angles or an angle of 45° to it, to make squares or diamonds. The design can be left at this but is better with a third layer piped over the first lines to give a raised effect. With very fine lattice up to five layers can be worked. Let each layer dry before starting the next so that if a mistake is made, the wet layer can be easily lifted off with a skewer or small sharp knife. Lattice designs can also be worked using curved lines.

Curved lines These can be worked quite easily, once you have mastered control of the icing, to produce loops, plain scrolls, and so on. For curves you really need a template (see pages 51–3), and it is a good idea to practice on thin cardboard or wax paper. Draw a series of curves and pipe over these until you feel confident. Place the tip of the tube at the beginning of the curve, lift it up above the surface as for straight lines and allow the icing to follow the curve around, lowering the tube to touch the surface between each scallop.

Writing The design should be pricked or traced onto the cake to make sure it is central and will fit in. First write the words on wax paper, then position on the cake and carefully prick out on the surface using a pin. When the paper is removed the guide lines for the writing remain. Pipe the words in white icing first and then, when dry, overpipe with a color – mistakes in color on a white cake are difficult to cover up. It is best to begin with capitals. All styles of writing can be used as you progress.

Lacework Using a fine or medium writing tube, this is a very effective decoration. It is like scribbling and can be added to set designs on cakes. Lacework is as easy to apply to the top of a cake as it is to sides. Hold the tube almost upright and just above the surface so that the icing flows out and move the tube around quickly and easily to form the pattern.

Star Tubes

These vary widely in size and shape of the star they produce. Some have five points, others six or eight and even more points as they become larger. For beginners, concentrate on 5-point (No. 13) or 8-point (No. 8). Many designs can be made using star tubes.

Stars Place a star tube in the bag and fill with icing of the correct consistency. Hold the bag upright and just above the surface. Pipe out sufficient icing to form the star and sharply lift the tube away with a down and up movement. Stars should sit fairly flat on the surface, not pulled up into a central point.

Rosettes or whirls These are piped with star tubes but in a circular movement like making a large dot. Begin just above the surface and move the tube in a complete circle to enclose the middle. Finish off quickly to leave a slightly raised point in the center but not a "tail." Varying sizes and slightly differing shapes can be made with different tubes.

Shells Use either a star tube or a special shell tube (No. 12); both make good shells and are worked in the same way but the shell tube gives a rather fuller and fatter shell. Hold the pastry bag at an angle to the surface and a little above it. Start in the center of the shell and first move the tube away from you, keeping an even pressure of icing, then back toward you with a little more pressure for the "fat" part of the shell. Release pressure and pull off sharply to form a point. To make a shell edging simply repeat the shells, linking them in a line by beginning the next shell over the tail of the previous one. It is very important to finish off each shell and lift the tube between each one or a bulky and uneven border will result.

Scrolls These are useful for tops and sides of cakes but do need a lot of practice, particularly if you want to achieve graduated scrolls. A simple scroll edging can be worked using either a star or shell tube, but if they are to be larger or individual scrolls on the top of the cake, a template will ensure evenness (see pages 51–3). Hold the pastry bag as for a straight line and with the tube almost on the surface. Work a question mark shape beginning with a fairly thick head and gradually releasing the pressure while finishing off in a long pointed tail. A series of scrolls can be worked the same way or several variations can be worked to make attractive designs or double-ended scrolls. Other scrolls can be worked adding twists and graduating the width and size, and using larger and smaller tubes.

Coils This is a border or edging and is made using a star tube. Begin just touching the surface and continue making small circular movements in a counter-clockwise direction. Coils can be worked from left to right or vice versa as you prefer, and variations of a coiled border are numerous.

Ribbon or Basket Tube

This tube (No. 22) is thick, with either one or both sides serrated and is flat to produce a ridged ribbon of icing. Some tubes are evenly ribbed, others are uneven. A ribbon tube is used for a flat pleated ribbon edging, is worked continuously by overlapping each pleat, as well as for basket work or "weaving" on a cake. To do the latter you need one pastry bag fitted with a ribbon tube and another fitted with a medium or thick writing tube. Hold the ribbon tube sideways to the cake and at an angle and pipe three short lines the same length as each other, one above each other and with the width of the tip of the tube between each one. Pipe a straight vertical line with the writing tube along the edge of the three ribbon lines. Next pipe three more straight lines with the ribbon tube of the same length as the first ones to fill in the gaps but beginning halfway along those and covering the straight line. Pipe another vertical line at the end of these lines and continue building up first with the ribbon tube and then the vertical line.

Three-Point Star Tube (Trefoil)

This tube (No. 4) is used for borders or small stars on edges or at the base of cakes. It is unusual and very simple and can be worked either upright or upside-down.

Leaf Tube

This tube (No. 10) has a pointed tip sometimes with an indentation in the center of the point. You can make three overlapping movements for each leaf or if this sounds a little bit difficult, simpler leaves can be made in the same way but without the overlapping movement, and other shaped leaves can easily be devised. Leaves can be piped straight onto cakes, or onto non-stick parchment paper first , if preferred. Leave the leaves to dry before attaching to the cake with a dab of icing.

Petal or Rose Tube

This tube (No. 18) is used especially for making flowers. Flowers are made separately and when they are dry attached to the cake. Flowers need practice. (To pipe a rose see page 60.)

Top row, from left: fine writing tube; medium writing tube; thick writing tube; 3-point star tube; 8-point star tube; leaf tube.
Bottom row, from left: shell tube; fine 5-point star; petal or rose tube; ribbon tube; fancy star; forget-me-not tube; 3-thread tube

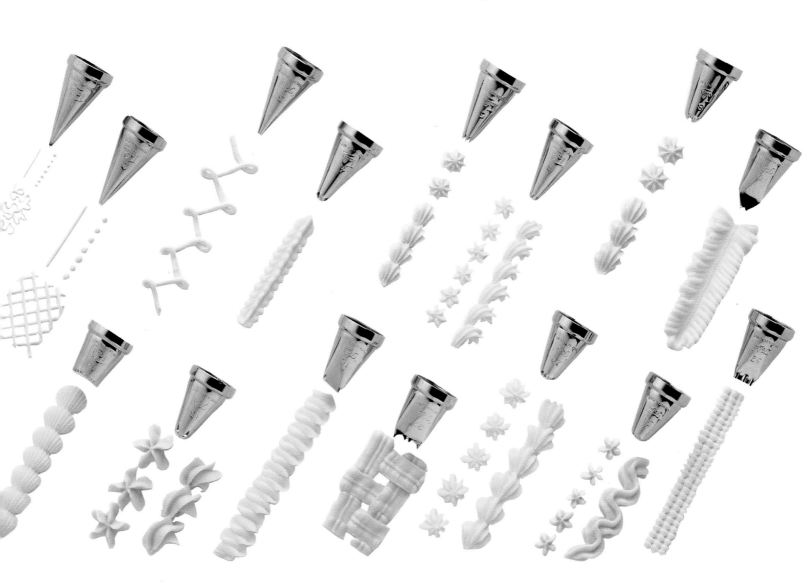

SPECIAL DECORATIONS

Special decorations can be made from royal icing, fondant molding paste and marzipan, to be attached to an iced cake when it is dry. These include piped flowers and leaves, all types of models, cut-outs and run-outs. All can be made 3–4 weeks in advance, covered in tissue or wax paper and kept in a dry atmosphere.

PIPED FLOWERS IN ROYAL ICING

All icing takes practice, but making flowers takes a lot of patience too, until you feel confident and can make all sorts of different flowers with ease. Roses are probably the most popular flower to make and are a good start if you are a beginner. There are numerous other flowers you can make by following instructions or by making your own shape.

To make flowers you need an icing nail or a cork impaled on a skewer, a quantity of non-stick parchment or wax paper cut into 1–2 inch squares, and a paper decorating cone or plastic pastry bag fitted with a large, medium or fine petal tube. For most flowers use a medium tube, which is the easiest to obtain and the easiest to use. Half fill the bag with icing and fold down ready to begin. Secure a square of paper to the icing nail with a dab of icing.

Leaves

Use a leaf tube and white or green royal icing. Place a sheet of wax paper on the work surface. Begin with the tube touching the paper and the end turned up a fraction. Press gently and as the icing begins to emerge, raise the tube slightly. When the leaf is large enough, break off sharply to leave a point. The bag can be gently twisted or moved up and down to give different shapes and the size can be increased by extra pressure.

A paper decorating cone without a tube can successfully be used for smaller leaves. Fill the cone to the halfway point with icing, but don't cut off the tip. Press the tip of the cone flat, then snip off the point in the shape of an arrow. Place the tip of the cone on the paper, holding it at a slight angle. Press out the icing and pull away quickly to make a tapering point. Mark on a vein with a toothpick. Serrated fern-like leaves can be made by moving the cone backwards and forwards. When you have had sufficient practice, leaves may be piped straight onto the cake.

Daisy

Probably the simplest of the piped icing flowers, the daisy is also the most effective. Pipe five or six or more slightly rounded but also pointed petals, each separate from the next. Then, using a No. 2 writing tube pipe a large dot in the center of the flower (if preferred several dots can be piped) using a contrasting color. These flowers can be made in a variety of colors, either with the petals in one color and the center white or yellow, or the petals white with a colored (or yellow) center.

Primrose

Use yellow icing and work with the thick edge of the petal tube to the center, keeping it flat. Pipe from the center outwards. Go halfway back in, then out again, then back to the center, to give a heart-shaped petal. Pipe five petals in all. Using a no. 1 writing tube and deep yellow or pale orange icing, pipe a dot in the middle.

Rose

Hold the pastry bag so that the thin edge of the tube is pointing upwards, then, squeezing evenly and twisting the nail at the same time, pipe a tight coil for the center of the rose. Continue to add five or six petals, piping the icing and twisting at the same time, but taking each petal only about three quarters of the way around the flower. Begin in a different part of the flower each time and make sure the base of the tube tips in toward the center of the flower or the rose will expand at the base and the top instead of just at the top.

For rose buds, keep the petals tight and only add two after the first central coil has been piped.

To make a rose, first pipe a tight coil for the center.

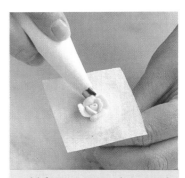

Add five or six petals around the center to complete.

RUN-OUTS

A run-out is a shaped piece of icing, such as an initial or animal. The outline is piped first, then the center filled using a technique called flooding. They are also suitable for plaques which can have a further decoration piped or placed on top. They are made from royal icing and can be piped straight onto a cake or onto non-stick parchment paper or wax paper and attached to the cake when dry. Outlines can be traced from the stencils on page 62 or from designs on greetings cards. Run-outs can be stored in an airtight container for a few months without discoloring.

For simple outline designs, follow the instructions for run-out hearts. If you are making a small number of a complex design proceed as follows. Draw or trace the outlines onto a piece of cardboard. Secure a piece of wax paper over the cardboard. Using a no. 2 writing tube and icing the same color as that to be used for flooding, trace the outlines of the drawing. Make more than you need – run-outs are very fragile.

To flood the shapes, thin down a little royal icing with lemon juice or egg white (see page 39 for a guide to the correct consistency) so that it flows. Spoon it into the center of the outline if it is large, or pipe it in using a no. 3 writing tube or a paper decorating cone with the end snipped off. Use a toothpick to ease the icing into corners and to prick any air bubbles. Leave to dry before completing the details. After 2–3 days, remove the paper; place the run-out on a thick book, slightly overlapping the edge. Pull the paper gently downwards, then turn the run-out around, pulling the paper away until all the edges are loose. Gently pull off the paper.

Butterfly

Use the template on page 62. Outline the wings and body separately. Pipe two antennae with a no. 1 writing tube. Decorate the wings with piped lines and dots around the edge using a no. 1 writing tube and a contrasting color. Attach the wings and antennae to the body with a little icing. The wings should tilt upwards slightly; rest them on a little plasticine until they are dry.

Flowers

Outline the edges and the lines of the petals. Flood with icing of the same color or tinted slightly lighter in tone. Pipe several tiny dots in the center with yellow icing and a no. 1 writing tube. Pansies are extremely pretty, especially when two shades are used in the same flower. Outline the large lower petal in each flower first, flood with icing and leave to dry. When set, outline the remaining petals and fill with a lighter shade. To finish, paint streaks from the center of the petals with food coloring.

Ivy Leaves

When the flooded leaf is dry, use a no. 1 writing tube to pipe a thin line down the center to make a vein and stalk.

To Make Run-out Hearts

1. Draw a 1½-inch heart shape and trace the number required plus extra for breakages on the underside of wax or parchment paper. Turn the paper over and fix it to a board.

2. Tint icing of the correct consistency (see page 39) to the desired color. Place a little icing in a parchment paper decorating cone fitted with a no. 2 writing tube.

3. Pipe around the outline of the heart design, making sure there are no breaks and that the corners are closed.

4. Thin a little icing with egg white or lemon juice until it is of a flooding consistency (see page 39). Place the icing in a paper decorating cone without a tube. Snip the point off the cone and fill in the design.

5. Use a toothpick to ease the icing into the corners and prick any air bubbles. The icing should be level and slightly raised from the outline.

6. Leave to dry for 2–3 days. Peel off the paper very carefully. Store the run-out hearts in an airtight container, layered between sheets of tissue paper.

Step 1
Tracing the outlines of the heart shape on to wax paper.

Step 3
Piping around the outlines.

Step 4
Flooding the outlines, using a paper decorating cone.

Step 6
Removing the dry run-out hearts from the paper.

Original Run-Outs

Once you have become proficient at making run-outs, you can progress from templates of simple shapes to inventing your own designs or using illustrations from greetings cards or magazines. This gives you the opportunity to decorate a cake with motifs particularly appropriate for an individual or a special event – two lovebirds for a wedding anniversary, a cradle for a new baby, a teddy bear, kitten or horse. Trace the design onto wax paper as described on page 61, and when it is dry pipe or paint details and features on as appropriate. If you have a steady hand with a fine paintbrush you can achieve sophisticated results with the range of food colorings now available.

You can make a run-out decoration from any fairly simple design traced onto wax paper.

Decoration Templates

MOLDED DECORATIONS

Both fondant molding paste and marzipan can be used for modeling, though molding paste is best for delicate shapes. It is easier to color molding paste to obtain true or bright colors because you start with a white base; but marzipan will turn a good color if you use a white or natural colored variety. This is available from some supermarkets, or cake decorating suppliers, or it can be made at home by substituting 2 egg whites for the egg or egg yolks. Knead food colorings into molding paste or marzipan until the mixture is evenly colored and no longer streaky. If the paste or marzipan becomes too soft or sticky, add extra confectioners' sugar. For dark colors use the concentrated colorings, which are available from specialist decorating suppliers. A touch of brown coloring or gravy browning will tone down an overbright color. Extra color or features can be painted on with fine paintbrush and liquid food colorings.

For rolling out, use a surface lightly dredged with confectioners' sugar or a mixture of confectioners' sugar and cornstarch, or roll out between sheets of plastic wrap. The latter method makes it easier to move the rolled-out paste or marzipan.

Egg cartons are a great help for resting models on as you make them. Wooden toothpicks and a fork are other useful implements.

Decorations from Fondant Molding Paste

This is an extremely pliable paste. It holds its shape even when paper thin, and is excellent for making flowers. Keep the paste to be molded wrapped in a plastic bag as it dries quickly if exposed to air. Leave the decoration for 24 hours to dry and harden.

Rose

Make a cone with a small piece of paste and press out the base to form a stand. Take a piece of paste the size of a pea, dip it in cornstarch and roll it into a ball in the palm of your hand. Take a hard-boiled egg in your other hand and use it to flatten the ball of paste, working with quick gentle strokes. Use more cornstarch if it is too sticky. The edge of the petal should be paper thin.

Carefully wrap the petal around the cone, turning the edges outwards. Repeat this process, overlapping each petal, until you have the shape you want. Use a toothpick if necessary to help mold the petals. Leave to dry overnight then cut off the base. When using several roses together in a decoration (for example, the Rose Wedding Cake on pages 94–5), color some a shade darker for a more elaborate effect.

To mold a rose, attach thin petals to the basic cone.

Continue to add overlapping petals to complete the rose.

To make a daisy, make a base at one end of a ball of paste.

Painting the tips of the petals to complete the daisy.

Daisy

Make a small ball of paste and pinch the bottom to form a base. Flatten the ball (as for the petals of a rose) to make a thin round. Using small scissors, cut the edges of the round to form petals, then turn them upwards. Using a toothpick, make holes in the center. Paint the center with yellow food coloring. Using pink food coloring and a fine paintbrush, paint the tips of the petals. Leave to dry. This daisy is very realistic, unlike the stylized version obtained by piping.

Leaves

Color the paste green and roll out the icing thinly on a surface dusted with cornstarch. Cut out leaf shapes with a small knife. Lift the shapes one by one into the palm of your hand and flatten the edges (as for the rose) and pinch each end into a point. Leave to dry overnight.

Mark veins on each leaf, using a fine paintbrush or the point of a knife dipped into coloring.

Christmas Rose

Use the inside of an egg carton to mold this flower. Cut a small circle of wax paper for each compartment and cut a line through to the center to shape a cone. Line each compartment with a circle of paper. Using white paste, shape five petals as for the rose and place them overlapping inside the paper cone. (See illustration overleaf.)

Shape a small piece of yellow molding paste into a ball and press it lightly into the center. If liked, use yellow royal icing to pipe stamens in the center. Leave to dry.

For a Christmas rose, place five white petals overlapping.

To finish, place a ball of yellow paste in the center.

To shape the chick's beak, use a small pair of scissors.

Attach the mouse's ears to the head with a dab of paste.

Chick

Shape two balls of yellow paste, one half the size of the other. Stick the small ball on top of the large one for the head. Using small scissors, snip the small ball to form a beak shape and paint the mouth with yellow coloring. Position colored sugar balls for the eyes.

Rabbit

Mold a piece of paste into an egg shape. Mold a smaller piece into an oval and place on top of the narrow end of the egg shape to form the head. Shape two large ears and attach them to the head. Shape a small ball of paste for the tail and attach it to the body with a dab of paste. Paint the inside of the ears with a little pink coloring. For the eyes, use pink royal icing and pipe on with a No. 1 writing tube.

Mouse

Mold a piece of pink (or white) icing into a cone shape for the body. Shape two pieces of icing into ears, working them like the petals of the rose. Stick the ears onto the pointed (head) end of the body with a dab of paste. Roll a small piece of icing into a thin tail and attach it to the rounded end of the body. For the eyes, use pink royal icing and pipe them on with a No. 1 writing tube, or use silver candy balls.

Molded Marzipan Decorations

Almond paste (marzipan) used for modeling must be supple enough to bend without cracking but firm enough to hold its shape. Purchased ready-made marzipan is ideal to use for making decorations as you can simply break off the amount you need. If using homemade almond paste, make a large quantity and keep it in a plastic bag, breaking off small amounts as you need them; it will keep for several weeks. Care must be taken not to over-knead, as this will make the paste oily and difficult to handle.

To color the paste, add food coloring a little at a time (see color chart on page 57), kneading it in until it is evenly colored. Keep the paste not being worked in a plastic bag, as it dries out quickly if exposed to air. Leave the decorations for 2–3 days to dry before positioning them on the cake. Alternatively make them up to 4 weeks in advance and store them in an airtight tin.

Simple Flowers

To make daffodils, use yellow marzipan. Curl around a small strip for the trumpet and attach four or five petals to the base, curving outwards. For violets, make five small circles from purple marzipan. Mold one into a cone. Attach three to one side, and place the last circle underneath to the other side. Use yellow marzipan for stamens.

Oranges and Lemons

Color some paste orange or lemon. Roll into a ball for an orange and a plump oval for a lemon. Roll the shapes over the fine surface of a grater to get the texture of the skin. Press in a clove at one end for the calyx.

Apples

Color some paste green and roll it into a ball, making a slight indentation at the top and the base. Cut a clove in half and use the top for the calyx and the rest for the stalk. Paint pink coloring on one side, gradually blending it into the green.

Bananas

Color some paste yellow and form it into a banana shape. Paint with brown coloring to mark the characteristic stripes on the skin.

Cluster of Grapes

Color some paste green or purple and shape into a cone. Roll out small balls for the grapes and stick them neatly on to the cone. Press in a clove for the stalk.

Carrots

Color some paste orange and shape into small cones. Make stalks from a small piece of green-colored paste. Mark the skin lightly with a pointed knife.

Cabbage

Color some paste green. Shape about two thirds into a small ball for the heart. Shape the remainder into six or eight leaves. Arrange the leaves around the heart, overlapping each one. Press gently at the base to join them together.

Parsnips

Shape some natural-colored paste into a cone. Paint with a little brown coloring and make a stalk from a small piece of green-colored paste. If the shape is slightly imperfect it will look more realistic.

Peas

Shape tiny pieces of green-colored paste into balls.

Pears

Form some natural-colored marzipan into a pear shape. Use a clove for the stem and calyx as for apples. Paint with green and pink coloring, gradually blending in the colors.

Strawberries

Color some paste red and shape into a rounded cone. Roll over the surface of a grater or granulated sugar. Make a hull from a small piece of green-colored paste and press onto the top of the strawberry.

Plums

Color some paste purple, using pink and blue coloring. Roll into an egg shape and mark a line down one side. Press a clove into the top for the stalk.

Above: Molded marzipan fruits and vegetables

Marzipan Cut-Outs

These are decorations made from flat cut-out shapes of marzipan and colored and assembled as required. The designs below all use templates which can be found on page 62. You can also draw your own templates or use designs from greetings cards, wrapping paper, etc. And pastry cutters in unusual shapes will also make simple effective marzipan cut-out decorations.

Mistletoe	**Holly Leaves**	**Christmas Tree**	**Stars**
Mistletoe leaves are made from a paler green marzipan than that needed for holly leaves. Cut them into long thin tongue shapes with rounded ends. Mark a heavy vein down the center with a knife and leave to dry. White mistletoe berries can be rolled from white or natural colored marzipan.	Color some marzipan deep green. Roll it out evenly on a piece of wax paper. Cut each piece into rectangles. Use the template to cut out leaf shapes with a sharp pointed knife, or use the base of a decorating tube to cut out the leaf shape. Mark veins on the leaf with the point of a knife. Leave to dry, laying some of the leaves over a spoon handle to give a curved shape. Color a little marzipan red and roll into tiny balls for berries.	Using the template, trace the outline of the tree and tub onto wax paper and transfer to a piece of cardboard. Roll out a little green and a little red marzipan and place the templates on top. Cut out carefully around the pattern with the point of a sharp knife. Attach the tub to the tree and leave on wax paper to dry. Pipe dots of icing on the points of the tree and place colored sugar balls on top.	Make a template of a star. Roll out some natural or yellow marzipan evenly. Cut out stars using the template as a guide (or use a star-shaped pastry cutter). Leave to dry. Using white royal icing (see page 39) and a No. 1 writing tube, pipe lines around the edges of the stars. Decorate the points with silver candy balls.

SUGARED FLOWERS AND FRUIT

Sugar-frosting is easy to do and gives a pretty finish to cakes covered with buttercream, glacé icing or frosting, or as a decoration on cheesecakes. Sugared fruits should be used within 2 hours, leaves and flowers may be kept for up to 6 weeks. Store between layers of tissue paper in an airtight container. Use small non-poisonous spring flowers, heathers, roses or violets, herb leaves such as mint and fruits such as currants, grapes, cherries, and segments of mandarin orange. Put 1 egg white in a small bowl with 2 teaspoons of cold water and whisk until lightly frothy. Make sure the flower heads or fruit are clean and dry, then paint all over with the egg white, or dip into the egg white, until evenly coated. Sprinkle with superfine sugar, or roll in sugar, and leave to dry on wax paper lightly dusted with sugar.

Crystallized Flowers

These attractive decorations keep well if made with care. Real flowers can be used as decorations at any time of year, instead of making them from marzipan or fondant molding paste. Always make more than you need and avoid using any flowers which are poisonous.

Use fairly small flowers, such as primroses and violets, which are not quite fully open. Remove all bruised petals and leaves. With roses, the petals can be crystallized individually and rearranged into flowers again. Mint leaves crystallize well too. There are two methods of crystallization.

Method 1

Put ½ cup triple-strength rosewater into a screwtop jar with 2 oz gum arabic (available from specialist suppliers) and leave overnight or longer, giving an occasional shake until the gum arabic crystals have dissolved. Hold the flower carefully by the stem (the stem can be removed when the flower is crystallized). Using a fine paintbrush, paint the rosewater mixture all over the petals on both sides. Quickly roll or dredge in superfine sugar, making sure the flower is

Sugared flowers and leaves

completely covered, then shake off the surplus sugar. Place on a wire rack or on wax or non-stick parchment paper and leave to dry in a fairly warm place for 1–2 days. Pack carefully between layers of tissue paper to store.

Method 2

Melt 2¼ cups granulated sugar in a heavy-bottomed saucepan. Bring to a boil, then strain through scalded cheesecloth into a clean pan to remove any impurities. Bring back to a boil and boil to 220°F on a candy thermometer. Leave to cool to about blood heat. Arrange the flowers on a wire rack over a shallow pan and pour the sugar syrup over each flower, using a fine paintbrush to ensure the whole flower is coated. Drain off excess syrup, then leave the flowers undisturbed in a warm place for 12–18 hours or until crystals begin to form on the surface. This means that crystallization is taking place. Pack away carefully as described far left.

CHOCOLATE

Whether used in elaborate cakes, rich puddings or simple confectionery, chocolate is one of the most versatile ingredients in baking and sweet-making. Unsweetened chocolate, semisweet chocolate and sweet or German chocolate are all suitable for cooking (see page 11, basic ingredients). All are sold in individually wrapped 1-ounce squares, in packages. For chocolate decorations, both semisweet and sweet chocolate may be used, although semi-sweet chocolate is preferable as it gives a nice contrast to sweet icings and frostings.

The simplest way to use chocolate is to grate it on a fine, medium or coarse grater for the top and/or sides of cakes and small cakes, cheesecakes and creamy desserts. Chill the chocolate square a little first, and rinse your hands in cold running water before you start. The warmth of your hands may make the chocolate melt as you work. Hold the chocolate in foil or wax paper. Almost as simple is to make chocolate curls by peeling thin strips off a large block of chocolate using a potato peeler. Peel the strips directly onto a cake or dessert, or chill after making and use to decorate the sides of a cream-covered or frosted cake.

Squares, Triangles and Circles

Spread a thin – ⅛ inch – even layer of melted chocolate on a sheet of wax or non-stick parchment paper using a long narrow spatula. Leave to set, but not completely hard.

Use a ruler and a sharp knife to mark out even-sized squares or rectangles. To make triangles, cut the squares in half. To make long-sided triangles, cut the rectangles in half. To make circles, cut the chocolate into small rounds using a pastry cutter. When they have set quite

hard, carefully lift the tip of the paper and peel it away from the chocolate. These shapes may be decorated with a piped chocolate design if desired. Fill a parchment paper decorating cone with melted chocolate. Snip off the end and pipe straight or zig-zag lines directly onto the shapes. Leave them in a cool place to set.

Rose Leaves

Pick fresh, undamaged leaves with clearly marked veins. Wash them thoroughly and dry carefully. Melt 2 squares semisweet or sweet chocolate in a *wide* heatproof bowl set over a pan of hot water. Stir until smooth, then cool to 92–110°F or until the chocolate has a smooth, glossy appearance. Using a fine brush, spread it over the underside of each leaf. You can also draw the underside of each leaf across the surface of the melted chocolate. Make sure the leaf is evenly covered right to the edge. Leave to set, chocolate side up. When the chocolate is hard, carefully peel away the leaf, starting at the stem. Make more than you will need for the design, as these fragile shapes may break in handling.

See the Rose Leaf Gâteau, page 172, for a sumptuous use of chocolate leaves.

Caraque and Scrolls

Spread a thin layer of melted chocolate onto a marble slab or cold work surface using a long narrow spatula. Leave until just firm but not hard. Using a sharp thin-bladed knife at an angle of about 45° push the knife across the chocolate with a slight sawing movement, scraping off a thin layer; this will form a long scroll. Take care not to cut too deeply into the chocolate or it will not curl. Place the curls on a plate and chill. Store in a

container between layers of wax paper.

Chocolate Easter Eggs

These are fun to make and the small ones make good decorations for Easter cakes. Molds are available in plastic, metal and china, and in various sizes. They can be obtained from kitchenware stores and specialist cake decorating suppliers. Brush the inside of the mold with melted chocolate to give it an even layer, then chill in the refrigerator until set. Repeat with another coat on small eggs or two further coats on larger ones. Chill thoroughly, then very carefully remove the eggs from the molds.

Paint melted chocolate on the underside of each leaf.

When the chocolate is set, carefully peel away the leaf.

Opposite: Simple homemade chocolate decorations

SIMPLE DECORATIONS

Melting Chocolate

To melt chocolate successfully, place the chocolate, broken into pieces, in the top of a double boiler or in a small heatproof bowl that will fit securely over the top of a saucepan. Partially fill the pan with hot water, making sure that the water does not touch the bowl or the top pan of the double boiler. Overheated chocolate becomes stiff and granular. Bring the water almost to a boil, then remove from the heat and place the bowl or top of the double boiler over the pan. Stir the chocolate with a wooden spoon until it is melted and smooth.

Chocolate can only be melted in a saucepan placed over direct heat when liquid is added at the beginning, for example when making some sauces. The minimum amount of liquid should be ⅔ cup and the sauce should be stirred vigorously while the chocolate is melting.

Some of the most tempting cakes can be achieved with ease. The Lemon Cake on page 78, pretty as it is, is simply a sponge covered in glacé icing – the easiest icing to make – decorated with sugar flowers and the sides coated in coconut. There are a number of ready-made edible decorations available which you can use to good effect such as silver and other candy balls, chocolate mint sticks, miniature macaroons, delicate cornet and wafer cookies, brightly colored chocolate candies, marrons glacés, and candied cherries and angelica. The sides of a cake can be coated in chopped or flaked nuts, toasted or colored flaked coconut or chocolate strands. Use tiny foil-covered chocolate eggs for an Easter cake, and silver and gold chocolate "money" for a children's party. For special cakes, a few chocolate-dipped strawberries or pieces of chocolate-dipped crystallized ginger clustered on top make a stylish finish.

Other simple decorations you can make yourself, include chocolate shapes (pages 68–9), praline (page 49), crystallized flowers and sugared fruits (pages 66–7), and molded figures (pages 63–5). Decorative extras can be a successful element in cake design if carefully used. These are the non-edible features such as ribbons, silver leaves and so on. The important thing to remember is to use them in moder-

ation – a cake is ultimately to be eaten, not a sculpture, and non-edible decorations should be subsidiary parts of the whole. When buying ribbons, candle-holders, candles and cake frills, buy them before making the cake, so that if you need to color the icing you can make sure it tones in well with the decorations. Paper cake frills come in various designs, ornate silver ones for weddings and anniversaries, printed ones for other occasions. If you make your own frill from fabric or broad lace remember to back it with a strip of wax paper, to prevent staining from the cake. Silver horse-shoes and leaves are useful, especially if used in conjunction with piped or molded flowers on a wedding cake. Tiered wedding cakes will need pillars to support them and a tiny silver vase for the top to hold a posy of fresh – they *must* be fresh – flowers on top. There is no reason why other celebration cakes should not also be decorated with a rosebud, a sprig of violets or primroses: but keep it light.

INTRODUCTION
PART 2

In the tempting variety of cakes in this section you are sure to find something for every occasion. The recipes – which range from those which are quick and easy to prepare to others which are more demanding of time and effort – all prove that cakes are just as much fun to make as they are to eat. The first chapter in this section includes a selection of simply constructed Family Cakes; it is here that you'll find well-established favorites such as Chocolate Battenburg or a Jelly Roll made luxurious with swirls of buttercream. Instructions for standard cake batters are given, while in subsequent chapters reference is made to the basic recipes in Part 1.

In the next chapter, Celebration Cakes, there are some stunning ideas for formal cakes such as weddings, special birthdays, Christmas and many more. In this area of cake decorating the classic craft of piping with royal icing comes into its own. Novelty Cakes includes a number of fantastic ideas for children's parties – but there are also many adults who'd love to celebrate getting older with an unusual birthday cake such as a Clock, a Hat or a Basket of Chocolates. All the cakes in this book are delicious, but those in the Fancy Cakes chapter are made with particularly irresistible ingredients: fresh cream, chocolate, nuts and exotic fruits. And the chapter on Cheesecakes demonstrates the versatility of this popular type of cake.

Part 2 concludes with a selection of delectable Small Cakes and Pastries, deliciously pretty little mouthfuls just right for after-dinner coffee, Sunday tea or children's parties. Whatever its size, a cake makes every day special.

FAMILY CAKES

*A homemade cake is always a special pleasure. Included here
are recipes to satisfy all tastes – from simple butter cakes to
feather-iced and decorated cakes.*

Most modern cooks are busy people, increasingly dependent on
ready-made dishes which – though reliable – can be monotonous.
There is no nicer way to brighten up your family's weekly menu than
with a homemade cake, spoiling them a little and at the same time
enjoying creating something that is both good to look at and
delicious to eat.

An indispensable part of successful cake-making is the pleasure it
gives to the cook as well as those who are lucky enough to eat the
finished product. Perhaps this is because, however simple, every cake
adds a touch of luxury to life. Luxurious they may be, but cakes can
be easy to prepare, as is clearly shown in this chapter. Here are a
range of recipes to satisfy everyone's idea of the perfect cake whether
it's Apricot Butterscotch Cake (page 86) by the fireside or Lemon
Cake (page 78) on a summer day. Most are based on butter or
sponge cake batters, some with different flavors such as chocolate,
coffee or orange. The frostings used are easy to make and work with,
and the decorations are uncomplicated but carefully applied. If you
have never covered a cake with marzipan, make the Chocolate
Battenburg (page 74) to get an idea of its texture and flexibility
before progressing to its use on a rich fruit cake under royal icing.
Make the Lemon Jelly Roll (page 76) one of your specialties and you
will have mastered a skill which will enable you to make fragile
roulades with ease. To get the feel of working with a pastry bag,
make a cake like Hazelnut Coffee Cake (page 80) that is decorated
with swirls of buttercream. Practicing in this way will build up your

skills for the highly decorative effects that are achieved with piped royal icing. For an invaluable and versatile decoration, try Strawberry Feather Bar (page 82) with its attractive and stylish patterned glacé icing.

There is no mystery to making perfect cakes: the "secret" is simply a combination of patience and confidence, two qualities that will be sure to increase the more cakes you make. As you try out these recipes, you will find that two or three become favorites with you and your family, the ones that you always enjoy making and which become part of your repertoire.

Whatever your preference, there is an example here to fit the bill, whether it's a sticky Dark Ginger Cake (page 87), sophisticated Chocolate Mint Cake (page 84) or fruity St Clement's Ring (page 80). Delicious cakes like these can be relied on to transform a dull table, and yet are relatively straightforward to prepare.

Coffee mornings, afternoon tea, an unexpected visit from friends: all these occasions take on a festive air when a cake appears. Once you have enjoyed the delighted response a good cake always receives, you will be encouraged to experiment with your own variations and to progress to some of the more demanding recipes in the following chapters.

Although cakes have always been part of traditional family fare, the combination of busy modern life and the current emphasis on healthy living and a careful diet have tended to push them to the sidelines of the menu.

This is a double misfortune, since life should not be so hectic that we cannot find time to practice the art of cooking as well as the joys of eating; and the indulgence of a fine homemade cake – especially if you use the Healthy Sponge Cake recipe on page 22 – is scarcely harmful if it is occasional. If it is to be occasional, then let it be special, and that means homemade.

Preparing traditional cakes for your family is the ideal way to develop confidence in the skills that can ultimately be displayed in the creation of wonderful celebration cakes.

Chocolate Battenburg

Battenburg is the perfect cake to serve with coffee or tea. Rectangular cakes like this are easy to serve, and the two-color pattern is easy to achieve by halving two cakes lengthwise and arranging them with the colors diagonally opposite.

½ cup sugar
1 stick butter or hard
  margarine
2 eggs
1 cup self-rising cake flour,
  sifted
1 teaspoon coffee essence
2 teaspoons cocoa powder
Chocolate buttercream:
4 tablespoons butter, softened
1 cup confectioners' sugar,
  sifted
1 tablespoon cocoa powder,
  sifted
2–3 teaspoons milk
a few drops of vanilla extract
Topping:
6–8 oz white marzipan
To decorate:
16 chocolate-coffee candysticks

Preparation time: about 40 minutes
Cooking time: about 30 minutes
Oven: 350°F

1. Grease and line an 8-inch square cake pan with greased wax paper or use non-stick parchment paper. Make a pleat down the center of the paper which stands up about 1½ inches. This divides the pan so that the two flavors of cake can be baked at the same time but kept separate.

2. Use the sugar, butter or margarine, eggs and flour to make a butter cake (see page 18).

3. Divide the batter in half and add the coffee essence to one portion and the cocoa to the other. Place one of the mixtures in one section of the pan and the other mixture in the other, and smooth the tops level with a round-bladed knife.

4. Place in a preheated oven and bake for about 30 minutes or until the cakes are well risen and firm to the touch. Unmold them carefully onto a wire rack without removing the paper. Leave until cold.

5. To make the chocolate buttercream, cream the butter, confectioners' sugar and cocoa together, adding the milk a little at a time to give a spreading consistency. Add a few drops of vanilla extract to enhance the flavor.

6. Remove the paper from the cakes and stand them one on top of the other. Trim the cakes so that they are equal in size. Cut them in half lengthwise and arrange the pieces so that the chocolate and coffee cakes are opposite.

7. Spread a little buttercream over the pieces of cake and stick them together. Spread a little buttercream around the sides – not at the ends – and set the remainder of the cream aside for decoration.

8. Roll out the marzipan to a rectangle just large enough to enclose the cake. Stand the cake on top of the marzipan. Wrap the marzipan around the cake, keeping the seam underneath.

9. Trim the ends of the marzipan level with the cake and pinch a "finger-and-thumb" design along the two top edges of marzipan. Mark a criss-cross pattern along the top of the cake with a sharp knife. Leave the marzipan to dry.

10. Place the remaining buttercream in a pastry bag fitted with a star tube. Pipe a line of buttercream along the top of the cake. Decorate with chocolate candysticks arranged in pairs.

Variations

Leave one half of the cake batter plain and tint the other half and the marzipan with a little pink food coloring. For a chocolate and lemon cake, flavor one half with cocoa powder and the other with grated lemon zest; sandwich the cakes with lemon cheese and decorate with crystallized lemon slices.

Caribbean Rum Layer Cake

This impressive cake is, in fact, quick and easy to make. The cake layers can be frozen, wrapped in foil, for up to 3 months, but once assembled the cake should be served on the same day.

¾ cup sugar
¾ cup soft margarine
3 eggs
1½ cups self-rising cake flour
1½ teaspoons baking powder
1 tablespoon rum

Filling:
1½ cups canned crushed
  pineapple
1½ teaspoons arrowroot
⅔ cup heavy or whipping
  cream
1–2 tablespoons rum
½ cup sliced flaked almonds,
  toasted

To decorate:
pieces of candied pineapple

Preparation time: about 30 minutes
Cooking time: about 15 minutes
Oven: 375°F

1. Grease and base-line three 8-inch round layer cake pans.

2. Put the sugar, margarine and eggs into a bowl and sift in the flour and baking powder. Add the rum.

3. Beat the mixture by hand or with an electric mixer for 2–3 minutes, until it is quite smooth.

4. Divide the batter between the pans and smooth the tops level with a round-bladed knife. Place in a preheated oven and bake for about 15 minutes or until the cakes are well risen and firm to the touch.

5. Unmold the cakes onto a wire rack to cool completely. When they are cold, remove the paper.

6. To make the filling, strain off 1–2 tablespoons of pineapple juice into a small bowl and blend in the arrowroot. Heat the remaining crushed pineapple and juice to just below boiling point. Add the blended arrowroot and bring to a boil, stirring continuously until thickened and clear. Leave to cool.

7. Whip the cream and rum together. Fold half the flavored cream into the cooled pineapple mixture with half the almonds.

8. Spread the cream and pineapple mixture over two layers of cake and place them one on top of the other. Place the third cake on top and spread the remaining cream over it, swirling it into an attractive pattern with the knife.

9. Sprinkle the remaining toasted almonds in the center of the cake and arrange pieces of candied pineapple around the edge.

Left: Chocolate Battenburg
Right: Caribbean rum layer cake

Strawberries and Cream Layer Cake

A cake with strawberries and cream is perfect for a summer tea party. Genoese sponge cake is a variant on the whisked mixture used for the jelly roll which has better keeping qualities because of the added butter. The cake can be made several days in advance of assembling and will keep very well in an airtight tin.

Genoese sponge cake:
4 tablespoons butter or
*   margarine*
3 eggs
6 tablespoons sugar
¾ cup cake flour, sifted twice
Filling and decoration:
1 ¼ cups heavy cream, lightly
*   whipped*
1 pint strawberries, hulled

Preparation time: 30 minutes
Cooking time: 25 minutes
Oven: 375°F

1. Grease and line two 7-inch layer cake pans with greased wax paper or non-stick parchment paper.

2. Place the butter in a bowl set over a pan of hot water to melt without becoming hot. Set it aside for 2–3 minutes.

3. Put the eggs in a mixing bowl set over a pan of hot water and beat for a few seconds. Add the sugar and continue beating until the mixture is thick and pale in color and forms a trail when the beater is lifted. Remove from the heat and beat until the mixture is cool. (If you use an electric mixer, no added heat is necessary.)

4. Fold in half the sifted flour with a metal spoon. Pour in half the melted butter in a thin stream at the side of the bowl. Fold in the remaining flour and add the remaining butter in the same way.

5. Pour the batter into the prepared pans and bake in a preheated oven for 25 minutes until the cakes are golden brown, well risen and firm to the touch. Unmold carefully and leave to cool on a wire rack. Carefully peel off the lining paper.

6. Slice the strawberries in half, keeping one strawberry whole for the center of the cake. Mix together one third of the cream with half the fruit and spread over one of the cakes. Place the other cake on top.

7. Spread some of the remaining cream over the top of the cake and make a pattern with the tip of a knife. Place the remaining cream in a pastry bag fitted with a star tube and pipe swirls around the top edge. Arrange strawberry halves around the swirls of cream and place the whole strawberry in the middle of the cake.

Lemon Roulade

Covering a jelly roll with buttercream turns it into a special treat. Roll the cake up the moment it comes out of the oven: if it is allowed to cool it will crack. Let it cool and set while rolled up before unrolling it to add the filling.

¼ cup sugar
2 eggs
½ cup cake flour
½ teaspoon baking powder
grated zest of ½ lemon
sugar, for dredging
Lemon buttercream:
1 stick butter, softened
1½–2 cups confectioners'
*   sugar, sifted*
1–2 tablespoons lemon juice
Filling:
3–4 tablespoons lemon cheese
To decorate:
chocolate triangles (see page
*   68)*

Preparation time: about 15 minutes
Cooking time: 10–12 minutes
Oven: 400°F

1. Grease and line an 11- × 7-inch jelly roll pan with greased wax paper or non-stick parchment paper.

2. Place the sugar and eggs in a mixing bowl set over a saucepan of hot, not boiling, water. Beat until the mixture is thick and pale in color and the beater leaves a heavy trail when lifted. Remove the bowl from the saucepan and continue beating until the mixture is cool. (If you use an electric mixer no added heat is necessary.)

3. Sift the flour and baking powder together. Sift them again over the beaten mixture. Fold the flour quickly into the mixture using a metal spoon.

4. Turn the batter into the prepared pan and spread it out evenly, making sure the corners are filled. Place in a preheated oven and bake for 10–12 minutes or until the cake springs back when gently pressed with the fingertips and has begun to shrink slightly from the sides of the pan.

5. While the cake is in the oven, place a damp dish towel on the working surface and lay a sheet of wax paper or non-stick parchment paper on it. If using wax paper, sprinkle it liberally with sugar.

6. When the cake is cooked, unmold it onto the sugared paper. Quickly peel off the lining paper and trim the edges of the cake with a sharp knife. Make an indentation with a round-bladed knife about 1 inch from the edge along the short side nearest to you. Starting at this end, roll up the cake loosely with the paper inside. Fold back the top of the paper so that it does not stick to the cake as it cools.

7. To make the lemon buttercream, cream the butter and confectioners' sugar together, adding the lemon juice a little at a time to give a spreading consistency.

8. Unroll the cooled cake carefully and remove the paper. Spread the cake with the lemon cheese and roll it up again.

9. Place the buttercream in a pastry bag fitted with a star tube. Pipe rows of buttercream along the roll and one row of shells or rosettes on top. Decorate with chocolate triangles.

From the top: Strawberries and cream layer cake, Lemon roulade

Lemon Cake

¾ cup sugar
4 eggs
grated zest of 1 lemon
1 cup cake flour, sifted
6 tablespoons lemon cheese
Glacé icing:
2½ cups confectioners' sugar
2–3 tablespoons warm water
a few drops of yellow food
    coloring
1 drop orange food coloring
To decorate:
⅓ cup dried shredded coconut
sugar flowers

Preparation time: 20 minutes
Cooking time: 30–35 minutes
Oven: 375°F

1. Grease and line a 9-inch round cake pan with greased wax paper or non-stick parchment paper.

2. Place the sugar, eggs and lemon zest in a mixing bowl set over a saucepan of hot, not boiling, water. Beat until the mixture is thick and pale in color and the beater leaves a heavy trail when lifted. Remove the bowl from the saucepan and continue beating until the mixture is cool. (If you use an electric mixer no added heat is necessary.)

3. Sift the flour over the mixture and fold it in quickly using a metal spoon.

4. Turn the batter into the prepared pan and place in a preheated oven. Bake for 30–35 minutes or until the cake springs back when lightly pressed and shrinks slightly from the sides of the pan. Unmold onto a wire rack to cool.

5. When the cake is cool, remove the lining paper and cut the cake in half horizontally. Put the two layers back together with 4 tablespoons of the lemon cheese. Spread the remaining lemon cheese around the side of the cake.

6. Place the shredded coconut in a small bowl and add a drop of yellow food coloring. Stir until the coconut is evenly colored.

7. Place the coconut on a sheet of wax paper. Hold the cake between the palms of your hand and roll it lightly in the coconut until the sides are covered. Place the cake on a 9-inch round board.

8. To make the glacé icing, sift the confectioners' sugar into a mixing bowl and very gradually add the water. The icing should be thick enough to coat the back of the spoon thickly. Add 2–3 drops of yellow food coloring. Immediately pour three quarters of the icing onto the top of the cake and spread it almost to the edge with a long narrow spatula. Gently bang the cake two or three times on the table to help the icing flow to the edge. Leave for a few minutes to dry.

9. Add a few more drops of yellow and a drop of orange coloring to the remaining icing. Place in a parchment paper decorating cone fitted with a No. 2 writing tube. Pipe parallel lines across the top of the cake, then more lines across them to form diamond shapes. Place a sugar flower in each diamond and leave to set.

Mocha Layered Cake

Mocha is a delicious blend of chocolate and coffee flavors. This is equally good with coffee mid-morning or after dinner.

6 tablespoons sugar
3 eggs
½ cup cake flour, sifted
1 tablespoon instant coffee
    powder
Chocolate buttercream:
1 stick butter
2 cups confectioners' sugar,
    sifted
2 tablespoons cocoa powder
    blended with 2 tablespoons
    boiling water and cooled
1 tablespoon milk
To decorate:
3 squares semisweet chocolate,
    grated
chocolate candies

Preparation time: 20 minutes
Cooking time: 20–25 minutes
Oven: 375°F

1. Grease and line 8- × 12-inch jelly roll pan with greased wax paper or non-stick parchment paper.

2. Place the sugar and eggs in a mixing bowl set over a saucepan of hot, not boiling, water. Beat until the mixture is thick and pale in color and the beater leaves a heavy trail when lifted. Remove the bowl from the saucepan and continue beating until the mixture is cool. (If you use an electric mixer no added heat is necessary.)

3. Sift the flour with the cocoa powder over the mixture and fold it in quickly using a metal spoon.

4. Turn the batter into the prepared pan and place in a preheated oven. Bake for 20–25 minutes or until the cake springs back when lightly pressed and shrinks from the sides of the pan. Unmold onto a wire rack to cool.

5. To make the chocolate buttercream, cream the butter and confectioners' sugar together, adding the cocoa powder dissolved in water and the milk a little at a time to give a spreading consistency.

6. When the cake is cool, remove the lining paper and cut the cake into 3 equal pieces. Put the layers back together using one third of the chocolate buttercream.

7. Spread more buttercream on the sides of the cake and coat with the grated chocolate. Place on a cake board.

8. Spread more buttercream over the top of the cake and mark out lines lengthwise with a knife. Place the remaining buttercream in a parchment paper decorating cone fitted with a fluted tube and pipe a border along the edges of the cake. Decorate with chocolate candies.

Variation

Make your own chocolate decorations such as triangles or leaves (see page 68). Caraque is a good choice for a rectangular cake, the strips laid closely side by side and lightly dusted with confectioners' sugar.

From the top: Lemon cake, Mocha layered cake

St Clement's Ring

A light butter cake becomes extra special with the tangy flavor of citrus fruit and baked in an attractive ring shape.

1 ½ sticks butter or margarine
¾ cup sugar
3 eggs
1 cup self-rising cake flour, sifted
½ cup ground almonds
grated zest of 1 orange
grated zest of 1 lemon
Glacé icing:
2 cups confectioners' sugar
2–3 tablespoons lemon juice
a few drops of yellow food coloring (optional)
To decorate:
shredded orange and lemon zest

Preparation time: 20 minutes
Cooking time: 40–45 minutes
Oven: 325°F

1. Grease and flour an 8-inch ring mold.

2. Cream the butter and sugar together until light and fluffy. Beat in one egg and mix well. Beat in the second egg, adding a little flour. Add the third egg with a little more flour and beat till smooth.

3. Fold in the remaining flour with the ground almonds and the grated orange and lemon zests.

4. Pour the batter into the prepared pan and bake in a preheated oven for 40–45 minutes until well risen and golden brown. Unmold carefully and leave to cool on a wire rack.

St Clement's Day Feast

Until recently the feast of St Clement, which falls on November 23, was a popular celebration in many parts of the British Isles. St Clement is the patron saint of blacksmiths. On their special day spiced cakes and apples were part of the traditionalfare, and children would bob for apples. There are a number of variations on clementing cakes. Among the simplest are little tarts made of pie pastry. These pastry cases were filled with a creamed mixture of butter, sugar and egg yolk, into which the finely chopped flesh of an orange and a lemon were blended with the juice and strips of zest, and finally beaten egg white. The result is a light well-risen cake on a crip pastry base – very popular with children at teatime.

5. To make the glacé icing, sift the confectioners' sugar into a mixing bowl and gradually stir in the lemon juice. The icing should be thick enough to coat the back of the spoon thickly. Add 2–3 drops of yellow food coloring, if used.

6. Immediately pour the icing over the cake, allowing it to run down the sides. Strew the shredded orange and lemon zest over the icing and leave to set.

Hazelnut-Coffee Cake

Piping the border of buttercream rosettes as evenly and close together as you can gives this delicious cake its luxurious effect. It is a particularly easy mixture – and ideal for the food processor – as all the ingredients are combined simultaneously.

1 stick butter or margarine
1 cup light brown sugar
2 eggs
6 tablespoons milk
1 tablespoon coffee essence or 1 tablespoon instant coffee dissolved in 1 tablespoon boiling water and cooled
¾ cup chopped hazelnuts
½ cup raisins
2 cups self-rising cake flour
1 teaspoon baking powder

Coffee buttercream:
6 tablespoons butter
2 cups confectioners' sugar
1 tablespoon milk
1 tablespoon coffee essence or 1 tablespoon instant coffee dissolved in 1 tablespoon boiling water and cooled
To decorate:
toasted hazelnuts

Preparation time: 20 minutes
Cooking time: 30–40 minutes
Oven: 325°F

1. Grease and line two 8-inch layer cake pans with greased wax paper or non-stick parchment paper.

2. Place all the ingredients in a mixing bowl and beat with a wooden spoon until well mixed.

3. Pour the batter into the prepared pans and bake in a preheated oven for 30–40 minutes, or until well risen. Unmold and cool on a wire rack.

4. To make the coffee buttercream, cream the butter and confectioners' sugar together, adding the milk and coffee essence a little at a time to give a spreading consistency.

5. Put the cake layers together with a little of the buttercream. Spread some more of the buttercream over the top of the cake and draw parallel lines across it with a long narrow spatula.

6. Place the remaining buttercream in a parchment paper decorating cone fitted with a star tube and carefully pipe a border of rosettes around the top edge of the cake. Top each rosette with a toasted hazelnut.

Variations

Make a little extra buttercream to coat the sides of the cake and cover with crushed hazelnuts. Substitute walnuts for hazelnuts in the recipe for a more sophisticated cake.

From the top: St Clement's ring, Hazelnut-coffee cake

Strawberry Feather Bar

The delicate patterns of feather icing look best when there is a strong color contrast between the icing and the base. The pink and white effect of this cake is particularly pretty, but dark chocolate feathers against coffee glacé icing are also attractive.

½ cup sugar
½ cup soft margarine
2 eggs
1 cup self-rising cake flour
1 teaspoon baking powder
Filling:
6 tablespoons unsalted butter, softened
1½ cups confectioners' sugar, sifted
1 tablespoon milk
red food coloring
2 tablespoons strawberry jam
To decorate:
1 cup confectioners' sugar
1–2 tablespoons boiling water
strawberry-flavor dessert sauce

Preparation time: 15 minutes
Cooking time: 30–35 minutes
Oven: 325°F

1. Grease and line an 8-inch square cake pan with greased wax paper or non-stick parchment paper.

2. Place all the cake ingredients in a mixing bowl and beat with a wooden spoon for about 2 minutes until light and fluffy.

3. Spoon the batter into the prepared pan, making sure the corners are filled, and smooth the top. Bake in a preheated oven for 30–35 minutes until golden brown and firm to the touch. Unmold onto a wire rack, remove the lining paper and leave to cool completely.

4. To make the buttercream filling, place the butter, confectioners' sugar and milk in a bowl. Beat together to give a light texture and spreading consistency. Tint the buttercream pink with a few drops of red food coloring.

5. Cut the cake in half and split each half horizontally. Put the split layers together with strawberry jam. Put the two cakes together with a little buttercream to form an 8-inch bar.

6. To make the glacé icing, sift the confectioners' sugar into a bowl and gradually beat in the water until the icing thickly coats the back of the spoon. Immediately spread the icing over the top of the cake, being careful not to let it drip over the sides (you can wrap a strip of wax paper around the cake to prevent this).

7. Place a little strawberry-flavor dessert sauce in a parchment paper decorating cone fitted with a thin writing tube. Pipe lines of sauce widthwise on the icing on top of the cake. Draw a fine skewer across the lines of sauce in alternate directions to form a feather pattern (see page 43).

8. Place the remaining buttercream in a pastry bag fitted with a shell or star tube. Pipe a border around the top edge of the cake and leave to set.

Feather-iced cakes

When you have mastered the feather icing pattern you will find it an invaluable technique for quickly decorating simple butter cakes of all sizes. Its most classic application is in a more complex but deservedly famous recipe. This is *Mille Feuilles*, which is made from layers of puff pastry filled with whipped cream, or cream and crème pâtissière, and glacé-iced on top feather fashion. The whole cake is then cut into fingers to serve as elegant pastries (Napoleons). The name means "thousand leaves" from the numerous layers of fine pastry.

Lacy Sugar Cake

For the filigree pattern of sugar on top of the cake to have its full effect, the sides must be well coated with chopped nuts. Simple to achieve, this decoration is very impressive.

¾ cup sugar
¾ cup soft margarine
3 eggs
1½ cups self-rising cake flour
1½ teaspoons baking powder
finely grated zest of 1 orange
Filling and decoration:
6 tablespoons apricot jam, warmed and sieved
¾ cup chopped nuts (hazelnuts, almonds or walnuts), toasted
confectioners' sugar, sifted

Preparation time: 15 minutes
Cooking time: 30–35 minutes
Oven: 325°F

1. Grease and line two 8-inch layer cake pans with greased wax paper or non-stick parchment paper.

2. Place all the cake ingredients in a mixing bowl and beat with a wooden spoon for about 2 minutes until light and fluffy.

3. Divide the batter equally between the prepared pans and smooth the tops level. Bake in a preheated oven for 30–35 minutes until golden brown and firm to the touch. Unmold onto a wire rack, remove the lining paper and leave to cool completely.

4. Put the cake layers together with two thirds of the apricot jam. Spread the remaining jam evenly around the side of the cake. Strew the chopped nuts on a sheet of wax paper. Holding the cake between the palms of your hands, roll it in the nuts to coat the sides.

5. Place the cake on a serving plate. Put a patterned doily on top of the cake. Dredge the cake with confectioners' sugar using a fine sieve and covering the cake evenly. Very carefully lift off the doily to reveal the sugar pattern.

From the top: Lacy sugar cake, Strawberry feather bar

Chocolate Mint Cake

If there's one cake which is by tradition everybody's favorite, it's chocolate. This chocolate cake with two kinds of mint icing is sure to appeal to all the family.

2 sticks butter or margarine
1 cup sugar
1 tablespoon cocoa powder blended with 1 tablespoon hot water and cooled
4 eggs
2 cups self-rising cake flour, sifted
1 tablespoon hot water
Mint buttercream:
1 stick butter
2 cups confectioners' sugar, sifted
2 tablespoons milk
a few drops of green food coloring
a few drops of peppermint extract
Glacé icing:
1 cup confectioners' sugar
1–2 tablespoons warm water
a few drops of green food coloring
a few drops of peppermint extract
To decorate:
1 cup chocolate sugared strands
2 squares semisweet chocolate

Preparation time: 30 minutes
Cooking time: 25–30 minutes
Oven: 350°F

1. Grease and line two 8-inch layer cake pans with greased wax paper or non-stick parchment paper.

2. Cream the butter and sugar together until light and fluffy. Beat the cocoa powder paste in to the mixture.

3. Beat in one egg and mix well. Beat in the other eggs one at a time, adding a little flour with each one. Fold in the remaining flour with a metal spoon. Add the hot water.

4. Turn the batter into the prepared pans and bake in a preheated oven for 25–30 minutes until well risen. Unmold carefully and leave to cool on a wire rack.

5. To make the mint buttercream, cream the butter and confectioners' sugar together. Add the milk, green food coloring and peppermint extract and beat until creamy.

6. Use half the mint buttercream to put the cake layers together. Cover the sides with more buttercream. Place the chocolate strands on a sheet of wax paper and holding the cake carefully between the palms of your hands, roll it in the chocolate strands until it is well covered. Place on a cake board.

7. Place the remaining buttercream in a pastry bag fitted with a ¼-inch fluted tube and pipe a border around the top of the cake.

8. To make the glacé icing, sift the confectioners' sugar into a mixing bowl and gradually add the water. (You may find you do not need as much as 2 tablespoons.) The icing should be thick enough to coat the back of the spoon thickly. Add 1–2 drops of green food coloring (the color should be subtle). Immediately pour the glacé icing on top of the cake and spread it almost to the edge with a knife, taking care not to touch the piping. Gently bang the cake on the table two or three times to help the icing flow smoothly to the edge.

9. Melt the chocolate in a small bowl placed over a saucepan of hot water. Place the melted chocolate in a paper decorating cone, cut off the tip and dribble the chocolate across the top of the cake.

Sugared Fruit Cake

There's nothing complicated in the preparation of this cake, but it is mouthwateringly pretty, and the orange-flavored liqueur sprinkled over the cake gives it a special lift. Bake and serve this cake on the same day. The sugared decorations, however, can be made up to 2 weeks in advance if kept in an airtight container between layers of tissue paper.

6 tablespoons sugar
3 eggs
¾ cup cake flour
4 tablespoons Cointreau
2 cups heavy cream, whipped
To decorate:
Sugared grapes
sugared mint leaves

Preparation time: 15 minutes, plus sugaring the fruit
Cooking time: 30–35 minutes
Oven: 375°F

1. Grease and flour a 9-inch ring mold.

2. Place the sugar and eggs in a mixing bowl set over a saucepan of hot, not boiling water. Beat until the mixture is thick and pale in color and the beater leaves a heavy trail when lifted. Remove the bowl from the saucepan and continue beating until the mixture is cool. (If you use an electric mixer no added heat is necessary.)

3. Sift the flour into the mixture and quickly fold it in with a metal spoon.

4. Turn the batter into the prepared pan and place in a preheated oven. Bake for 30–35 minutes until the cake springs back when lightly pressed with the fingertips and has begun to shrink slightly from the sides of the pan. Unmold onto a wire rack to cool.

5. Cut the cake in half horizontally and sprinkle with Cointreau. Put the two layers together with a quarter of the cream. Place on a cake board. Cover the cake with the remaining cream and mark with a knife into a swirl pattern.

6. Decorate with clusters of sugared grapes and mint leaves. Keep the cake in the refrigerator until you are ready to serve it (because of the fresh cream).

Variation

For a luscious mocha variation, bake a chocolate Quick Mix Cake using the same size ring mold and following the instructions on pages 16–17. Sprinkle the horizontally cut halves with coffee liqueur. Put back together and top with cream as above. Decorate with marrons glacés halves.

From the top: Chocolate mint cake, Sugared fruit cake

Apricot Butterscotch Cake

This delicious cake demonstrates the versatility of the basic butter cake. Adding molasses and lemon juice enriches the flavor without making it excessively sweet, giving it a pleasant nuttiness that combines really well with the apricots.

1½ sticks butter or hard margarine
½ cup light brown sugar
½ cup dark brown sugar
3 eggs
1½ cups self-rising cake flour, sifted
1 tablespoon molasses
1 tablespoon lemon juice
Filling:
16-oz can apricot halves, drained
⅔ cup heavy or whipping cream
3 tablespoons milk or medium white wine

Preparation time: 30 minutes
Cooking time: 20–25 minutes
Oven: 375°F

1. Grease and base-line two 8-inch square cake pans with greased wax paper or non-stick parchment paper.

2. Place the butter or margarine in a mixing bowl and beat until soft. Add the two kinds of brown sugar and beat together until the mixture is very light and fluffy.

3. Beat in the eggs one at a time, following each with 1 tablespoon of the flour to prevent the mixture from curdling. Fold in the remaining flour. Beat in the molasses and lemon juice, combining the ingredients smoothly.

4. Divide the mixture between the pans, leveling the tops and making sure the corners of the pans are filled.

5. Place in a preheated oven and bake for about 20–25 minutes or until well risen, golden brown and firm to the touch. Unmold onto a wire rack and leave to cool. Peel off the paper.

6. To make the filling, chop half of the apricots and then cut the remaining half into quarters.

7. Whip the cream and milk or wine together until stiff. Put

almost half into a parchment paper decorating cone or pastry bag fitted with a ½-inch plain tube. Fold the remainder into the chopped apricots.

8. Use the apricot cream to put

Dark Ginger Cake

the cake layers together. Place the cake on a serving plate.

9. Pipe a lattice of cream over the top of the cake and fill alternate squares with pieces of apricot. Keep the cake in the refrigerator if it is not to be served immediately (because of the fresh cream).

The spiciness of this cake is well matched by its rich texture. It must be made 24 hours or more before eating for the flavors to blend.

½ cup molasses
¼ cup light brown sugar
6 tablespoons butter or hard
  margarine
1½ cups cake flour
2 teaspoons ground ginger
1 teaspoon apple pie spice
½ teaspoon baking soda
2 eggs
½ cup milk or buttermilk
Ginger crème au beurre:
2 egg yolks
6 tablespoons sugar
4 tablespoons water
1½ sticks butter
pinch of ground ginger or apple
  pie spice
To decorate:
a few pieces of stem or
  crystallized ginger

Preparation time: 45 minutes, plus standing
Cooking time: about 1¼ hours
Oven: 325°F

1. Grease and line a 9- × 5-inch loaf pan with greased wax paper or non-stick parchment paper.

2. Put the molasses, sugar and butter or margarine into a saucepan. Heat gently until the ingredients have melted. Set aside to cool slightly.

3. Sift the flour, ginger, apple pie spice and baking soda into a bowl and make a well in the center. Add the eggs and milk or buttermilk and the melted molasses mixture and beat until smooth.

4. Pour the mixture into the prepared pan and place in a preheated oven. Bake for about 1¼ hours or until a skewer inserted in the center comes out clean. Unmold onto a wire rack and leave until cold. Wrap the cake in foil and store for at least 24 hours before eating.

5. To make the crème au beurre, beat the egg yolks in a bowl until smooth.

6. Place the sugar and water in a small heavy-bottomed saucepan and heat gently until the sugar dissolves. Boil steadily until the syrup reaches the thread stage, 230°F on a candy thermometer.

7. Remove the syrup from the heat and immediately pour it onto the beaten egg yolks, beating well all the time. Continue to beat until the mixture is very light and fluffy.

8. Cream the butter until it is soft, and gradually beat in the egg and sugar mixture. Flavor the cream with a pinch of ground ginger or apple pie spice.

9. Place the crème au beurre in a pastry bag fitted with a star tube and pipe a pattern of swirls on top of the cake (alternatively spread the cream on top of the cake with a long narrow spatula and make a pattern with the spatula). Decorate with pieces of stem or crystallized ginger.

From the left: Dark ginger cake, Apricot butterscotch cake

Orange Cake

Like the Strawberries and Cream Layer Cake on page 76, this cake is based on a Genoese sponge cake batter (also known as a Torten) and so has good keeping qualities. This gives you the opportunity to make the cake a few days ahead of assembling. Use a small thin-skinned orange for making the glazed orange slices.

4 tablespoons butter
¾ cup self-rising cake flour
3 eggs
½ cup sugar
finely grated zest of ½ orange
Filling and decoration:
¾ cup orange jelly or orange
*   marmalade without peel*
2 cups heavy or whipping
*   cream*
½ cup sliced almonds, toasted
Glazed orange slices:
10 orange slices, ¼ inch thick,
*   or 5 slices cut in half*
6 tablespoons sugar

Preparation time: about 1 hour
Cooking time: about 30 minutes
Oven: 375°F

1. Grease and line a deep 8-inch round cake pan with greased wax paper or non-stick parchment paper.

2. Heat the butter in a small saucepan until it has just melted. Remove the pan from the heat and leave to stand so that the sediment sinks to the bottom.

3. Sift the flour twice.

4. Place the eggs, sugar and grated orange zest in a mixing bowl set over a pan of gently simmering water. Beat until light and creamy, so that the beater leaves a heavy trail when lifted. Remove the bowl from the heat and continue beating until the mixture is cool. (If you use an electric mixer no added heat is necessary.)

5. Fold the sifted flour lightly and evenly through the mixture.

6. Carefully pour in the butter, without the sediment, and fold it in lightly and carefully.

7. Turn the batter into the prepared pan and bake in a preheated oven for about 30 minutes until well risen, golden brown and firm to the touch. Unmold and cool on a wire rack. Remove the lining paper.

8. Glaze the orange slices. Remove any seeds from the slices and place them in a skillet. Cover with cold water and set over a gentle heat. Poach for about 20 minutes or until the slices are tender, adding more water if necessary.

9. Lift the orange slices out of the pan with a slotted spoon and transfer them to a baking sheet.

10. Add the sugar to the water left in the skillet and stir to dissolve. Bring the syrup to a boil and continue to boil until it is reduced to a thick glaze. Pour the glaze over the orange slices and leave them to cool.

11. Cut the cooled cake into three equal layers. Place the base layer on a serving plate and spread it with half the orange jelly or marmalade.

12. Whip the cream until it is stiff and spread a thin layer over the orange jelly. Place the second cake layer on top and spread with the remaining orange jelly and a little cream. Top with the third cake layer.

13. Use most of the remaining cream to cover the top and sides of the cake completely. Put the rest of the cream into a pastry bag fitted with a medium star tube.

14. Press the toasted almonds onto the sides of the cake, using a round-bladed knife or a long spatula.

15. Arrange the glazed orange slices in an overlapping circle on top of the cake. Pipe a border of shells around the top of the cake with the cream. A similar border can be piped around the base of the cake if you wish.

Variation

For a lemon cake, replace the orange zest in the cake batter with lemon zest; the orange jelly with lemon jelly, and glazed orange slices with glazed lemon slices.

Fruit Variety

Using a Genoese cake as the basis, build up a repertoire of cakes on the tried-and-tested combination of fruit, cream and nuts, adding a little liqueur to the whipped cream when serving cake as a dessert. In season, strawberries and raspberries are unbeatable. Alternatively, make a square cake and arrange closely packed rows of dark loganberries on top with a border of piped whipped cream and chopped hazelnuts on the side.

Orange cake

CELEBRATION CAKES

Formal cakes with fine and intricate piping work and decoration feature here. Simpler, but equally effective, are cakes for Christmas and Easter with marzipan decoration.

All the important occasions in life – whether they are times of personal happiness, such as a wedding or special birthday, or great days in the calendar, like Christmas – are celebrated with a feast, and an essential part of that feast is a grand and formal cake. Although a number of conventions are associated with cakes in this category, the scope for an imaginative and skillful cake decorator is enormous.

Occasions of this kind will tend to be well-planned, so there is usually plenty of time to design and create the cake. Most formal cakes are based on a rich fruit mixture, because its flavor, firmness of texture and keeping quality is best suited to this type of icing and decoration as well to the occasion itself. Indeed a rich fruit cake should be made several weeks before it is to be iced and eaten, in order for the flavors to mature and blend.

Wedding cakes can be elaborately designed and decorated but sometimes an element of restraint is useful. What would look wonderful on a single layer may well be over-fussy on a second and third. Don't be caught out making special decorations the night before! Tiny piped or run-out decorations can be made some time in advance and stored in an airtight container between sheets of tissue paper. Delicate items like this need to be handled with care. The separate tiers of the cake should also be well-packed before transporting them to be assembled before the reception.

With celebration cakes it is vital to know how many people the cake will feed. As a rough guide, a 1-pound baked rich fruit cake without marzipan or icing should cut into about 10 portions when completed. Therefore, for every 45–50 people you will need about 5 pounds basic rich fruit cake. Square cakes usually weigh heavier than round ones of the same size, although the depths can vary slightly as well.

The diagram below shows how to cut a square and a round wedding cake.

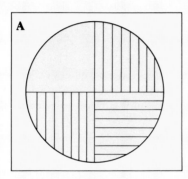 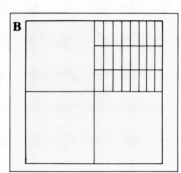

Because this chapter includes cakes for every significant occasion, the range of techniques involved is all-embracing. The finest piped royal icing work is used, for example, on the Hexagonal Wedding Cake – one of the most romantic designs imaginable – and the Eighteenth Birthday Cake. Pretty molded flowers feature on many of the cakes – spectacularly on the Rose Wedding Cake – and marzipan fruits make a colorful display on the Harvest Cake.

A wide range of ideas for Christmas is included, expanding on the traditional white-iced cake with red and green decorations to take in an unusual Santa's Stocking and some delightful miniature designs. Easter is as important a feast day as Christmas, and has its own cake customs as well as the conventional chocolate eggs. The French Pâques Cake is a marvelous cake for this springtime celebration.

Birthdays, anniversaries, engagements, retirement parties: these and many other occasions are milestones in life that deserve to be honored with a cake.

WEDDING CAKES

A once-in-a-lifetime event calls for a beautifully crafted cake to match the occasion. Strictly traditional designs at their best are represented by these classic cakes which embrace a broad range of intricate techniques. Traditional or modern, wedding cakes represent the pinnacle of decorative skills as a vital part of an unforgettable day.

Hexagonal Wedding Cake

If you are able to buy or rent hexagonal cake pans, bake the cakes in sizes of 10 and 6 inches. If you bake round cakes as directed in the recipe, cut them out as described on page 53. If you are unable to buy or make hexagonal cake boards, use round boards 13 and 8 inches in diameter.

1 11-inch and 1 7-inch round
Rich Fruit Cake (pages 24–5)
1 quantity apricot glaze (page 38)
3 1/2 lb marzipan (page 37)
about 26-cup (6 1/2-lb) sugar quantity royal icing (page 39)
mauve liquid food coloring
a little egg white or lemon juice
about 120 piped fans (see below)
about 40 run-out heart shapes (page 61)
4 white cake pillars

Preparation time: icing and decoration of the cake, plus time for making and drying the fans and hearts

1. Brush the tops and sides of the cakes with apricot glaze and coat with marzipan (see page 38). Leave to dry.

2. Make up some royal icing. Attach each cake to the appropriate board with a dab of icing. Flat ice the cakes with three coats all over and a further coat to the top of the larger cake. Leave to dry for 24 hours.

3. Tint a little of the icing pale mauve and put into a pastry bag fitted with a fine writing tube (No. 1 or 0). To make the fans, take a sheet of cardboard and draw a continuous line along the length of it, then draw a second line 1/2 inch below it broken into short lines of 3/4 inch with about 1/2 inch gap between. Repeat these lines all over the card. Using each short line as a base, draw 5 petal shapes as a guide to making the fan. Repeat this 2–3 times (once you have piped two or three fans no extra guidelines will be necessary). Cover the cardboard with a sheet of non-stick parchment paper, attaching it firmly with cellophane tape.

4. To pipe the fans, start in the center of one of the short lines, work around the petals, moving up to the tallest central point and back down again the other side, keeping to the short line for length and to the continuous line to give the height. Make some extra as some may break as they are moved. Leave to dry in a warm place. If you cannot get them all on one sheet, make another.

5. For the run-out hearts, draw heart shapes, each fitting into a 1 inch square, all over a sheet of cardboard or stiff paper. Cover with a sheet of non-stick parchment paper and using a No. 1 or 2 writing tube and mauve icing, outline at least 40 heart shapes. Leave to dry. For 10 of the hearts, work a lattice pattern to fill the shapes. For the others, thin a little mauve icing with egg white or lemon juice until it flows, then put into a paper decorating cone without a tube. Cut off the tip and use to flood the hearts. Prick any air bubbles and leave to dry.

6. Make up the rest of the icing as and when necessary. Take a pastry bag fitted with a No. 1 writing tube and white icing and pipe a series of dots all around the run-out hearts just in from the edge (but not on the lattice ones).

7. At the base of the large cake mark each section equally into four with small dabs of icing as markers. Divide the small cake into three sections in the same way. Fill a pastry bag fitted with a medium star tube with white icing. Pipe twisted scrolls in a clockwise movement, graduated in size from small to large and back to small again, all around the base of both cakes between the markers. Leave to dry.

8. Attach three hearts (two run-outs and one lattice) centrally to each side of the large cake and two hearts (both run-outs) on the small cake. Use just a small dab of icing to attach each one.

9. On top of the large cake, prick out a 2 1/4-inch long line, 1 inch in from the edge of the cake on each section. Using tweezers, attach three fans upright to each of these lines with icing.

10. For the smaller cake, prick a line 1 1/2-inches long and again 1 inch in from the edge. Attach two fans to each line and leave to dry.

11. Take a pastry bag fitted with a No. 2 or 3 writing tube and filled with white icing. Pipe three dots centrally inside the fans on top of the cake, as shown. Next pipe one centrally on the outer side of the fans with a slightly smaller one each side of it. Finally take a No. 1 writing tube and white icing and complete the central design by piping four graduated dots toward the center of the cake from the middle dot, and two graduated dots from the outer ones. On the outer side of the fan, pipe three more graduated dots to reach the end of the fans. On the smaller cake fewer dots will be required for only two fans, but keep to the same pattern.

12. Attach fans all around the top edge of the cakes, facing outwards. You need seven for each section on the large cake and five for the smaller cake.

13. Take the No. 1 writing tube and white icing and pipe a large dot at the bottom and in the middle of each fan on the top of the cake with a smaller one on each side. Do the same under the fans on the side.

14. Finally, using the same tube, pipe a squiggly white line of icing along the top of each scroll at the base of the cakes and attach a fan at each corner. Leave to dry.

15. Assemble the cake, positioning the smaller tier on top with the sides matching. Top with a silver vase of small flowers.

Hexagonal wedding cake

Rose Wedding Cake

Traditionally, American wedding cakes have three tiers, but there are no pillars supporting the middle and top tiers. This means that the icing on the base cake needs to be hard enough to take the weight of the other two cakes. Do not add glycerin to the icing which you use for the four coats on the base cake. The advantage is that designs for these wedding cakes can embrace the whole cake, like these cascading roses. For instructions on cutting the cake for ease of serving, see step 15.

1 13-inch thick round silver cake board
1 9-inch and 1 7-inch medium thick or thin but extra firm round silver cake boards
1 6-inch round, 1 8-inch round and 1 10-inch round Rich Fruit Cake (pages 24–5)
2 quantities apricot glaze (page 38)
4 lb marzipan (page 37)
about 24-cup (6-lb) sugar quantity royal icing (page 39)
cream and golden yellow liquid food colorings
about 50 white molded roses of varying sizes (page 63)
about 60 cream molded roses of varying sizes
about 60 pale golden yellow molded roses of varying sizes
about 30 purchased silver or white molded leaves

Preparation time: icing and decoration of the cake, plus making and drying of the roses

1. Brush the tops and sides of the cakes with apricot glaze and coat with marzipan (see page 38). Leave to dry.

2. Make up some of the royal icing and attach each cake to the appropriate board with a dab of icing. Flat ice the cakes, giving three coats all over and a further coat to the top of the base coat. Leave to dry completely.

3. Make the roses, using about 1 lb fondant molding paste (see page 44) and leave them to dry. Also make the leaves if using molded ones.

4. On the tops of the base and middle cakes, mark the size of the boards which will stand on them (for the next cake up) with pinpricks or dabs of icing.

5. Draw some scroll shapes on non-stick parchment paper to fit around the top space outside the cake boards on the middle and bottom tiers, the scroll for the base being rather more elongated. Place the paper patterns at four equal points on each cake and prick out the scroll design.

6. Make up the rest of the royal icing as necessary. Fill a pastry bag fitted with a No. 2 writing tube with white icing and outline the scrolls, then pipe a second scroll shape beside the first. Leave to dry, then overpipe one line of the scrolls.

7. For the sides of all the cakes, draw vertical scroll shapes which work as a mirror-image pair on non-stick parchment paper. Prick these shapes onto the sides of the cakes.

8. Using the writing tube, pipe double lines in white icing as for the first scrolls, dry, then overpipe one scroll with white icing. Leave to dry.

9. Fill a pastry bag fitted with a medium star tube with white icing. Pipe a fairly heavy shell border around the top edge of the three cakes. Leave to dry.

10. Fill a pastry bag fitted with a fine writing tube (No. 1 or 0) with pale gold icing and pipe a continuous slightly looped line to fit around the shells both on top of the cake and on the sides. Leave to dry.

11. To assemble the cakes, stand the base on a flat surface, then put the middle tier carefully on top, so that the scrolls correspond.

12. Work a white shell border to match the one on the top edges of the cakes, to attach the base cake to the board and middle tier to the base cake. Do the same to the top tier.

13. With the fine writing tube and gold icing, pipe a slightly scalloped line above and below the shell borders as on the tops of the cakes.

14. Starting on top of the cake, arrange a cluster of roses of varying colors and sizes, attaching each one with a dab of icing. Continue attaching roses to build up a heavy swirling cascade of roses down the sides and over the tops of each of the cakes to the base. Keep the colors mixed and fill in the gaps with leaves. On each of the tiers, midway between the scrolls on the sides of the cake, attach one rose and three rose buds. Allow to dry.

15. To cut the cake, begin at the lowest tier. Run a knife vertically downwards all around where the lowest tier meets the bottom edge of the second tier. Take out a wedge from the bottom cake (see diagram) and cut it into slices. Continue this process with the middle tier, removing another wedge of slices until a cylindrical core remains. Cut the remainder in slices starting centrally from the top, working around and down.

Rose wedding cake

Two-Tier Wedding Cake

The lower tier of this handsome cake is unusually large, so that although there are only two tiers you can expect it to provide enough slices. Flat-ice the top of the lower tier before adding glycerin to the royal icing: it must be hard enough to take the weight of the top tier without cracking. For the best results, the cake must be kept at least 2–4 weeks, preferably up to 3 months, after baking.

1 13-inch and 1 9-inch square
    silver cake board
8 cups (3 lb) currants
3 ½ cups (1 ¼ lb) golden raisins
4 cups (1 ½ lb) raisins
2 cups candied cherries,
    quartered, washed and dried
1 ½ cups blanched almonds,
    chopped
1 ½ cups chopped mixed
    candied peel
grated zest of 2 lemons
grated zest of 1 large orange
7 cups cake flour
2 ½ teaspoons ground
    cinnamon
2 teaspoons apple pie spice
½ teaspoon ground nutmeg or
    allspice
6 ½ sticks (1 lb 10 oz) butter
4 ⅓ cups (1 lb 10 oz) dark
    brown sugar
12 eggs (extra large)
2 tablespoons molasses
1 tablespoon gravy browning
about ⅔ cup brandy
1 quantity apricot glaze (page
    38)
3 ½ lb marzipan (page 37)

Royal icing:
7 egg whites
about 20 cups (5 lb)
*   confectioners' sugar, sifted*
3 tablespoons lemon juice,
*   strained*
3–4 teaspoons glycerin
To decorate:
yellow and orange liquid food
*   coloring*
64 pale gold molded roses (see
*   page 63)*
4 white square pillars

Preparation time: about 4 hours, plus making the roses
Cooking time: about 2¾ and 5 hours
Oven: 300°F

1. Grease and line a 7-inch and a 10-inch square cake pan (see page 14).

2. To make the cakes, put the currants, raisins, cherries, almonds, peel and fruit zests into a bowl and mix well.

3. Sift the flour with the spices into a separate bowl.

4. Cream the butter until soft. Add the sugar and cream again until the mixture is light and fluffy and pale in color.

5. Beat in the eggs one at a time following each with 1 tablespoon of the flour mixture; fold in the remaining flour, then the molasses. Finally add all the fruit and mix well.

6. Put about two thirds of the batter into the larger pan. Add the gravy browning to the remaining batter and put it into the smaller pan. Level the tops and make a slight hollow in each.

7. Tie a treble thickness of brown paper or newspaper around the outside of the cake pans and place in a preheated oven. Bake (separately if necessary), allowing about 2½–2¾ hours for the smaller cake and 4¾–5 hours for the larger cake, or until a skewer inserted in the center of the cakes comes out clean. Leave the cakes to cool in the pans and then unmold them carefully. Prick all over the surface with a skewer and pour over about half the brandy. Wrap in foil and leave for 2 weeks.

8. Repeat the dosing with brandy after 2 weeks and rewrap in foil. Leave for a further 2–4 weeks or up to 3 months before proceeding.

9. Prepare the apricot glaze. Use the glaze and the marzipan to cover both the cakes as described on page 38. A square cake is covered in just the same way as a round cake. Leave to dry for 3–4 days.

10. Make up the royal icing, in two batches for ease (see page 39). Place the icing in airtight plastic containers.

11. Position the cakes on the cake boards with a dab of icing. Put two flat coats of icing on the tops of the cakes (see page 40), omitting the glycerin from the first layer on the base cake. Leave to dry between coats.

12. Flat ice the sides of the cakes, working opposite sides at a time to get good square corners (see page 40). Spread some icing onto one side of each cake, making it as even as possible with a long narrow spatula. Using an icing comb or the spatula draw the icing toward you, keeping it at an angle, and making sure the cake is stable to give it an even finish. Using the spatula, cut off the icing down the corners in a straight line and also off the top edge and around the base of the cake. Repeat with the two opposite sides and leave to dry.

13. Add a second coat of icing to the sides in the same way and then give a final coat to the tops of the cakes. Leave to dry.

14. Draw a pattern for decorating the cakes. Cut a square of wax paper the size of the top of each tier. Fold into quarters and then draw a bracket sign on the paper across the corner (see diagram). Place this paper on the cake itself and prick out the shape with a pin on two opposite corners. Turn the paper around and prick out the other two corners. Half-fill a pastry bag fitted with a medium writing tube with white icing and pipe over the outlines. Allow to dry and then overpipe.

15. For each corner draw a fancy "W" shape on paper and prick out this shape on to the cake (see diagram). Pipe over the outlines and leave to dry, then overpipe.

Two-tier wedding cake

16. On the sides of the large cake, make three evenly spaced marks along each side. On the small cake make just two marks. Using the writing tube and white icing, pipe two loops from each mark. When dry, overpipe. Attach three roses to the top of the center loops on the large cake and two roses to the side loops and the loops on the small cake.

17. Using a small star tube and white icing, pipe a shell pattern all along the top edges of the cakes so it falls over the edge slightly. Leave to dry.

18. With the same tube and white icing pipe alternate small stars and elongated stars around the lower edges which reach about ¾ inch up the sides.

19. Tint a little icing a pale gold using yellow and orange food colorings and put into a pastry bag fitted with a medium writing tube. Pipe loops between alternate shells all around the top edges.

20. Pipe a loop or double loop from the top of the elongated star to the next, around the base of the cakes. Leave to dry.

21. Attach a gold rose to the center of each decorative "W" on top of the cakes and another one or two at the lower corners of each cake.

22. To assemble the cake, place the pillars evenly on the lower tier and stand the smaller cake on top. Place a small flower arrangement of white freesias and/or small yellow roses in a tiny silver vase on top.

Use this template as a guide for drawing up the decorative pattern in step 14.

Three-Tier Wedding Cake

In purest white – apart from the centers of the daisies – and decorated with delicate lace-work, this magnificent cake is the perfect centerpiece for a grand wedding.

3 round silver cake boards 7-inch, 10-inch and 14-inch
1 5-inch round, 18-inch round and 1 11-inch round Rich Fruit Cake (pages 24–5)
2 quantities apricot glaze (page 38)
4½ lb marzipan (page 37)
32- to 36-cup (8- to 9-lb) sugar quantity royal icing (page 39)
pink and green liquid food colorings
about 120 piped daisies with pink centers
about 25 white and pink butterflies
7 or 8 white cake pillars

Preparation time: icing and decoration of the cake, plus making and drying the daisies and butterflies

1. Brush the tops and sides of the cakes with apricot glaze and coat with marzipan (see page 38). Leave to dry.

2. Make up the royal icing in two batches for ease and place in airtight plastic containers. Attach each cake to the appropriate board with a dab of icing. Flat ice the cakes giving three coats all over and a further coat to the tops of the cakes, especially the large one (see pages 40–41). Leave to dry for 24 hours.

3. Make the daisies (see page 60) and butterflies (see page opposite) and then leave them to dry.

4. On thin cardboard, draw three circles 1 inch smaller than the top of each of the cakes for templates and cut them out. Fold each circle into eighths, then draw a deep petal from the folded edge and a shallow curve shape (see page 51).

5. Place the templates centrally on each cake according to size. Carefully prick out the pattern with a pin on each cake. Remove the templates. Place some white royal icing in a pastry bag fitted with a fine writing tube (No. 1) and use to outline the patterns. Pipe two further lines, one inside and one outside the first. Leave to dry. (Keep the pastry bag in a plastic bag for later use; see step 7.)

6. Make templates for the sides of each cake. Take a strip of paper the depth and circumference of the iced cake and fold it into quarters, then in half again. Draw a shallow curve, then a deep curve to the folded edge keeping to about half the depth of the cake. Cut out, open up the papers and place them around the cake to correspond with the top design.

Prick out the pattern as before (step 5).

7. Using the white icing, pipe just inside the pattern using the writing tube. Pipe two further lines below the first.

8. To make the template for the cake boards, cut a circle the size of each board, then cut off ½ inch all around. Cut out a circle the size of each cake and discard. Fold the remaining rings into quarters, then eighths and draw a petal shape to correspond with that on the sides of the cakes but shallower. Cut out the pattern. Make one cut into each template and place them around the cakes on the boards. Outline the pattern with white icing. Leave to dry and remove the template.

9. Tint a little icing pale soft green or pink if preferred, and put into a pastry bag fitted with a No. 1 tube. Use to overpipe all the center outlines on the tops and sides of the cakes.

10. For the lacework, fill a pastry bag fitted with a No. 0 tube with white icing. Work a lacework pattern (see page 58) to fill the spaces between the icing outlines on the tops and sides of the cakes and on the boards between the icing outline and base of the cakes. Leave to dry.

11. For the base border, fill a pastry bag fitted with a large writing tube (No. 3 or 4) with white icing and pipe a border of plain large dots all around the base of the cakes to attach to the board.

12. To complete the decoration, on the small cake add one daisy to each point of the shallow curve on top of the cake, one at the join of deep curves on the sides and one centrally opposite the deepest part of each curve

on the board, attaching each with a dab of icing. Add two daisies in each matching place on the middle tier and three daisies on the large tier. Attach one butterfly (on each tier) on the top edge of the cake at the point of the curves and where the lacework joins the cake on the base. Leave to dry.

13. To assemble the cake, place four cake pillars evenly in the middle on the largest cake and place the middle tier on top. Place three or four cake pillars on the middle tier and put the small cake in place. Put a small arrangement of flowers in a silver vase on the top tier.

Simple butterflies

Draw the butterfly wings separately on a piece of stiff cardboard, tracing from a picture if you can't manage freehand. Place a piece of non-stick parchment paper over the drawing and attach it firmly, so that it is quite flat. Using a writing tube and white icing, outline the wings. Thin a little royal icing with the lemon juice or egg white until it just flows. Put into a paper decorating cone without a tube, cut off the tip and pipe into the outline until it is filled. Prick any air bubbles and leave to dry. Repeat by moving the parchment paper over the pattern. Outline the wings in pale pink icing using a fine writing tube (No. 0) and pipe a little lacework over them. Leave to dry. To assemble: use pink icing and a No. 2 writing tube to pipe a squiggle the length of the wings onto parchment paper. Press on a pair of wings, one each side of the body, and leave to set.

Three-tier wedding cake

CHRISTENING CAKES

A christening is the happiest of family celebrations. Like a wedding, it's a time for champagne and a beautiful cake, one of the most welcome gifts you could make for the new arrival. An attractive way of adding the baby's name to the cake is to pipe the letters on little cubes of molding icing like toy bricks and arrange them on top.

Christening Cake for a Girl

Christening cakes look best in pastel colors or in white. This pretty example with yellow roses is traditionally perfect for a baby girl. As the christening ceremony involves the bestowing of the baby's name, it should be a prominent feature of the cake.

1 10-inch round silver cake board
1 8-inch round Rich Fruit Cake (pages 24–5)
1 quantity apricot glaze (page 38)
1¼ lb marzipan (page 37)
8-cup (2-lb) sugar quantity royal icing (page 39)
yellow food coloring
¼ lb fondant molding paste (page 44)
about 40 piped yellow roses (page 60)
2 feet yellow ribbon about 1½ inches wide

Preparation time: icing and decorating the cake

1. Brush the top and sides of the cake with apricot glaze and coat with marzipan (see page 38). Leave to dry.

2. Make up the royal icing. Attach the cake to the cake board with a dab of icing. Flat-ice the cake, giving two coats all over and a third coat to the top if necessary (see pages 40–41). Leave to dry for 24 hours.

3. Make a template for an 8-point scallop (see page 51).

4. Tint about 2 tablespoons of the royal icing with yellow food coloring and put into a pastry bag fitted with a medium writing tube.

5. Position the template on the cake and prick out the pattern. Outline the pattern using the yellow icing. Remove the template. Pipe two more outlines, each a little inside the former. Leave to dry, then overpipe the center line, again using yellow icing.

6. Write the name of the child on a piece of paper and prick out the name a little above the center of the cake. Pipe with yellow icing; when dry overpipe and leave to dry again.

7. Make the crib. Using about 2 oz white molding paste, mold the crib base. Use about 1 oz white paste to mold the hood, and attach it to the base with a dab of water. Make a small pillow of white paste and place it in position. Tint the remaining paste pale yellow with a drop of yellow food coloring and roll it out to make a cover. Lay this over the base to cover it completely. Mark a criss-cross design on the yellow cover with a sharp pointed knife. Leave the crib to dry.

8. Using a fine star tube and white royal icing, pipe a continuous twisted edging to the top of the cake so it begins on the side of the cake and just overlaps on to the top.

9. Using a medium star tube and white icing, pipe another continuous twisted edging to the base of the cake to attach it to the board.

10. While the base border is still wet, attach a yellow rose to every alternate twist. Leave to dry.

11. Attach a yellow rose to each point of the scallops on the top of the cake.

12. Tie the ribbon around the sides of the cake, finishing with or without a bow.

13. Finally, attach the crib with a little icing so it stands inside the yellow outline just below the name.

Christening Cake for a Boy

If the child is being given a first name that is too long to fit attractively on the cake, use only the initials instead and design a monogram.

1 10-inch square silver cake board
1 8-inch square Rich Fruit Cake (pages 24–5)
1 quantity apricot glaze (page 38)
1¾ lb marzipan (page 37)
12-cup (3-lb) sugar quantity royal icing (page 39)
green or blue food coloring
a little egg white, lightly beaten, or lemon juice, strained
silver candy balls
1 yard white and/or mid-green or blue ribbon

Preparation time: icing and decorating the cake

1. Brush the top and sides of the cake with apricot glaze and coat with marzipan (see page 38). Leave to dry.

2. Make up the royal icing. Attach the cake to the cake board with a dab of icing.

3. Tint two-thirds of the icing pale green or blue with food coloring. Use to flat ice the cake, giving two coats all over and a third coat to the top if necessary (see pages 40–41). Leave to dry for 24 hours.

4. Draw a small train with two or three cars, or trucks, on non-stick parchment paper so it will fit on the cake. Place a little white icing in a paper decorating cone fitted with a fine writing tube. Outline the train and trucks and leave to dry. Thin a little icing with egg white or lemon juice until it flows. Spoon this into the outlines to fill them completely, using a skewer to help guide the icing to the edge. Burst any bubbles which appear and leave until dry.

5. Write the child's name on a piece of non-stick parchment paper and prick out the letters in a gently curving line on the cake. Make a double outline using white icing and a medium writing tube. When the letters are dry, overpipe them and leave to dry completely. A neat row of tiny touching dots may also be piped on top of the outline of the name.

6. Position the train or trucks on the cake beneath the name and attach them carefully with a little icing. Outline it all with white icing, adding windows and wheels with simple spokes.

7. Pipe three straight lines in white icing in graduated lengths above the name and below the train, parallel to the edge of the cake. Pipe two small dots at the end of each line.

8. Using a fine star tube and white icing, pipe a zigzag border all around the top edge of the cake.

9. Work another zigzag on the side of the cake to join the first row and decorate the points with silver candy balls.

10. Work a heavier zigzag border around the base of the cake, again decorating with silver candy balls. Leave to dry.

11. Tie the ribbon or ribbons around the side of the cake, finishing with a bow, or attaching the ends of the ribbon with a dab of icing.

Christening cakes

VALENTINE CAKES

Whether it's tea for two or a romantic candlelit dinner, commemorate the day dedicated to lovers with a cake that is sure to melt the hardest heart. Here are two very different but equally delectable cakes designed to inspire undying affection from the object of your attentions – and what better reward for such a labor of love?

Chocolate Valentine Cake

This irresistible cake is made up of four layers filled with strawberries, cream and grated chocolate, covered with melted chocolate cream, or *crème ganache*. The crème should be poured over the cake while it is hot, so that it will set evenly. The Genoese sponge cake can be made several days in advance if kept in an airtight container, but once assembled the cake should be served on the same day.

1 9-inch round silver cake
    board
4 eggs
½ cup sugar
1 cup cake flour
2 tablespoons butter, melted
⅓ cup finely ground hazelnuts
1¼ cups whipping cream
2 squares semisweet chocolate,
    grated
1 pint firm strawberries
crème ganache:
10 squares semisweet chocolate,
    broken into pieces
⅔ cup heavy or whipping
    cream
To decorate:
chocolate leaves (page 68)
confectioners' sugar, for
    dusting (optional)

Preparation time: 1 hour, plus cooling
Cooking time: 15–20 minutes
Oven: 350°F

1. Grease and flour two 7-inch heart-shaped pans, measured at the widest part.

2. Beat the eggs and sugar together in a bowl, then place the bowl over a saucepan of very hot (not boiling) water. Beat until the mixture becomes thick and creamy and leaves a

trail when a little of the mixture is pulled across the surface. Remove from the heat and continue to beat until the mixture is cold. (If using an electric beater, added heat is not necessary.)

3. Sift half the flour over the surface of the mixture. Add half the melted butter. With a metal spoon, fold in the flour using a cutting figure-of-eight action until all the flour has been incorporated. Repeat with the remaining flour, the hazelnuts and the remaining butter. Fold as lightly and as little as possible.

4. Pour the batter into the prepared pans and tilt until the batter spreads evenly over the tins.

5. Place in a preheated oven and bake for 15–20 minutes until the cake is well risen and golden brown, and springs back when lightly pressed with a finger. Unmold onto a wire rack to cool.

6. When the cakes are cool, split each heart into two layers. Whip the cream, fold in the grated chocolate and spread one third of the cream on one heart.

7. Reserve three strawberries with stems for decoration. Slice some of the remaining even-sized strawberries to obtain 24 thin slices. Chop the remaining strawberries roughly.

8. Spread the chopped strawberries over the first layer of cream, smooth over a little more cream and put on a second layer of cake. Divide the remaining cream in two and put together the remaining cake layers, leaving the top layer plain. Stand the cake on a wire rack with a large plate underneath.

9. To make the *crème ganache*, place the chocolate in a heatproof bowl set over a pan of hot water. When the chocolate has melted, stir until smooth. Meanwhile, pour the cream into a separate pan and bring just to a boil. Gradually pour the cream into the melted chocolate, stirring vigorously until the mixture is smooth.

10. Pour the hot *crème ganache* over the cake and smooth it over quickly with a small narrow spatula. Leave to set for about 15 minutes.

11. Arrange the sliced strawberries in a row around the base of the cake. Place the three whole strawberries in a cluster on top and surround with chocolate leaves.

12. Leave the cake to set for about 2 hours. If liked, give it a very light sprinkling of confectioners' sugar just before serving.

Above: Chocolate valentine cake

Sweetheart Cake

If the Chocolate valentine cake is dark and dangerous, this one is all sweetness and light! For a less formal effect, 7-minute frosting can be used. Swirl the frosting over the top and sides and make circular shapes with a narrow spatula.

1 12-inch round silver cake board
1 cup sugar
1 cup soft margarine
4 eggs
2 cups self-rising cake flour
2 teaspoons baking powder
finely grated zest of 1 lemon
1½ quantities fondant molding paste (page 44)
3 tablespoons raspberry jam
a few drops of red food coloring
confectioners' sugar and cornstarch, for dredging
To decorate:
royal icing for piping (page 39)
sugared rose petals (page 66)
sugared mint leaves (page 66)

Preparation time: 35 minutes, plus setting time
Cooking time: 45–55 minutes
Oven: 325°F

1. Grease and line a 9- to 10-inch heart-shaped pan with greased wax paper or non-stick parchment paper.

2. Place the sugar, margarine, eggs, flour, baking powder and lemon zest in a mixing bowl. Beat to combine the ingredients, then beat for a further 2 minutes until the mixture is light and fluffy. Turn the batter into the prepared pan, making sure it is filled right to the edge. Smooth the top.

3. Place in a preheated oven and bake for 45–55 minutes, until the cake is golden brown and firm to the touch. Unmold onto a wire rack, remove the lining paper and leave to cool before icing.

4. Split the cake in half horizontally and put the layers together with raspberry jam.

5. Tint the molding paste pink with a drop or two of red food coloring. Roll out the paste on a work surface or a sheet of plastic wrap dredged with a mixture of confectioners' sugar and cornstarch. Dredge the rolling pin with the same mixture. Roll to the width of the top of the cake, plus the sides, plus about 1 inch extra.

6. Support the paste on the rolling pin and place it centrally over the top of the cake. Press the paste onto the sides of the cake and down the sides, using a gentle circular movement to give an even covering. Dip your fingers in a mixture of confectioners' sugar and cornstarch while you work. When the finish is smooth, trim the base edge of the cake with a sharp knife. Place on a cake board and leave to dry for 24 hours.

7. Place two thirds of the royal icing in a paper decorating cone fitted with a small star tube and pipe a border around the top and base borders of the cake. Tint the remaining icing pink with a drop of red food coloring and overpipe the base border.

8. Decorate with sugared rose petals and mint leaves.

Above: Sweetheart cake

MOTHER'S DAY CAKES

A bouquet of flowers and breakfast in bed are essential gifts for Mother's Day, but it's a lovingly decorated cake that best conveys your affection. Whatever your skills, these two cakes – one simple, one splendid – provide you with the opportunity to say thank you in the sweetest way to the one who's at the heart of the family.

Daisy Cake for Mother's Day

This Mother's Day cake is decorated with an appropriately springtime air. The fondant and royal icings can be made in advance, as can the molded daisies, but once assembled the cake should be eaten on the same day.

1 9-inch round silver cake board
1 4-egg quantity Butter Cake batter (page 18)
⅓ cup strawberry jam
4 tablespoons apricot glaze (page 38)
1 quantity fondant icing (page 46)
½ quantity pink crème au beurre (page 47)
½-cup sugar quantity pink royal icing (pages 39)
To decorate:
18 molded daisies (page 63)

Preparation time: 25 minutes
Cooking time: 25–30 minutes
Oven: 350°F

1. Grease and line two 8-inch layer cake pans with greased wax paper or non-stick parchment paper.

2. Make up the cake batter and pour it into the prepared pans. Place in a preheated oven and bake for 25–30 minutes. Unmold, remove the lining paper and leave to cool on a wire rack.

3. Put the layers together with the jam. Replace on the wire rack and brush the top and sides with apricot glaze. Place the wire rack over a large plate.

4. Place the fondant icing, divided into small pieces, in a bowl set over a pan of hot water. Warm gently, stirring, until the fondant is smooth and has the consistency of thick cream. If the icing is too thick, add a little water.

5. Pour the icing over the cake, allowing it to run down the sides and tilting the cake a little if necessary to help coat it evenly – the icing should not be spread with a knife or the gloss will be spoiled. Leave to set, then trim off any excess icing. Place the cake on a board.

6. Place the crème au beurre in a nylon pastry bag fitted with a ¼-inch fluted tube and pipe a decorative border around the base of the cake.

7. Place the royal icing in a parchment paper decorating cone and snip off the end. Use the icing to write "Mother" on the cake.

8. Arrange the daisies in clusters of three around the top edge of the cake. Using royal icing, pipe a looped border between the clusters.

Ideas for Children

A simplified version of the Daisy Cake can be made by children as a present for Mother's Day. A Quick Mix cake (page 16) is easier to prepare and rises well. Glacé icing is quickly made and easier than fondant icing, and can be tinted to a pale pink or lemon with food coloring. Instead of piping the name, "Mother" can be written out with silver candy balls and a border of sugar flowers arranged around the edge.

Mother's Day Cake

All the family will want a slice of this sumptuous cake, even if it is meant for mother. It incorporates a number of the techniques for using chocolate described on page 68. It's best to make a few extra rose leaves.

1 9-inch cake board
1 4-egg quantity chocolate Butter Cake batter (page 18)
2 quantities simple coffee buttercream (page 46)
To decorate:
8 squares semisweet chocolate
2–3 artificial flowers

Preparation time: about 45 minutes
Cooking time: about 20–25 minutes
Oven: 375°F

1. Make up the cake batter and place in three greased 8-inch round layer cake pans, lined with greased wax paper or non-stick parchment paper. Bake in a preheated oven for 20–25 minutes or until well risen and firm to the touch. Unmold and cool on a wire rack. Remove the lining paper.

2. Make up the coffee buttercream. Use some to put the cake layers together.

3. Spread a layer of coffee buttercream over the top of the cake and use a round-bladed knife to smooth the top with a backward and forward action. Turn the cake at right angles to the first lines and pull the same knife straight across in 7 or 8 equidistant lines to complete the pattern.

4. Using a potato peeler, pare off mini chocolate curls from the chocolate, using about 5 squares of it.

5. Spread a thin layer of buttercream around the sides of the cake and carefully press on the chocolate curls, using a narrow spatula. Stand the cake on the board.

6. Melt the remaining chocolate in a bowl set over a pan of hot water. Take some clean, dry and unblemished rose leaves and paint the underside of each with melted chocolate. Leave to dry, add a second coat and chill thoroughly.

7. Attach a sheet of non-stick parchment paper to a board, then spread out the remaining melted chocolate on it. Leave until set but not quite dry, then, using a sharp knife and ruler, cut it into strips about 1½ inches wide. Quickly cut these into squares, then cut again to make into triangles. Leave to dry and set completely. Reserve the chocolate trimmings.

8. Melt the trimmings in a bowl set over a pan of hot water and put into a paper decorating cone. Cut off the tip of the bag and carefully write "Mother" across the cake.

9. Put the remaining butter-cream in a pastry bag fitted with a large star tube and pipe a continuous twisted line of icing all around the top of the cake about 1 inch in from the edge.

10. Carefully separate the chocolate into triangles and place one between each of the buttercream whirls on top of the cake.

11. Peel the real rose leaves carefully from the chocolate ones. Arrange two chocolate leaves on either side of the artificial flowers in front of "Mother." Leave to set.

Opposite: Daisy cake for Mother's Day
Below: Mother's Day cake

CHRISTMAS CAKES

Of the many traditions observed at Christmas, few are as central as a suitably iced cake, bearing the season's symbols of holly, mistletoe and tidings of glad joy. Here are some inspiring variations on the green and red theme; but for a stunning new idea to ring the changes, see the delicately colored cake with angels on page 114.

Square Christmas Cake

This impressive cake calls for a steady hand when applying the peaked icing on the side corners to make sure the ribbons stay clean. The rounded shape of the mistletoe leaves softens the angles of a square cake, but if you wished they could be replaced by the plaque bearing "Season's Greetings" on the round cake.

1 10-inch square silver cake board
1 8-inch square Rich Fruit Cake (pages 24–5)
1 quantity apricot glaze (page 38)
1¾ lb marzipan (page 37)
2 lb fondant molding paste (page 44)
a little egg white
confectioners' sugar and cornstarch, for dusting
To decorate:
about 20 green mistletoe leaves, 20 natural marzipan mistletoe berries and 4 green marzipan holly leaves (see opposite, step 5 and page 66)
4-cup (1-lb) sugar quantity royal icing (page 39)
about 1¾ yards, ¾-inch wide red or green ribbon

Preparation time: to make, bake, marzipan and ice the cake and make the decorations plus about 45 minutes for the final decoration

1. Brush the cake with apricot glaze and use the marzipan to cover the cake (see page 38). Stand the marzipaned cake on the board and leave for at least 24 hours for the marzipan to dry thoroughly.

2. Brush the marzipan with egg white. Roll out the fondant paste on a surface dusted with confectioners' sugar and cornstarch and use to cover the cake (see page 44). Mold it to fit the cake and give a rounded edge on the top edge (not the sharp edge achieved with royal icing). Trim off around the base and smooth all over with fingers dipped in sugar and cornstarch. Leave to dry for 24–48 hours.

3. Make the holly and mistletoe leaves and berries and leave to dry.

4. Make up the royal icing. Lay the ribbon diagonally over one corner of the cake, and then take it down to the base at the center of the cake on the board and attach with a pin and a dab of icing. Take it up to the next corner and so on all around the cake. When you bring the ribbon back to the beginning, trim both ends evenly with an inverted "V."

5. Using a long narrow spatula, add a thin layer of royal icing to the corners at the sides of the cake up to the ribbon, over the top edge corners of the cake and covering the cake board. Pull the icing up into peaks using the spatula or a spoon handle. Take care not to get any icing on the ribbon. Leave the icing to dry. (The rough icing may be added before the ribbon if preferred.)

6. Put the remaining royal icing into a pastry bag fitted with a No. 2 writing tube and pipe a continuous looped border inside the ribbon on top of the cake. Leave to dry.

7. Attach a decoration of holly leaves and mistletoe berries and leaves to the center of the cake with small dabs of icing.

8. Finally add bunches of three mistletoe leaves and some berries to the cake board where the ribbon meets it, attaching them with icing and removing the pins from the ribbon.

Variation

Make a marzipan Christmas tree cut-out to place in the center of the cake and decorate around the cake with cut-out stars (see page 66). Press gold and silver candy balls along the edges of the cut-outs to emphasize their shape.

Round Christmas Cake

Christmas wouldn't be the same without a snowy white Christmas cake to mark the occasion. The cake itself should be made up to three months in advance for the best results. Once the marzipan has been applied, leave at least 24 hours or up to 1 week before icing the cake.

1 10-inch round silver cake board
1 8-inch round Rich Fruit Cake (pages 24–5)
1 quantity apricot glaze (page 38)
1½ lb marzipan (page 37)
8-cup (2-lb) sugar quantity royal icing (page 39) or 1½ lb fondant molding paste (page 44)
little egg white if using fondant paste
red and green food colorings

Preparation time: to make, bake, marzipan and ice the cake and make decorations plus about 1 hour for final decorations.

1. Brush the cake with apricot glaze and use 1¼ lb marzipan to cover the cake (see page 38). Stand the cake on the board and leave to dry.

2. Flat ice the cake with the royal icing (see page 40) giving it two coats all over and a third on top (see page 41), allowing it to dry between each coat. Alternatively, brush the marzipan with egg white and cover with fondant molding paste (see page 44). Leave the cake to dry completely – a minimum of 24 hours for royal icing and up to 48 hours for molding paste.

3. Divide the remaining marzipan in half and color one portion red with food coloring and the other half dark green, kneading to color evenly. Use some of the red marzipan to make 40 holly berries.

4. Roll out the remaining red marzipan and cut to a 3-inch square. Place on a sheet of non-stick parchment paper with the holly berries and leave to dry in a warm place.

5. Roll out the green marzipan thinly and cut into 20–30 holly leaves using a special cutter of about 1–1½ inches in length. Mark a vein down the center, then put each leaf over a wooden spoon handle to curve it. Leave to dry for at least 24 hours, so that the coloring will not seep on to the top of the cake and mark it. If you do not have a special-shaped cutter, follow the instructions on page 66 for holly leaf cut-outs.

6. To make a template for the top of the cake, cut a circle of thick paper about ½ inch smaller than the top of the cake. Fold it in half, then carefully into three, making sure each piece is exactly even. Draw a curve across the folds. Cut around the curve. Open and press flat.

7. For the sides, cut a strip of paper long enough to reach right around the outside of the cake and the same depth of the cake. Fold it evenly into six. Cut ½ inch off the top, then make a curved cut to correspond with the curve on the cake top.

8. Place the circular template on the top of the cake. Put some royal icing into a parchment paper decorating cone fitted with a medium star tube and pipe a row of small shells to outline the template without touching it. Leave the icing to dry, then remove the template.

9. Put the side template around the side of the cake so that it matches the top design, attaching it with a dab of icing. Pipe a similar row of shells to outline the top edge of this template. Remove the template carefully and allow the icing to dry.

10. Using a slightly larger star tube, put some more royal icing into a pastry bag. Pipe a row of medium to large shells around the base of the cake.

11. Put some more icing into a pastry bag fitted with a No. 2 writing tube (or a finer No. 1 tube if you prefer) and pipe a lacework design between the icing shells made with the templates to fill in the shapes. (See page 58.)

12. Attach the square of red marzipan centrally to the top of the cake with a dab of icing, then, using a No. 2 writing tube, pipe a suitable Christmas message, such as the words "Season's Greetings," on top.

13. Decorate the top of the cake with the holly leaves and berries, arranging them around the piped design. Secure with a little royal icing if necessary. Leave to dry.

From the left: Round Christmas cake, Square Christmas cake

Ribbon and Holly Cake

*1 10-inch square silver cake
board*
*1 7- or 8-inch square Christmas
cake (see Merry Christmas
Cake, page 110)*
*1 quantity apricot glaze (page
38)*
1½ lb marzipan (page 37)
*8-cup (2-lb) sugar quantity
royal icing (see page 39)*
To decorate:
*about 1 yard green ribbon, 1½-
inches wide*
*about 1 yard red ribbon, not
more than ¾-inch wide*
silver candy balls
*about 7 marzipan holly leaves
and berries (page 66)*

Preparation time: icing and
decorating the cake

1. Brush the top and sides of
the cake with apricot glaze, then
cover with marzipan (see page
38). Leave to dry for a minimum
of 24 hours.

2. Make up the royal icing.
Attach the cake to the board
with a dab of icing. Flat ice the
cake all over (see page 40)
giving it two coats. Leave to dry.

3. Attach the center of the green
ribbon to the center base of
one side of the cake with two
pins. Place the red ribbon in the
center of the green and secure
with a dab of icing. Fold the
ribbons up and over the top of
the cake as in the picture and
down the other side; attach with
icing.

4. Put some white icing in a
pastry bag fitted with a medium
writing tube and pipe evenly
spaced straight lines across the
cake between the ribbons and
almost up to them, leaving
space for a row of dots. Leave to
dry completely.

5. Turn the cake around and
complete the lattice by piping
groups of four lines at right
angles to the first with about
½ inch between the groups,
almost up to the ribbons. Leave
to dry.

6. Using the same tube, pipe a
row of small dots between the
lattice and ribbon to give it an
edging. Wrap the pastry bag in
plastic wrap to use later.

7. Put some more icing in a
pastry bag fitted with a thick
writing tube and pipe a continuous looped edging around
the top edge of the cake
(except where the ribbon
overlaps the edge).

8. Under each alternate loop
pipe a large dot on the side of
the cake with a smaller one
under it. Complete with a third
dot using the medium writing
tube.

9. Pipe large dots with the larger
tube around the base of the
cake to seal it to the board. Put
a silver candy ball in every
second or third dot. Pipe two
smaller dots above alternate
base border dots to match
those on the top border.

10. Pipe a line of dots down
each corner of the cake.

11. Complete the top decoration by adding bunches of two
or three holly leaves and berries
on the lattice each side of the
ribbon. Leave to dry.

Chocolate Yule Log

The yule log is as much a part
of the Christmas celebration as
the presents and the tree. This
chocolate cake makes a light
and delicious alternative to the
heavier fruit cake, but will not
of course keep longer than a
day because of the fresh cream.

3 eggs
6 tablespoons sugar
*10 tablespoons self-rising cake
flour*
*1 tablespoon cocoa powder,
sifted*
*⅔ cup heavy or whipping
cream, whipped*
Chocolate frosting:
*4 squares semisweet chocolate,
broken into pieces*
4 tablespoons butter
2 egg yolks
*1 cup confectioners' sugar,
sifted*
To decorate:
little confectioners' sugar
*marzipan holly leaves and
berries (page 66)*
*marzipan robin (page 110) or
Christmas roses (page 63)*

Preparation time: 20 minutes,
plus frosting and decorating the
cake
Cooking time: 10–15 minutes
Oven: 400°F

1. Beat the eggs and sugar
together in a heatproof bowl set
over a pan of simmering water
until the mixture is very thick
and the beater leaves a heavy
trail when lifted. (If using an
electric mixer, no heat is
needed.) Remove from the heat
and continue to beat until the
mixture is cool.

2. Sift the flour and cocoa
together twice, then fold lightly
and evenly into the beaten
mixture.

3. Pour into a greased and lined
12- × 9-inch jelly roll pan,
spreading the batter right into
the corners.

4. Bake in a preheated oven for
10–15 minutes or until just firm
to the touch.

5. Unmold the cake onto a
sheet of non-stick parchment
paper or onto wax paper
sprinkled with sugar.

6. Trim the edges of the cake
while it is still hot and immediately roll it up with the paper
inside. Cool on a wire rack.

7. Carefully unroll the cooled cake and remove the paper. Spread all over with most of the whipped cream. Re-roll carefully and place on a foil-covered oblong board or a plate.

8. If you want a branch on the log, cut a 2-inch piece from the end of the cake at an angle and position it on one side of the cake.

9. To make the chocolate frosting, put the chocolate and butter in the top of a double boiler or heatproof bowl over a pan of gently simmering water, and heat until the chocolate melts. Remove the bowl from the heat and beat the mixture until smooth. Beat in the egg yolks and enough sugar to give a thick, smooth, spreading consistency. Spread the frosting all over the cake, including the ends.

10. Mark with a fork or narrow spatula along the length of the roll and branch to resemble the bark of a tree and leave to set.

11. Put the remaining whipped cream in a pastry bag fitted with a thick writing tube and pipe the filling on the ends to resemble rings. Leave to dry.

12. Sprinkle lightly with sifted confectioners' sugar and decorate with holly leaves and berries and a robin or roses.

From the left: Chocolate Yule log, Ribbon and holly cake

Merry Christmas Cake

This enriched fruit cake mixture, with extra spices and brandy in the mixture, makes a Christmas cake to remember.

1 9-inch square silver cake board
1 1/3 cups golden raisins
1 1/3 cups raisins
1 1/3 cups currants
2/3 cup chopped mixed candied peel
1/2–2/3 cup ground or finely chopped almonds
1/3 cup candied cherries, quartered, washed and dried
grated zest of 1 lemon
2 sticks butter, softened
1 cup light or dark brown sugar
4 eggs (extra large)
2 cups cake flour, sifted
pinch of salt
1 teaspoon apple pie spice
1/2 teaspoon ground cinnamon
good pinch of ground nutmeg
2 tablespoons brandy or sherry
3–4 tablespoons brandy for soaking (optional)
1 quantity apricot glaze (page 38)
1 3/4 lb marzipan (page 37)
8-cup (2-lb) sugar quantity royal icing (page 39)
To decorate:
red and brown food colorings
2 silver candy balls
about 30 marzipan holly leaves and berries (page 66)

Preparation time: about 20 minutes plus icing and decorating the cake
Cooking time: 3 1/2–3 3/4 hours
Oven: 300°F

1. Grease and double-line an 8-inch square cake pan with greased wax paper or non-stick parchment paper.

2. Mix together the dried fruits, peel, almonds, cherries and lemon zest.

3. Cream the butter and sugar together until light and creamy.

4. Beat in the eggs one at a time, following each with a tablespoon of flour.

5. Sift the remaining flour with the salt and spices and fold into the creamed mixture, followed by the brandy or sherry. Add the fruit mixture and combine the ingredients well.

6. Turn the batter into the prepared pan, level the top and make a slight hollow in the center.

7. Wrap several thicknesses of brown paper or newspaper around the outside of the pan and bake in a preheated oven for 3 1/2–3 3/4 hours or until a skewer inserted into the center of the cake comes out clean.

8. Cool in the pan, then unmold onto a wire rack. Store in an airtight container or wrapped in foil until required. If using extra brandy, pierce the cake all over with a fine skewer and drizzle 3–4 tablespoons of brandy over it before storing.

9. To prepare the cake for decoration, brush the top and sides with apricot glaze, then cover with marzipan (see page 38), reserving about 1/4 lb for the central decoration. Leave the marzipan to dry for a minimum of 24 hours.

10. Make up the royal icing and attach the cake to the board with a dab of icing. Flat ice the cake all over, giving it two coats (see pages 40–41). Leave to dry.

11. To make the robin for the decoration, use 1/2 oz of the reserved marzipan. Color a small piece of it red and the remainder brown. Mold two small flat pieces for wings and mark feathers with a knife. Mold the remainder into a bird shape with head and pointed beak, and a tail. Use red marzipan to mold over the robin's breast, up to his beak. Attach the wings, mark the tail feathers with a knife and add one silver candy ball on each side of the head for the eyes. Leave to dry.

12. Roll out about 2 oz of the remaining marzipan and cut to a rectangle measuring about 5 × 3 inches. Position the rectangle on the cake diagonally across the center and attach with a dab of icing at each corner.

13. Place some royal icing in a parchment paper decorating cone fitted with a medium writing tube and pipe the words "Merry Christmas" on the plaque. Pipe one or two outlines onto the cake to surround the plaque.

14. Color the remaining marzipan red with food coloring. Roll it out thinly and cut out a small lantern. Attach the lantern to the plaque together with the robin, using a dab of icing.

15. Pipe three lines of "corners" on the cake making each a little shorter than the last one, using the medium writing tube. Add dots to each corner and three more dots in a line toward the center as shown.

16. Attach a set of three holly leaves with berries above and below the plaque.

17. Arrange a border of holly leaves and berries around the side of the cake, attaching each with a little icing.

18. Using a medium star tube, pipe a sloping shell edging around the top edge of the cake, with each shell beginning on the top of the cake and ending on the side.

19. Use a thicker star tube to pipe a shell border around the base to seal the cake to the board. Leave to set.

Holly and Ivy Christmas Cake

The Christmas roses for this elegant cake can be made from bought fondant molding paste (follow instructions on page 63) or piped freehand in royal icing adapting instructions for Primrose, page 60.

1 8-inch round silver cake board
1 8-inch round Christmas cake (see Merry Christmas Cake, above)
1 quantity apricot glaze (see page 38)
1 1/2 lb marzipan (page 37)
8-cup (2-lb) sugar quantity royal icing (page 39)
lemon juice or beaten egg white

To decorate:
5 Christmas roses (page 63)
4 marzipan ivy leaves (page 62 for template)
12 marzipan holly leaves and berries (page 66)

Preparation time: icing and decorating the cake

1. Brush the top and sides of the cake with apricot glaze, then cover it with marzipan (see page 38). Leave to dry for a minimum of 24 hours.

continued

From the top: Merry Christmas cake, Holly and ivy Christmas cake

2. Make up the royal icing. Attach the cake to the board with a dab of icing. Flat ice the top of the cake only (see pages 40–41), giving it two coats. Leave to dry.

3. Draw a cross shape on a piece of paper the same size as the top of the cake, making the cross about 1¼ inches wide. Cut out the cross and place it on top of the cake.

4. Prick out the outline of the cross on top of the cake and remove the paper pattern.

5. Place some royal icing in a parchment paper decorating cone fitted with a medium writing tube and outline the cross with royal icing. Leave to dry.

6. Thin a little of the royal icing with lightly beaten egg white or strained lemon juice until it just flows, then spoon it inside the lines of icing to fill the cross completely. Burst any air bubbles which appear with a pin. Leave to set.

7. Thicken the rest of the icing slightly with extra confectioners' sugar, then use most of it to rough ice the sides of the cake. Pull the icing up into peaks all over, using a spoon handle or small narrow spatula. Let the peaks of icing just overlap on to the top of the cake to give it an edging.

8. Put the remaining icing into a pastry bag fitted with a small star tube and pipe a narrow line of stars or shells to outline the cross.

9. Arrange a bunch of Christmas roses and ivy leaves in the center of the cross, and holly leaves and berries along the spokes of the cross. Attach the decorations to the cake with a little icing. Leave to dry.

Santa's Stocking

This is an idea for a Christmas party cake for those who prefer a lighter Christmas cake but still favor marzipan. For a smaller stocking use an 11- × 7- × 1½-inch pan and a 4-egg quantity of Pound Cake batter. Bake for about 50 minutes.

1 5-egg quantity Pound Cake batter (page 19)
1 quantity apricot glaze (page 38)
1 lb marizpan (page 37)
red and green food colorings
To decorate:
narrow gold, green and/or red Christmas ribbons
chocolate money
½ quantity simple vanilla buttercream (page 46)

Preparation time: decorating the cake
Cooking time: about 1 hour 15–20 minutes
Oven: 325°F

1. Grease and line a 12- × 10- × 2-inch jelly roll pan with greased wax paper or non-stick parchment paper.

2. Turn the batter into the prepared pan and bake in a preheated oven for about 1 hour 15–20 minutes or until well risen and firm to the touch. Unmold onto a wire rack and leave to cool.

3. Draw a "stocking" on a sheet of paper the same size as the cake, following the diagram. Cut out and place on the cake.

4. Cut around the stocking shape with a sharp knife and place the stocking-shape cake on a cake board. Cut two or three packages from the cake trimmings (see diagram).

5. Brush all over the stocking and packages with apricot glaze.

6. Take three-quarters of the marzipan and color it red with food coloring. Roll out between two sheets of plastic wrap and use to cover the stocking completely. Make a few holly berries from the marzipan trimmings.

7. Color half the remaining marzipan green. Roll out and cut out six holly leaves (see page 66). Use the remaining green marzipan to cover the largest of the cake packages.

8. Roll out the remaining uncolored marzipan and use it to cover the other cake packages. Tie the appropriate colored ribbons around the packages.

9. Position the parcels and chocolate money at the top of the stocking as if spilling out.

10. Put some of the buttercream into a pastry bag fitted with a thick writing tube and pipe "Happy Christmas" along the stocking.

11. Put the rest of the butter-cream into a pastry bag fitted with a star tube and pipe several rows of stars or shells at the top of the stocking to represent fur.

12. Attach the holly leaves and berries to the stocking with buttercream. Leave to set.

Cut out stocking shape. Cut "presents" from trimmings.

Snowman Christmas Cake

The evenly peaked rough icing around the sides of this cake provides a suitably wintry looking setting for the little snowman. The snowman and the decorations for this cake are made from molding icing, not marzipan.

1 10-inch round silver cake board
1 8-inch round Christmas cake (see Merry Christmas Cake, page 110)
1 quantity apricot glaze (page 38)
1½ lb marzipan (page 37)
9-cup (2¼-lb) sugar quantity royal icing (page 39)
½ quantity fondant molding paste (page 44)
food colorings (red, green, orange and brown)
extra confectioners' sugar, sifted

Preparation time: icing and decorating the cake

1. Brush the top and sides of the cake with apricot glaze, then cover with marzipan (see page 38). Leave for a minimum of 24 hours to dry.

2. Make up the royal icing. Attach the cake to the board with a dab of icing.

3. Flat ice the top of the cake only with half the royal icing, giving it two coats (see pages 40–41). Leave to dry.

4. Thicken the rest of the icing with extra confectioners' sugar, then use most of it to rough ice the sides of the cake, pulling the icing up into evenly spaced peaks with a long narrow spatula.

5. Tint one quarter of the molding paste green and use to make into four cut-out holly leaves (see instructions for marzipan cut-outs, page 66). Reserve the trimmings. Color a

little of the remaining molding paste red and make some small berries, reserving the remainder. Leave the holly and berries to dry.

6. Shape some of the uncolored molding paste into two balls one larger than the other, for the head and body of the snowman. Press them gently together. Make a hat with the remaining red paste, and place on the head. Tint a little of the uncolored molding paste orange. Make three thin ropes of red, green and orange paste and twist them together to form a scarf, snipping the ends with scissors for tassels. Wrap the scarf around the neck of the snowman. Make a nose with a small piece of orange paste and three buttons with red paste. Color a little of the uncolored paste brown and shape a broomstick and eyes.

7. Place the snowman with the broomstick in the center of the cake and make snowballs with the remaining uncolored paste. Place the snowballs on top of the cake in piles around the snowman and arrange groups of holly leaves and berries around the top of the cake. Dust the snowman with a little confectioners' sugar, for snow. Leave to set completely.

Opposite page: Santa's stocking
Left: Snowman Christmas cake

Christmas Cake with Angels

It may depart from the traditional in shape and color, but this Christmas cake is still very much in spirit with the season. If you are unable to buy a cake board of the correct size, cover a board or a piece of thick cardboard with silver foil.

1 13- × 7-inch silver cake board
1 8-inch square Rich Fruit Cake (pages 24–5)
1 quantity apricot glaze (page 38)
2 lb marzipan (page 37)
a little egg white, beaten lightly
about 2 lb fondant molding paste (page 44)
confectioners' sugar and cornstarch for dusting
4-cup (1-lb) sugar quantity royal icing (page 39)
yellow and blue liquid food colorings
a little lemon juice (optional)
90 piped snowflakes (see below)
14 run-out angels (see below)

Preparation time: icing and decorating the cake, plus making and drying the angels and snowflakes

1. Cut the cake in half, then cut one piece in half crosswise to give two small squares. Stand the larger strip of cake on the cake board, brush one short end with apricot glaze and attach one of the small squares, to give a cake of 12 × 4 inches. (Use the remainder of the cake for another purpose as it will not be needed here.)

2. Brush the top and sides of the cake with apricot glaze and cover with marzipan (see page 38). Leave to dry for 24 hours.

3. Brush the marzipan lightly with egg white. Roll out the molding paste on a surface dusted with confectioners' sugar and cornstarch, and use to cover the cake smoothly and evenly. Dip your fingers in sugar and cornstarch as you smooth the molding paste over the cake. Leave to dry.

4. To make the snowflakes, make up the royal icing and, using a No. 1 writing tube and white icing, pipe out snowflake designs (they should have six sides but the patterns can differ) on non-stick parchment paper. Make about 90 and leave them to dry.

5. Make 14 angels (see right) and leave to dry completely.

6. Attach four angels with a little royal icing centrally to the top of the cake in a circle with the heads facing inward, then attach one more at each end of the top. Next attach one angel on each short side and three along each long side, all with their heads pointing in the same direction.

7. Using a No. 1 writing tube and white icing, pipe a series of slanting straight lines from the top of the cake over the edge, keeping them about ¼ inch apart. Leave to dry. When dry, pipe over the lines to give a trellis effect, taking them from the top of one line on the cake over two slanting lines and attaching to the base of the third one. Continue as evenly as possible all the way around the top edge and leave to dry completely.

8. For the base border, fill a pastry bag fitted with a medium star tube with white icing and pipe alternate stars and elongated stars, which spread onto the cake board. At each corner pipe a very much larger pointed and elongated shape which reaches further up the corner of the cake and down on to the board.

9. Finally attach snowflakes with a little royal icing all around the angels on the sides and on top of the cake use tweezers to move the snowflakes and arrange them informally around the angel shapes. Leave to dry.

To make angels

Draw angel shapes using the template on page 62 on stiff cardboard. Cover with non-stick parchment or wax paper, then outline the various parts of the body with a pastry bag fitted with a No. 2 writing tube and white icing. Fill in the hands. Leave to dry. Tint a little icing pale yellow with food coloring and put into a pastry bag fitted with a No. 2 writing tube. Fill in the hair with a squiggly pattern and leave to dry.

Tint a little more of the icing pale blue with food coloring, then thin it down with a little egg white or lemon juice and put into a parchment paper decorating cone without a tube. Cut off the tip and use to flood the dress. Leave to dry. Thin a little white icing with egg white or lemon juice and put into a paper decorating cone without a tube. Cut off the tip and use to flood the face and wings. Leave to dry.

Christmas cake with angels

Miniature Christmas Cakes

*4 7-inch round silver cake
    boards
1 quantity Christmas cake
    batter (see Merry Christmas
    Cake, page 110)
1 quantity apricot glaze (page
    38)
1½ lb marzipan (page 37)
6-cup (1½-lb) sugar quantity
    royal icing (page 39)
½ quantity fondant molding
    paste (page 44)
confectioners' sugar and
    cornstarch for dusting
silver candy balls
food colorings (red, yellow and
    green)
1 yard Christmas ribbon*

Preparation time: icing and
decorating the cakes
Cooking time: 1¾–2 hours
Oven: 275°F

Gifts for Christmas

These little cakes – only 4
inches in diamter – have a
multiplicity of festive uses.
They make wonderful
presents for people living
alone, or to add to a
Christmas hamper full of
seasonal homemade fare. At
a special Christmas party for
all the family, why not make
a little cake for each pair of
guests? They are perfect for
church bazaars too. Best of
all for the cake decorating
enthusiast, they give the
opportunity to try out a
number of designs on a
single theme.

1. To make the individual cake
cases, cut out 4 10-inch circles
of double thickness foil. Mold
each circle of foil around the
base and sides of a 1 lb 14 oz
can to make a 4-inch foil case.
Remove the can carefully and
place the foil cake cases on a
baking sheet covered with a
double thickness of brown
paper.

2. Divide the cake batter evenly
among the foil cases and
smooth the tops. Place in the
preheated oven and bake for
1¾–2 hours. Remove from the
oven and allow to cool slightly.
Remove the foil and leave the
cakes to cool completely.

3. Brush the tops and sides of
the cakes with apricot glaze,
then cover with marzipan (see
page 38), reserving the trimmings. Leave to dry for a
minimum of 24 hours.

4. Make up the royal icing.
Attach each cake to a board
with a little dab of icing.

5. Decorate cake 1: Flat ice the
top of the cake (see page 40)

and leave to dry a little. Rough ice the sides, swirling the peaks with a narrow spatula. Make a template (see diagram) to fit the top of the cake. From a sheet of paper cut a circle 4 inches in diameter. Fold the circle evenly into 8 and cut off a diagonal piece to form a star shape. Open out the paper and prick out the design on top of the cake. Fill a paper decorating cone fitted with a star tube with royal icing. Pipe along the outline of the star. Press a silver candy ball into each point of the icing stars. Pipe a star border around the edge of the cake. Use molding paste trimmings from cake 3 to make a Christmas rose (page 63). Place in center of the cake.

6. Decorate cake 2: Rough ice all over the cake with royal icing. Use marzipan trimmings to make holly leaves and berries (page 66) and place three clusters on top of the cake.

7. Decorate cake 3: Roll out half the molding paste on a surface dusted with confectioners' sugar and cornstarch to a circle large enough to cover the top and sides of the cake plus 1 inch. Supporting the paste with the rolling pin, place the paste centrally on the cake and smooth it into place with the fingers, dipped in sugar and cornstarch. Trim the edges, reserving the trimmings. Using royal icing in a pastry bag with a plain tube, pipe "Merry Christmas" on top of the cake. Color a little royal icing red and overpipe the letters. Use the trimmings to make holly leaves and berries. Tie a 20-inch length of Christmas ribbon around the cake.

8. Decorate cake 4: Roll out the remaining molding paste and cover the cake as described for cake 3. Use the trimmings to make a red candle shape with a yellow flame, and holly leaves and berries. Finish by tying the remaining length of ribbon around the cake.

Variations

Some of the other Christmas cakes in this chapter can be adapted successfully to smaller dimensions. Those that work best in miniature are the lacework round cake on page 98, the Holly and Ivy Cake on page 100 and the Snowman Cake on page 103.

Miniature Christmas cakes

EASTER CAKES

The festival of Easter brings to an end the sober days of Lent, heralding the spring with cakes for a great feast day. As well as a British Simnel Cake, try a delicious Pâques Cake, glistening with crystallized fruits. And at summer's end, set a new tradition with a cake to celebrate the fruits of the field at harvest-time.

Simnel Cake

This cake derives its name from the Latin word for "the best flour" used in it. Although long associated with Easter in Britain, in the seventeenth century this was the cake that young women in service made to take home on Mothering Sunday in March, showing off their culinary skills. The eleven small paste balls on top of the cake symbolize the faithful apostles of Christ.

2 cups cake flour
pinch of salt
1 teaspoon baking powder
1 teaspoon ground cinnamon
¼ teaspoon ground nutmeg or
*   mace*
1½ sticks butter or hard
*   margarine*
1 cup light brown sugar
3 eggs
2 tablespoons lemon juice
⅔ cup raisins
1 cup golden raisins
⅓ cup chopped mixed candied
*   peel*
⅓ cup candied cherries,
*   quartered, washed and dried*
grated zest of 1 orange
1 lb marzipan
a little apricot jam or egg white
To decorate:
about 1 yard of yellow ribbon
*   about 1-inch wide*

Preparation time: about 40 minutes
Cooking time: about 2 hours
Oven: 325°F

1. Grease and line a deep 7-inch round cake pan with greased wax paper or non-stick parchment paper.

2. Sift together the flour, salt, baking powder, cinnamon and nutmeg or mace into a bowl.

3. Cream the butter or margarine and sugar together until very light and fluffy and pale in color. Beat in the eggs, one at a time, adding 1 tablespoon of the flour mixture after each one. Fold in the remainder of the flour alternating with the lemon juice.

4. Combine the dried fruits, peel, cherries and orange zest and stir into the mixture.

5. Spread half the batter in the base of the prepared cake pan. Roll out one third of the marzipan and trim it to a 7-inch round to fit the cake pan. Lay the marzipan round on the cake batter and cover with the remaining cake batter.

6. Place in a preheated oven and bake for about 2 hours, or until cooked, and the cake has shrunk slightly from the sides of the pan. Leave to cool in the pan for 10 minutes, then unmold onto a wire rack until quite cold.

7. Roll out just over half of the remaining marzipan to a round to fit the top of the cake. Brush the top of the cake with jam or egg white and position the marzipan on top. Mark a criss-cross pattern all over with a sharp knife and crimp the edge.

8. Roll the remaining marzipan into 11 equal-sized balls. Attach them around the edge with a dab of jam or egg white.

9. Cut a strip of wax paper the same width as the ribbon and circumference of the cake. Line the ribbon with the paper and tie it around the cake, securing the strip of wax paper against the cake with a little jam or egg white to prevent the marzipan filling from staining the ribbon.

Pâques Cake

Pâques is actually the French word for Easter, but once you have tried this stunning cake you will be sure to want to use it for many other special occasions.

2 quantities Genoese Sponge Cake batter (page 22)
Filling:
2 cups (1 lb) full or medium fat cream cheese
½ cup sugar
finely grated zest of 1 lemon
1¼ cups confectioners' cream, whipped until stiff
To decorate:
sifted confectioners' sugar
a selection of crystallized or candied fruits

Preparation time: about 40 minutes
Cooking time: 30–35 minutes or 1–1¼ hours
Oven: 375°F

1. Grease and line two deep 9-inch round cake pans with greased wax paper or non-stick parchment paper.

2. Make up the cake batter and put into the pans. Place in a preheated oven and bake for 30–35 minutes or until well risen and just firm to the touch. Make up and bake the cakes separately if your oven shelf will not take both together.

3. Unmold onto a wire rack and leave until cold.

4. To make the filling, cream the cheese until soft. Add the sugar and continue to beat until light and fluffy. Beat in the lemon zest. Fold the whipped cream into the cheese mixture.

5. Split the cakes in half horizontally and use the filling to put the four layers together.

6. Stand the cake on a plate and dredge the top heavily with sifted confectioner's sugar. Arrange a ring of whole, sliced or pieces of crystallized or candied fruits around the top of the cake and serve.

Variation

Flavor the cakes with the finely grated zest of 1 lemon or orange to each batch of batter. For the filling: whip 2½ cups heavy cream with 2–3 tablespoons orange liqueur until stiff. Peel 4 large oranges (free of white pith) and slice very thinly. Fill the split cakes with a layer of cream and then with orange slices. Assemble the cake and sprinkle the top with 2–3 tablespoons orange liqueur. Mask the cake in most of the remaining cream and press about ¾ cup toasted chopped hazelnuts around the sides. Pipe whirls of whipped cream on the top and decorate each with 3 toasted hazelnuts. Sprinkle a few chocolate mini curls (page 68) over the center. Chill before serving.

From the left: Simnel cake, Pâques cake

Easter Egg Cake

These cakes are much more satisfying than hollow chocolate eggs! To make the smaller Easter egg use a 2-egg cake batter and smaller dishes.

1 3-egg quantity chocolate Quick Mix Cake batter (page 16)
1½ quantities simple chocolate buttercream (page 46)
red, yellow or green ribbon
selection of marzipan flowers (page 64), e.g. daffodils, violets, and cut-out marzipan leaves

Preparation time: about 30 minutes, plus frosting and decorating
Cooking time: about 45 minutes
Oven: 325°F

1. Divide the cake batter between two greased and floured oval 2½-cup capacity ovenproof glass dishes.

2. Bake in a preheated oven for about 45 minutes or until well risen and firm to the touch. Unmold onto a wire rack and leave to cool.

3. Use a little of the buttercream to put the cake layers together to give an egg shape. Stand the cake on a cake board.

4. Use the remaining buttercream to mask the whole cake. Smooth the surface with a narrow spatula.

5. Cut a strip of wax paper the same width as the ribbon and lay across the cake, molding it around as if the cake were tied up. Place the ribbon over the wax paper. If preferred, complete with a ribbon bow on the side.

6. Arrange a spray of marzipan flowers and leaves on each side of the ribbon, attaching them to the buttercream. Leave to set.

Variations

The cake may be flavored vanilla, coffee or any other flavor, if preferred, or a Pound Cake batter (pages 18–19) may be used.

For a children's party, make tiny individual egg cakes. Divide the Quick Mix Cake batter between paper cup cake cases (see chart pages 16–17). After cooling, peel off the cup cake cases. Put the cakes together in pairs and coat them in chocolate buttercream.

Alternatively make up plain buttercream and tint it a bright shade of pink, green, blue or yellow. Then for a simple finish, roll the little eggs in colored candies or in chopped nuts. Brightly colored sugar-coated chocolate candies or white chocolate disks could also be used as a covering to the buttercream, or use a mixture to make individual patterns on each egg.

The Healthy Sponge Cake recipe on page 22 could be substituted for the Quick Mix to give a more interesting texture to the little eggs.

Easter egg cakes

Easter Basket

The basketweave design on the sides of this cake looks complicated, and takes a little time to do, but once you get the rhythm of it it is relatively easy. Make the marzipan daffodils in advance if you wish.

1-cup flour quantity coffee Quick Mix Cake batter (pages 16–17)
Chocolate buttercream:
2 tablespoons cocoa
2 tablespoons boiling water
1 stick unsalted butter, softened
2 cups confectioners' sugar, sifted
To decorate:
3 oz marzipan
a few drops of yellow food coloring
1 yard narrow yellow ribbon

Preparation time: 20 minutes, plus making the decorations
Cooking time: 50 minutes
Oven: 325°F

1. Grease a 1-quart pudding basin or steaming mold. Place the mixture in the basin and smooth the top. Bake in a preheated oven for 50 minutes until firm to the touch. Unmold onto a wire rack and cool.

2. To make the chocolate buttercream, blend the cocoa and boiling water to make a smooth paste. Leave to cool slightly. Place the paste in a bowl with the butter and confectioners' sugar and beat to combine the ingredients. Continue to beat for 2 minutes, until the buttercream is light and fluffy.

3. Split the cake in half horizontally and put the layers back together with a little buttercream. Place the cake, smallest end down, on a serving plate or board. Spread a little buttercream over the top and sides.

4. Place the remaining buttercream in a pastry bag fitted with a ribbon tube. Pipe a basketweave design all around the sides of the cake (see page 59). Pipe a decorative border around the top edge of the cake.

5. Tint the marzipan yellow with a drop or two of food coloring and shape into daffodils (you will need about 20 – see page 64). Leave to dry a little and arrange on top of the basket.

6. To make the basket handle, take a strip of foil about 15 inches long and fold it over several times to form a thick strong band. Wrap half with the ribbon around the foil, securing it at each end with a little cellophane tape. Curve the band into shape and place it on the cake, fixing each end to the buttercream. Make a bow on one side with the remaining length of ribbon.

Harvest Cake

Here is a splendid cake to celebrate one of the happiest times of the year. There's plenty of fruit inside, as well as the goodies on top.

1 10-inch square silver cake board
1 8-inch square Rich Fruit Cake (pages 24–5)
1 quantity apricot glaze (page 38)
1¾ lb marzipan (page 37)
1 egg white
¾ lb fondant molding paste (page 44)
a few drops of yellow food coloring
1-cup sugar quantity royal icing (page 39)
a little confectioners' sugar and cornstarch, for dusting
To decorate:
an assortment of marzipan fruits and vegetables (pages 64–5)

Preparation time: icing and decorating the cake

1. Brush the top and sides of the cake with apricot glaze and cover with marzipan (see page 38). Place the cake on the cake board and leave to dry for a minimum of 24 hours.

2. Color the molding paste yellow with a drop or two of food coloring.

3. Roll out the molding paste on a surface dusted with confectioners' sugar and cornstarch to make a 10-inch square.

4. Brush the marzipan with a little egg white. Supporting the molding paste with the rolling pin, place it centrally over the top of the cake. Smooth it over the top and down the sides with a circular motion, dipping your fingertips in sugar and cornstarch as you work. Work the surplus to the base of the cake and trim the edges.

5. Color the royal icing with a drop of yellow food coloring and place a little in a parchment paper decorating cone fitted with a medium writing tube. Pipe the word "Harvest" with a flourish across the top of the cake as shown (prick the letters out first if you wish).

6. Arrange the marzipan fruits and vegetables in a cluster in one corner. Place them carefully to occupy about a quarter of the cake, leaving about 1 inch clear at the sides to set them off. Group each type together balancing color and size.

7. Place the remaining icing in a pastry bag fitted with a ¼-inch fluted tube and pipe a shell border around the bottom edge of the cake to attach it to the board. Leave to dry before serving.

Opposite page: Easter basket
Below: Harvest cake

SPECIAL OCCASIONS

Many special days in life are made even nicer with a glorious cake. When you want to say congratulations on an anniversary, to wish a loved one good luck in a new venture or on retirement, or to celebrate a child's confirmation, choose one of these cakes. The designs can be adapted as you wish to suit a variety of different occasions.

Confirmation Cake

1 11-inch round silver cake board
1 9-inch round Rich Fruit Cake (pages 24–5)
1 quantity apricot glaze (page 38)
1¾ lb marzipan (page 37)
12-cup (3-lb) sugar quantity royal icing (page 39)
deep purple or other food coloring
9 white piped roses (page 60)
6 silver leaves
white or silver and white 1½- to 2-inch wide ribbon
For the Bible:
½ lb marzipan (page 37)
deep red food coloring

Preparation time: icing and decorating the cake

1. Brush the top and sides of the cake with apricot glaze, then cover with marzipan (see page 38). Leave to dry.

2. Make up the royal icing and attach the cake to the cake board with a dab of icing. Flat ice the cake, giving two coats all over and a third coat to the top if necessary (see page 40). Leave to dry for 24 hours.

3. To make the Bible, knead the marzipan and shape it into a rectangle. Place between sheets of plastic and roll out carefully into an open book shape, making a depression in the center and at the ends as with an open book. This is done by pressing fairly firmly at each end, reducing the pressure until you come to the center and then giving firm pressure in the center again. Trim off the overhanging edges of the "pages" and straighten the sides. Trim to give a border which represents the cover of the book. Make cuts into the sides of the book with a sharp knife to represent the pages.

4. Roll out the marzipan trimmings and cut them into a cross to fit one of the pages; position on the left-hand page and attach with a dab of icing. Using a fine paintbrush and deep purple food coloring, paint the cross and the "cover" of the book. Transfer the book to a sheet of wax paper and leave in a warm place to dry. If necessary, add a second coat of coloring.

5. Make a hexagonal template (see page 51), making the points about 1 inch from the edge of the cake. Place some royal icing in a parchment paper decorating cone fitted with a medium writing tube and outline the hexagonal shape on top of the cake. Make two more outlines inside the first, leaving a small gap between them. Leave to dry, then overpipe the center line.

6. Position the Bible a little above the center of the hexagon and attach with icing. Using the writing tube, pipe words of your choice on the plain page of the book.

7. Write the name of the child on paper, then prick out the letters on the cake in front of the Bible. Outline this in white icing and overpipe when dry.

8. In front of alternate sides of the hexagon write the initials of the child; in front of the other sides, arrange a spray of roses and silver leaves, attaching them with icing.

9. Mark the top edges of the cake evenly into 12 or 18 portions, putting a small dot of icing on the cake and keeping it even with the lines of the hexagon on the top. Using a fine or medium star tube and white icing, pipe graduated twisted scrolls around the top edge of the cake between the dots (page 58) increasing pressure of icing in the center of each scroll to make it larger and decreasing as you tail it off.

10. Work the same type of border around the base of the cake, making it a little heavier if preferred. Leave to dry.

11. Tie the ribbon around the side of the cake, with or without a bow.

Good Luck Cake

With its ornate icing patterns and delicate flower sprays, this handsome alternative to a horseshoe good luck cake could be used for other occasions with a change of wording (such as a 45th – sapphire – wedding anniversary).

1 10-inch square silver cake board
1 8-inch square Rich Fruit Cake (pages 24–5)
1 quantity apricot glaze (page 38)
1¾ lb marzipan (page 37)
14-cup (3½-lb) sugar quantity royal icing (page 39)
blue food coloring
little egg white, lightly beaten, or lemon juice, strained
length of ¾- to 1-inch wide blue ribbon
silver candy balls

Preparation time: icing and decorating the cake

1. Brush the top and sides of the cake with apricot glaze, then cover with marzipan (see page 38). Leave to dry.

2. Make up the royal icing and attach the cake to the cake board with a dab of icing.

3. Color about three-quarters of the icing blue and use this to flat ice the cake, giving two coats all over and a third coat to the top if necessary. Leave to dry for 24 hours.

4. On a piece of non-stick parchment paper write the words "Good Luck".

5. Place a little white or colored icing in a parchment paper decorating cone fitted with a medium writing tube and outline the words on the paper. Thin a little matching icing with egg white or lemon juice until it flows. Use this icing to flood the letters. Burst any bubbles that

appear and leave the words to dry.

6. Place the ribbon over the cake as shown in the photograph and attach it to the board with a dab of icing.

7. Using a fine writing tube and white icing, work rows of lattice on the cake between the ribbon and the corners, taking care to start and end each row of icing neatly as it acts as a border.

8. Position the words of greeting on the cake and attach them with a little icing.

9. Using the medium writing tube and white icing, pipe sprays of lily of the valley on each side of the writing. This is done by piping slightly curved lines for both stems and leaves and then adding dots to each side of some of the lines to represent flowers.

10. Pipe two sprays of lily of the valley on each side of the cake in the same way.

11. Using a fine star or a rope or scroll tube, pipe a line of shells just inside the ribbons on top of the cake and along the top edge of the cake where there is no lattice. Place a silver candy ball in between the shells on the lines across the top of the cake.

12. Pipe a heavier shell edging all around the base of the cake and down the corners. Leave to dry.

From the left: Confirmation cake, Good luck cake

Good Luck Horseshoe Cake

This is a useful cake to include in your repertoire as it is appropriate for a number of occasions: a retirement party, a new job, moving house, an important exam or a new school term.

If you cannot find a horse-shoe cake pan, make a large round cake and cut it out as explained on page 53.

A lighter cake could be made with a butter cake batter and covered with buttercream or molding paste. Such a cake would need to be eaten sooner than an iced fruit cake.

1 13-inch round silver cake board
1 10-inch round quantity Rich Fruit Cake mixture (pages 24–5), baked in a 10-inch horseshoe cake pan
1 quantity apricot glaze (page 38)
2 lb marzipan (page 37)
16-cup (4-lb) sugar quantity royal icing (page 39)
To decorate:
about 50 piped yellow roses (page 60)
24 small silver leaves

Preparation time: icing and decorating the cake

1. Brush the top and sides of the cake with apricot glaze and cover with marzipan (see page 38). Leave to dry for a minimum of 24 hours.

2. Make up the royal icing and attach the cake to the board with a dab of icing.

3. Flat ice the cake, giving two coats all over and a third to the top, if necessary. Leave to dry. To cover the cake board, thin a little icing and place the cake on an icing turntable, smoothing the icing onto the board with a narrow spatula as you turn the cake. Leave to dry.

4. Fill a parchment paper decorating cone fitted with a star tube with royal icing and pipe a coiled border around the top and base edges of the cake, stopping the base border at the inside straight edge.

5. Using a little royal icing, attach five clusters composed of three yellow roses and two silver leaves to the top of the cake at evenly spaced intervals. Attach pairs of roses and leaves to the sides of the cake, one cluster on the inside and a single rose with a pair of leaves at each end. Leave to set completely.

Good luck horseshoe cake

Golden Wedding Cake

All wedding anniversaries call for celebration, but 50 years is something special – and this cake rises to the occasion. The piped and run-out decorations are as delicate as they are beautiful, so make extra in case some of them crack in handling.

1 12-inch square gold cake board
10- × 6-inch rectangular Rich Fruit Cake (pages 24–5) or a 10-inch square cake trimmed to the correct size
1 quantity apricot glaze (page 38)
about 16-cup (4-lb) sugar quantity royal icing (page 39)
a little egg white or lemon juice
¼ lb fondant molding paste (page 44)
gold candy balls
about 1 yard narrow gold ribbon (optional)

Preparation time: icing and decoration of the cake, plus making and drying of the collars, plaque, numbers and fans

1. Brush the top and sides of the cake with apricot glaze and coat with marzipan (see page 38). Leave to dry for 24 hours.

2. Make up some of the royal icing and use a good dab to attach the cake to the board.

3. Flat ice the cake giving it two coats all over and a third coat to the top if necessary (see pages 40–41). Leave to dry. Make up the rest of the royal icing as needed.

4. Meanwhile make the collars. On a sheet of paper, cut out a corner to fit the corners of the cake exactly. Draw a curved shape as in the picture which measures 1½ inches along each side. Cut this shape out and transfer the shape to a sheet of cardboard. Also draw shapes for the collars for the long sides of the cake, which should be 2 inches long.

5. Lay a sheet of non-stick parchment paper over the collar templates. Using a No. 2 writing tube and white icing, outline them, making at least eight collars for the corners and four for the sides to allow for breakages.

6. Next place the paper collar templates around the base of the cake on the board and outline with white icing and the same writing nozzle.

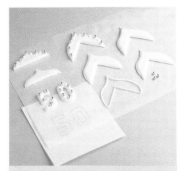

Making the decorated run-out collars and numbers.

Golden wedding cake

7. Draw the figures 5 and 0 on the card, cover with parchment or wax paper and outline, making three of each, again to allow for breakages. (You only need one of each for the cake.)

8. Thin a little of the icing with egg white or lemon juice and put into a paper decorating cone without a tube. Cut off the tip and use to flood the collars and numbers. Prick any air bubbles that come to the

surface and leave undisturbed until quite dry.

9. At the same time flood the collar shapes on the cake board, prick any air bubbles and leave to dry.

10. Roll out the fondant molding paste thinly on non-stick parchment paper and trim evenly to a rectangle of approximately 5 × 2 inches. Leave to dry completely.

11. To make the fans, using white icing and a No. 1 or 0 writing tube, follow the directions for fans on the Hexagonal Wedding Cake (page 92) but make the shape different by piping four shallow loops for the first row; three for the second row; two for the third and one final loop to complete it, keeping the basic pattern the same size and shape. Make at least 40 fans to allow for breakages. Leave to dry.

12. When the collars are dry, carefully pipe a series of dots all around the outer edge using the fine writing tube, and add gold candy balls to every other dot. When dry, attach the collars carefully to the corners and sides of the cake with icing and stand something underneath them to hold in position while they dry.

13. Pipe dots around the collars on the board, again adding gold candy balls to every alternate dot. Do the same to the 5 and 0, adding gold candy balls to every alternate dot.

14. Using the medium writing tube, pipe "Happy Anniversary" on the fondant plaque. When dry, overpipe. Leave to dry completely, then attach the plaque centrally to the cake with icing. (Measure up first and prick out marks to help you place the plaque centrally.)

15. Stand the 50 up at the back of the plaque and attach with icing, holding it in position until dry.

16. On a piece of paper, draw a semicircle a little wider than the side collar on the board and prick it out on the side of the cake. Take a pastry bag fitted with a No. 2 writing tube and pipe a series of dots to outline this shape. Also pipe a series of dots all around the plaque on top of the cake, adding a few gold candy balls if liked.

17. Using a pastry bag fitted with a No. 3 writing tube, pipe a border of dots all around the base of the cake except over the run-outs. Next pipe a series of small dots just each side of the outlined semicircle above three alternate dots, with two graduated ones each side and three in the center. Pipe another series of dots centrally on the short sides of the cake.

18. Pipe a smaller border of dots around the top edge of the cake and a series of three, four and three graduated dots on the long sides under three alternate main dots between the two collars and centrally on the short sides of the cake.

19. Finally attach three icing fans in each corner of the cake as shown, and three by each central collar. Attach five fans around each semicircle and one fan at each corner, pointing outwards.

20. Add a small bow of gold ribbon at each corner on top of the cake, if liked.

Variations

For a silver wedding, simply change the numbers to 25 and substitute silver candy balls and ribbon for the gold, placing the cake on a silver board. To get a good red for a ruby wedding you will need to color the icing for the plaque, collars and fans with a paste color. Add a few sugared red rose petals. The list of wedding anniversaries and corresponding materials is as follows (though not all of them are equally inspiring!).

Wedding anniversaries

1st	Paper
2nd	Cotton
3rd	Leather
4th	Fruit
5th	Wood
6th	Candy
7th	Wool
8th	Bronze
9th	Pottery
10th	Tin
11th	Steel
12th	Linen
13th	Lace
14th	Ivory
15th	Crystal
20th	China
25th	Silver
30th	Pearl
35th	Coral
40th	Ruby
45th	Sapphire
50th	Gold
55th	Emerald
60th	Diamond

BIRTHDAY CAKES

Everyone enjoys birthdays, no matter what their age, and seizes the opportunity for a party where the centerpiece is a beautifully decorated cake, such as the pretty one opposite.

The Sporting Birthday Cake on page 134 can easily be adapted for a different purpose, while the most elaborate decorations are reserved for special celebrations like an 18th birthday.

Square Birthday Cake

The fondant molding paste used to cover this cake and to make the frill around the edge gives a soft finish so that the cake looks like a satin cushion with flowers embroidered on top.

1 10- or 11-inch square silver cake board
1 8- or 9-inch square Rich Fruit Cake (page 24–5)
1 quantity apricot glaze (page 38)
1¾–2 lb marzipan (page 37)
a little egg white
2–2½ lb fondant molding paste (page 44)
about 50 piped royal icing pink tea roses with white or pale green centers (step 3)
about 24 piped royal icing small pale green leaves (page 60)
2-cup sugar quantity royal icing (page 39)
pink and green liquid food colorings

Preparation time: icing and decoration of the cake, plus time for making and drying the flowers, leaves and frills

1. Brush the top and sides of the cake with apricot glaze and coat with marzipan (see page 38). Stand on the cake board and leave to dry for 24 hours.

2. Brush the marzipan lightly with egg white. Roll out most of the fondant molding paste and use to cover the cake smoothly and evenly (see page 44). Leave to dry.

3. Make the royal icing pink roses adapting freehand from the instructions for primrose (page 60) to give an open petal shape. Make the leaves. Allow to dry.

4. Make a template for the design of the flowers on top of the cake. Fold a 7½-inch square into a triangle, fold the triangle in half, then in half once again. Draw a small curve from the folded edge, then a deep petal shape to within about ¾ inch of the top of the paper. Cut out. Position the template on the cake and prick out the design.

5. Tint the royal icing pink to match the flowers and put into a pastry bag fitted with a small writing tube. Outline the template.

6. Prick out the words "Birthday Greetings" and the name of the person inside the piped line. Pipe over with pink or green icing. Let dry, then overpipe.

7. Arrange the pink flowers and green leaves over the outlined shape made by the template, attaching with a dab of icing.

8. Make a template for the sides of the cakes. Cut out a strip of paper the length of the side and two-thirds of the depth. Fold into quarters and draw a shallow curve on it. Don't make this too deeply curved or it will be difficult to add the frills without breaking them.

9. For the frilling on the side of the cake, tint the remaining fondant paste the same pink or a little paler than the flowers

and roll out thinly. Cut into strips about ¾ inch wide, then mark a line along the length of each strip about ¼ inch down from the top edge. Next, take a wooden toothpick and roll it gently from side to side below the marked line, to thin out the icing. This should make the frilling. Do not attempt to make the frills too long or they will break as you try to pick them up.

10. Fit the template around the sides of the cake and pipe a line of pink icing onto the side of the cake to follow the scallop lines. Attach the frilling to this line. Make joins as and when necessary by slightly moistening the ends of the frills, pressing together and rubbing over the joins with the fingertips. The frilling must be added while still soft or it will become brittle and be difficult to handle.

11. Using a medium writing tube and pink icing, pipe a series of dots all around the base of the cake to attach it to the board. Next, pipe another dot directly under the point of the curved frill just above the base dot, then a smaller one still above that. Add a fourth dot with the fine tube. Add two dots of graduating sizes above the dots each side of the central one; and one dot over the one each side beyond that. Repeat under all the points of the frills.

12. Add a pink rose and two small leaves by every other dot decoration on the board, so that the flower tilts slightly up the cake but the leaves are on the board. Leave to dry.

Strips of fondant molding paste cut and ready to make the frills for the cake.

Gently rolling a toothpick along the strips below the marked line to "frill" them.

Square birthday cake

Eighteenth or Twenty-First Birthday Cake

This elegant cake will delight the most sophisticated young adult. The effect is achieved with subtle coloring and extremely delicate piping of the trelliswork on top of the cake and the curtainwork attaching it to the board.

1 11-inch round silver cake board
1 8- or 9-inch round Rich Fruit Cake (pages 24–5)
1 quantity apricot glaze (page 38)
1¾ lb marzipan (page 37)
10-cup (2½-lb) sugar quantity royal icing (page 39) or 3-cup sugar quantity royal icing and (2 lb) fondant molding paste (page 44)
peach liquid food coloring

Preparation time: icing and decoration of the cake, plus time for drying the run-out numbers

1. Brush the top and sides of the cake with apricot glaze and cover with marzipan (page 38). Stand the cake on the board and leave to dry.

2. Tint the royal icing a pale peach and use to give two coats all over the cake *or* tint the molding paste pale peach and use to cover the cake (page 44). Leave to dry.

3. Draw the number "18" or "21" eight times on a piece of cardboard, cover with parchment or wax paper and run-out the figures. To do this, tint all the remaining icing a deeper shade of peach and put some into a pastry bag fitted with a No. 0 or 1 fine writing tube. Outline the figures carefully. Next, thin a little of the icing with lemon juice or egg white, fit into a paper decorating cone, snip off the end and use to flood the figures (see picture, top right). Leave the numbers undisturbed to dry completely.

4. Make a template for the cake (see page 52). Draw a 7½-inch circle on thickish paper and cut it out. Fold the circle in half and draw a pencil line across the length of the semicircle ¾ inch up from the edge on each side. Next, fold the paper evenly to give three even portions. Open out and make a mark ½ inch each side of the folded line at the curved edge. Number these 1 to 4 working from left to right. Draw lines from points 1 and 4 to where the folds meet the penciled line. Next mark the center of the penciled line and draw two lines from here to the curved edge to join points 2 and 3. Repeat on the other side. Position the paper on the cake and prick out these shapes with a pin.

5. Using the writing tube, pipe out the name in the center of the cake in the space between the pricked-out shapes. Leave to dry, then overpipe. When dry again, decorate the letters with a series of tiny dots, if liked.

6. Pipe two long lines under and above the name, making the one nearest the writing about 1 inch shorter at each end.

7. Using the finest writing tube you have, work a 5-row trellis to fill the shapes pricked out on top of the cake. To do this, first pipe a series of parallel lines beginning with the two outer shapes of each set of three and keeping in line with the lines already piped on top of the cake, just over ¼ inch apart. For the central shape outline it, then pipe lines parallel with the left-hand side. Turn the cake around and work the remaining three shapes in exactly the same way.

8. Turn the cake back again and when the first piping is dry, pipe lines parallel to the other side of the shape, again spacing them evenly ¼ inch apart. Complete all the trellis in the same way. When the icing is dry continue to work the trellis up until you have five rows. If you find it very difficult to keep it neat and even, stop after completing three layers.

9. Fill a pastry bag fitted with a small writing tube with deep peach icing. Pipe a series of small dots all around the top edge at about ¾-inch intervals to make a border. Pipe a loop from each of these dots.

10. Pipe a second row of small dots all around in between the first ones. Again work a row of loops from each dot, with slightly deeper curves than the first ones.

11. For the curtain decoration base, first make a template for the curves. Cut a strip of stiff paper about ¾-inch deep. Fold into 1½-inch widths and cut out shallow curves. Open out the strip and place around the sides of the cake, so that it touches the board. Using the writing tube, pipe a series of almost touching tiny dots all around to outline the curves. Remove the template and with a medium writing tube, pipe a border of dots all around the cake to attach it to the board. Next with the small writing tube, pipe a series of dots all around the cake board about ½ inch from the end of the dots, matching one for one with those on the side of the cake.

12. With the fine writing tube, work straight lines from the dots on the cake to the corresponding dots on the board keeping it very neat and even. Leave to dry.

13. Attach either six or eight number 18s or 21s evenly all around the sides of the cake with tiny dabs of icing. Leave to dry.

Drawing, piping and filling the outlines for the run-out 18s for the Eighteenth Birthday Cake.

Piping straight lines from the dots on the side of the cake to the dots on the board, to create a curtain effect.

Eighteenth birthday cake

Sporting Birthday Cake

This design makes a good general birthday cake for men and boys, but it is distinguished enough to be adapted for a 21st birthday or a club celebration when your team has won the cup!

1 10-inch square silver cake board
1 8-inch square Rich Fruit Cake (pages 24–5)
1 quantity apricot glaze (page 38)
1¾ lb marzipan (page 37)
10-cup (2½-lb) sugar quantity royal icing (page 39)
yellow food coloring
a little egg white, lightly beaten, or lemon juice, strained

Preparation time: icing and decorating the cake

1. Brush the top and sides of the cake with apricot glaze, then cover with marzipan (see page 38). Leave to dry for 24 hours.

2. Make up the royal icing and attach the cake to the cake board with a dab of icing. Tint two thirds of the icing yellow with food coloring. Use to flat ice the cake, giving it two coats all over and a third coat to the top if necessary (see pages 40–41).

3. Draw the outline of two crossed baseball or cricket bats and two crossed tennis rackets, a yacht or other type of boat, or a car about 2 inches high on a sheet of paper. These sporting motifs can be drawn freehand, or by tracing a picture of the correct size. Place the drawings under a sheet of non-stick parchment paper.

4. Fill a parchment paper decorating cone fitted with a medium writing tube with white icing and outline the drawings five times each for bats and rackets or nine times for boats or cars, moving the pattern under the paper each time.

5. Thin about 6 tablespoons of the icing with a little egg white or lemon juice until it flows, then use to flood the outlines. Burst any air bubbles that appear and leave the run-out motifs to dry.

6. When dry, pipe details such as racket-strings, sails or car windows with white icing.

7. Using white icing and a pastry bag fitted with a medium tube pipe two square outlines on the top of the cake about 1 inch in from the cake's edge. When dry, overpipe the inner square.

8. With the same tube pipe "brackets" in each of the corners of the cake, making two lines of graduated lengths.

9. Midway between the brackets, along the sides, pipe five dots in a straight line. Then pipe three dots in front of these and finally two dots, one in front of the other in the center.

10. Write the name or greeting on a piece of paper. Prick the words onto the cake and outline three times with white icing. When dry, overpipe and complete with dots. Leave to dry.

11. Using white icing and a thick writing tube, pipe a row of dots around the top edge of the cake. Pipe a second row on the side of the cake in between the first ones but so they just touch.

12. Pipe a row of large dots with a smaller one on top (by depressing the tube after piping the first part of the dot) all around the base of the cake.

13. Carefully stick a pair of bats and rackets or two boats on each side of the cake with a dab of icing. Leave to dry.

Draw the outlines for the tennis rackets or other sporting motifs. Pipe onto squares of non-stick parchment paper. Fill handle and frame outlines.

When you have filled in the outlines of the frames and handles, pipe in the racket strings working lengthwise and across the frames.

Sporting birthday cake

NOVELTY CAKES

Everyone loves a surprise cake, while for the cake-maker novelty cakes provide a wonderful opportunity to create imaginative cake designs.

When the occasion calls for fun, a novelty cake is the right choice. This chapter shows that there is nothing that cannot be represented in the form of a cake: all it takes is a sense of adventure and a lively imagination.

The focus of attention at children's parties is always a cake, the more amazing the better, and their delight in a special creation is particularly rewarding to the cook. The range of ideas is limitless: a well-loved nursery rhyme character, perhaps, like Humpty Dumpty (page 148), a Fairy Castle (page 141) or a friendly Lion (150). Children particularly enjoy the results of your inventiveness when you choose a theme that is a special favorite of the birthday girl or boy, such as Ballet Shoes (page 146) or a Spaceship Rocket (page 156) – and the cakes are great fun to make.

There are many other occasions, not only for children, on which a cake that is out-of-the-ordinary adds a sparkle to the proceedings. The Flower cake on page 152 could be made for an outdoor party, Mother's Day or the summer meeting of your local garden club. The Hat cake in the same page would also be fun for Mother's Day, or as a birthday cake for a teenage girl. While most men like cakes, they might not appreciate being presented with one that's covered with molded roses. The Executive Case on page 145 would be much more appropriate.

The most versatile novelty cakes are in the shape of numerals, which can be used for birthdays, wedding and other anniversaries and any occasion at which a number is significant. By using different icings and decorations you can achieve any effect you please.

Most of the cakes in this section are based on the Quick Mix batter (page 16, or use the Healthy Sponge Cake recipe on page 22), with one or two Pound and Whisked Sponge recipes. The cakes are baked in a variety of pans and molds with the minimum amount of trimming needed to achieve a particular shape.

As you work your way through the recipes you will realize how easy it is to construct special cakes from a few basic shapes. A butterfly, for example, could easily be made by cutting a around cake in half and turning each semi-circle around so that the curved edges are side by side.

The Peppermint Racer (page 157) is one example of the transport theme which is perennially popular: fire engines, tractors, trains and boats can all be constructed on the same principle.

Soft cakes are easier to cut and shape if they are made one or two days before required. It is easier to ice or frost if apricot glaze is applied over the whole cake and left to set overnight.

The most versatile covering is fondant molding paste, which can be colored in any shade and used to cover cakes and make models and fancy shapes.

Buttercream provides a good surface for small decorations and is also used for the basketweave pattern shown on the Basket of Chocolates (page 142) and the Summer Straw Hat (page 153). If you want to give buttercream a smooth surface, use a small narrow spatula dipped into hot water.

If you cannot buy a cake board of the size and shape you need, you can make your own by cutting several thicknesses of cardboard to the required size and covering the built-up board with foil. You can also use a wooden board or chopping block, covered with foil.

The techniques in this chapter can easily be adapted to other novelty ideas – a cake that looks like a book or a golf-course, a maypole or a bottle of champagne. Half the fun lies in thinking up the ideas. And once you have discovered the delights of making novelty cakes, your talents are sure to be much in demand.

Numeral Birthday Cakes

These cakes are especially fun for children and can be decorated in many ways to incorporate a hobby or child's special fancy. For a formally iced cake using marzipan and royal icing, a Rich Fruit Cake (page 24) can be used. Numeral cakes are fun for length of service parties, retirements, or the number of a new house. They make good anniversary cakes, especially for 25, 40 and 50 years. For a 40th or ruby wedding cake, decorate with chocolate buttercream, candied cherries and grated chocolate or chocolate curls.

Quick Mix Cakes (pages 16–17) or Pound Cakes (page 19)
⅔ cup jam or ¼ quantity simple buttercream, if necessary, for putting layers together
1¾–2 quantities simple buttercream (page 46)
food coloring and flavoring (optional)
candles and candle holders (optional)
colorful candies (optional)
marzipan flowers (page 64)
marzipan leaves (page 63)

Preparation time: frosting and decorating the cakes

1. If using cake layers, put them together with the jam or buttercream. Place on a cake board of the appropriate size.

2. Tint the buttercream and add flavoring, if using. Use to mask the whole cake, perhaps finishing with a swirling design all over or backward and forward lines made with a round-bladed knife.

3. Tint the remaining buttercream a darker shade and put into a pastry bag fitted with a star tube. Use to pipe a shell or star edging around the top edge and base of the cake.

4. Stick candles at intervals on the top of the cake. Alternatively, put sieved jam or jelly into a paper decorating cone (see page 56), without a tube, then cut off the tip. Pipe a message on the top of the cakes.

5. Stick candies in a line around the sides, or pipe stars of buttercream.

6. Finally, position the marzipan flowers and leaves on top of the cake, attaching with buttercream. Leave to set.

Shaping Numeral Cakes

Nought: bake one 9- to 12-inch round cake. When cold cut a 3- to 5-inch diameter hole in center.

One: bake one 6-inch square layer cake. When completely cold cut the cake in half and position one piece above the other.

Two: bake one 11½- × 8½- × 1½-inch sheet cake or a 12- × 10- × 2-inch sheet cake. Cut out a pattern, transfer to the cooled cake and carefully cut out.

Three: bake two 8-inch round layer cakes. Cut out a pattern, transfer to the cakes and cut out. Stick the two cakes together with jam or buttercream.

Four: bake one 7- to 10-inch square layer cake. Cut out a pattern, transfer to the cake and cut out, taking care when removing the middle piece.

Five: bake one 11½- × 8½- × 1½-inch sheet cake or one 12- × 10- × 2-inch sheet cake. Cut a pattern, transfer to the cake and cut out.

Six or Nine: bake one 11½- × 8½- × 1½-inch sheet cake or one 12- × 10- × 2-inch sheet cake. Cut a pattern, transfer to the cake and cut out.

Seven: bake one 7- to 10-inch square cake, or one 11½- × 8½- × 1½-inch or one 12- × 10- × 2-inch sheet cake. Cut out a pattern, position on the cake and cut out.

Eight: bake two 8-inch round layer cakes. Cut out a pattern with a 3- to 3½-inch circle out of the center. Transfer to the cakes and cut out. Trim a piece off the side of each cake and put together with jam or buttercream to make an eight.

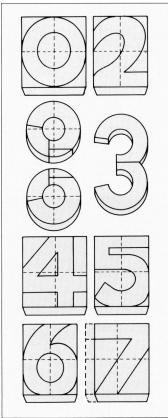

Numeral birthday cakes

Pirates' Treasure Chest

This cake sums up the best of "novelty" cakes in that it is as much fun to make as it is to serve – it won't be long before the party guests have run off with the treasure!

1 10-inch square gold cake board
1 3-egg quantity orange-flavored Quick Mix Cake batter (pages 16–17)
²⁄₃ cup chocolate chips
6–8 tablespoons chocolate fudge-type topping
gold candy balls
1 individual chocolate-covered jelly roll
diamond candy cake decorations
2 tablespoons apricot jam, warmed and sieved
sugar crystals, for sprinkling
assorted candies, including foil-covered chocolate coins, candy "jewelry" and gold "bullion"
pirates' treasure map (optional)

Opposite page: Sugar plum fairy castle
Below: Pirates' treasure chest

Preparation time: frosting and decorating the cake
Cooking time: about 55 minutes
Oven: 325°F

1. Grease and line a 9- × 5- × 3-inch loaf pan with greased wax paper or non-stick parchment paper.

2. Make the cake batter and stir in the chocolate chips. Pour into the prepared pan and bake for about 55 minutes, until golden brown and firm to the touch. Unmold onto a wire rack. Remove the lining paper and leave the cake the right way up to cool.

3. Cut a horizontal slice about ½-inch deep from the top of the cake to make the lid of the chest, and trim a narrow strip off one long side. Spread the sides of the base of the chest with chocolate fudge topping. Place the cake on the cake board.

4. Spread the top of the lid with chocolate fudge topping, leaving the underside uncovered. Using clean tweezers, arrange a row of candy balls around the top and bottom edges of the base and the lid and down each corner.

5. Cut a thick slice from the flat side of the jelly roll, then place the roll lengthwise on top of the base, towards the front of the center. Place the lid on the base, with the trimmed side at the back. (The jelly roll will help to keep it open.) Decorate the top of the lid with rows of candy diamonds.

6. Spread the area around the base of the cake with jam and sprinkle with sugar crystals. Stuff the chest with chocolate coins and candy "jewelry." Place a pile of coins, bullion and candies around the base of the chest. Place the map, if using, on the board with a gold coin or two to hold it in place.

Sugar Plum Fairy Castle

1 12-inch fluted round silver cake board
1 6-egg quantity Whisked Sponge Cake batter (pages 20–21)
6 tablespoons apricot glaze (page 38)
1½ lb fondant molding paste (page 44)
pink food coloring
1-cup flour quantity Quick Mix Cake batter (pages 16–17)
1¾ cups sugar
2 teaspoons cold water
a little cornstarch for sprinkling
pink food coloring pen
½ lb sugared almonds

Preparation time: 1 hour, plus cooling and drying
Cooking time: 40 minutes
Oven: 350°F

1. Place two thirds of the whisked sponge batter in a greased wax paper-lined 13- × 9-inch baking pan, and one third of the batter in a greased, wax paper-lined 11- × 7-inch baking pan. Bake in a preheated oven for 15–20 minutes until well risen and firm to the touch.

2. Use some of the apricot glaze as filling and roll up following the instructions for making a jelly roll (page 20) but roll the smaller jelly roll lengthwise to make a long thin roll.

3. Make the fondant molding paste and tint it very pale pink with a few drops of food coloring, then wrap it in plastic wrap.

4. Place the quick mix cake batter in a greased wax paper-lined 8-inch layer cake pan and bake in a preheated oven for 15–20 minutes until well risen and firm to the touch. Unmold and cool on a wire rack.

5. Place the sugar in a bowl and add a drop of pink food coloring to tint it the same color as the fondant molding paste. Reserve one third of the sugar and add the water to the remainder. Mix well together so that the sugar becomes damp.

6. Make three cone shapes out of paper (see small photograph, opposite). Fill the large cone with the dampened sugar and press firmly down. Place a piece of cardboard over the top and invert the sugar cone, then remove the paper shape. Use the other two papers to make one medium and two small cones and leave in a warm place to dry hard.

7. Trim the ends of each jelly roll, so that they are level. Cut one third off each roll to make four towers all of different heights (see diagram).

8. Unwrap the molding paste and cut it into five pieces. Roll out one piece thinly on a surface well sprinkled with cornstarch, the width of the largest roll and long enough to roll completely around it.

9. Brush the roll with some of the remaining apricot glaze. Place it on the molding paste, trim the molding paste to fit, then roll up, carefully sealing the seam by rubbing over it with fingers dipped in cornstarch. Repeat to cover the remaining rolls. Knead and re-roll the trimmings.

10. Place the reserved sugar on a piece of wax paper and roll each iced roll in it to coat evenly. Leave to dry.

11. Place the round cake on the cake board and, using plain cutters the same size as the base of each roll, cut out and remove four rounds (these will not be needed).

12. Brush the cake with some more of the apricot glaze and roll out the remaining molding paste to a circle large enough to cover the round cake. Place the molding paste over the cake, and gently press it into the holes. Smooth over and trim off the excess at the base. Sprinkle the molding paste and cake board with the remaining pink-tinted sugar.

13. Place each pink tower in position in the cut-out holes and carefully place the sugar cones on top of each.

14. Make the windows and doors for the towers with the fondant molding paste trimmings (as in the main photograph) and use the pink pen to mark the lattice work and door

panels. Place these in position and secure with the remaining apricot glaze.

15. Arrange the sugared almonds like a path and steps into the castle.

Using a paper cone to make the castle's sugar towers.

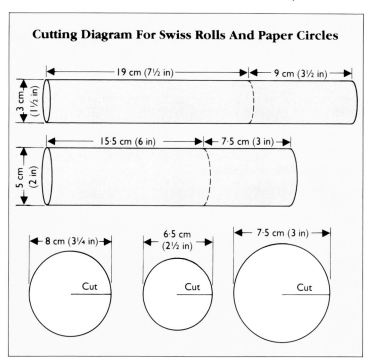

Cutting Diagram For Swiss Rolls And Paper Circles

19 cm (7½ in) — 9 cm (3½ in)
3 cm (1½ in)

15·5 cm (6 in) — 7·5 cm (3 in)
5 cm (2 in)

8 cm (3¼ in) — Cut
6·5 cm (2½ in) — Cut
7·5 cm (3 in) — Cut

Basket of Chocolates

Here is a sure way to a chocolate-lover's heart. Take your time building up the basketweave pattern and you will find it easy once you have done three or four lines.

1 11-inch round or heart-shaped heavy gold board
1 8- or 9-inch heart-shaped Quick Mix Cake (pages 16–17) or Pound Cake (page 19) (baked in a heart-shaped pan or cut to shape, see page 53)
brown food coloring
about 6 oz fondant molding paste (page 44)
1 quantity apricot glaze (page 38)
1–2 tablespoons coffee essence (optional)
2 quantities simple buttercream (page 46)
about ¾ lb assorted luxury chocolates
1 large gold bow
1 artificial flower

Preparation time: to make the cake, frosting etc. and about 1 hour for the final decoration

1. Add a touch of brown food coloring to the fondant paste to tint it to a pale coffee color. Roll out the paste on a surface dusted with cornstarch and confectioners' sugar and cut to a heart shape the same size as the cake. Cut in half down the center, place on a sheet of non-stick parchment paper and leave to dry in a warm place.

2. Stand the cake on the board. Brush the cake all over with apricot glaze.

3. Add a touch of brown food coloring or coffee essence to tint the buttercream a pale coffee color to match the lid. Spread a thin layer of buttercream over the top of the cake and neaten with a narrow spatula.

4. To work the basketweave, fit one pastry bag with a basket-weave tube and another with a No. 2 writing tube and fill both with buttercream. Beginning at the indentation at the back of the cake and holding the basketweave tube at an angle to the cake, pipe three or more horizontal lines about 1 inch long, one above the other and with the width of the tube left between them. Next, with the writing tube pipe a straight vertical line down the edge of the horizontal ribbon lines. Take the basket tube again and pipe more lines the same length as the first ones to fill the gaps but beginning halfway along those already piped and covering the straight lines. Pipe another straight vertical line down the edge and continue to build up the basketweave around the sides of the cake in this way, taking care to keep it even.

5. Work basketweave in the same way on the dried fondant paste heart pieces for the lid, and pipe a squiggly line with the writing tube around the edge. Leave to dry.

6. Arrange the chocolates (in their paper cases if preferred) around the top edge of the cake. Build up with more chocolates on the front half of the cake, but leave the center empty.

7. Carefully place the lids on the cake sticking the cut edge into the center and allowing the lids to rest on the chocolates as if they are peeping out. Place the gold ribbon bow and the flower in the center of the lid.

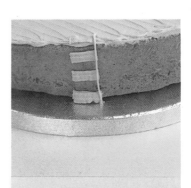

The first step in making the basketweave pattern.

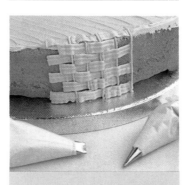

Building up the basketweave pattern around the cake.

Basket of chocolates

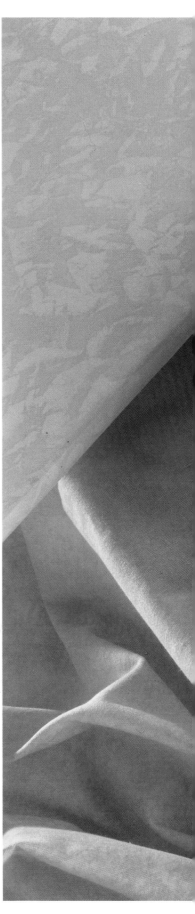

Hickory Dickory Dock Cake

If you cannot find a cake board of the right size for this large cake, cover a tray or chopping board with silver foil.

1 20- × 10-inch silver cake board
1 4-egg quantity Quick Mix Cake batter (pages 16–17)
1 quantity fondant molding paste (page 44)
a few drops of red food coloring
3 tablespoons blackberry jelly, warmed and melted
2 cups confectioners' sugar, sifted
boiling water
chocolate disks
2–4 silver candy balls (optional)
cornstarch and confectioners' sugar, for dusting
¾ cup dried shredded coconut

Preparation time: icing and decorating the cake, plus drying time
Cooking time: 35–40 minutes
Oven: 325°F

1. Grease and line an 8-inch round layer cake pan and a 7-inch square cake pan with greased wax paper or non-stick parchment paper. Divide the cake batter between the pans. Place in the preheated oven and bake for 35–40 minutes, until golden brown and firm to the touch.

2. Unmold the cakes onto a wire rack, remove the lining paper and leave to cool completely.

3. Knead the molding paste to make it pliable. Reserve a piece to make a mouse (or two small mice if you want to show the mouse running down the clock as well as up). Tint the remainder of the molding paste pale pink with a drop or two of red food coloring.

4. Using an 8-inch round cake pan or plate as a guide, cut a curved edge from one side of the square cake so that it fits snugly against the round cake. Separate the cakes and brush the top and sides of each with warm blackberry jelly.

5. Divide the pink fondant molding paste in half. Roll out

each half on a surface dusted with cornstarch and confectioners' sugar and use to cover both cakes, fitting it carefully around the sides. Place the two cakes on the tray and fit together.

6. Spread a little warm blackberry jelly on the board and sprinkle shredded coconut evenly over.

7. To make the piping icing, put three-quarters of the confectioners' sugar into a bowl with a little boiling water and stir to give a stiff piping consistency. Beat until smooth. Place the icing in a parchment paper decorating cone fitted with a star or shell tube and pipe shells around the top of the round cake and the three edges of the square cake. Pipe a border of shells around the base of both cakes.

8. Attach a chocolate disk to the center of the round cake and place 12 disks around the edge. Mix the remaining confectioners' sugar with a little water to give a piping consistency and place in a pastry bag fitted with a thin writing tube. Pipe numbers on the buttons and clock hands set at one o'clock.

9. Pipe two zigzag lines of icing on the lower cake to form the pendulum and finish it with two chocolate disks.

10. Shape the reserved uncolored piece of molding paste into the mouse or mice. Press in silver candy balls (if using) for eyes. Place on the lower cake as shown.

Hickory Dickory dock cake
Opposite page: Executive case

Executive Case

1 8-inch square thin silver cake board
1 3-egg quantity coffee Quick Mix Cake batter (pages 16–17)
1 quantity fondant molding paste (page 44)
food colorings (red, green, blue and gold)
2 tablespoons apricot glaze (page 38)
1 oblong wafer cookie
black food coloring pen
1 candy stick
2 sheets of rice paper

Preparation time: 40 minutes, plus setting
Cooking time: 50–55 minutes
Oven: 325°F

1. Place the cake batter in a greased and lined 10½- × 7½- × 2-inch baking pan and bake in a preheated oven for 50–55 minutes until well risen and firm to the touch. Unmold onto a wire rack, remove the paper and cool.

2. Make the molding paste. Reserve a small piece and color the remainder a deep brown color by adding red, green and a touch of blue food colorings.

3. Cut the cake in half across the width, put the layers together with apricot glaze and trim the top square. Brush with apricot glaze and place upright on the cake board.

4. Roll out one third of the dark brown colored molding paste to a 5-inch square. Cut the square in half and place each piece down the side of the case. Carefully trim along the edges to fit.

5. Roll out the remaining piece of dark brown paste large enough to cover the front, top and back of the case. Carefully fit the paste over the case and trim to fit, neatly joining the edges together.

6. Mark a line across the top and down the side for the opening seam.

7. Cover the cookie with trimmings of brown molding paste for the handle. Roll, cut and trim a 1½-inch square for the label.

8. Roll out the white molding paste and cut out two locks, two handle supports and the initials and paint with gold food coloring. Leave to set. Cut out the name tag from white paste. Reserve the trimmings. (See diagram, bottom.)

9. Secure the locks, the handle and supports in place with a little glaze. With a food coloring pen, write the name and address of the person on the white plaque then stick together with the label.

10. Fix the label in position under the handle.

11. Re-roll the dark brown molding paste trimmings into a 6-inch round. Place the candy stick in the center, then pleat the remaining paste around like an umbrella (see pictures, right).

12. With the remaining white paste, make a handle and top for the umbrella and trim with gold food coloring. Leave to set, then place on the cake board.

13. Using the rice paper and coloring pen, make a newspaper and write the day and date of the celebration, favorite newspaper title and a few lines written in columns. Place by the case.

Set out the candy stick, brown molding paste round, and white handle and top.

Pleating the circle of fondant molding paste for the umbrella.

Cutting Diagram For Locks And Handle

← 4·5 cm (1¾ inches) →

Handle

Lock × 2

2 cm (¾ in)

← 7·5 cm (3 inches) →

Ballet Shoes

As the jelly roll is very fragile when it is made, leave it to settle for a day first.

When rolling out the fondant molding paste, take care not to roll it out too thinly, otherwise the cake may show through and the molding paste will be difficult to handle when it is being molded into shape.

1 8-inch round thin silver cake board
1 3-egg quantity Whisked Sponge Cake batter (pages 20–21)
3 tablespoons apricot glaze (page 38)
1 quantity fondant molding paste (page 44)
cornstarch and confectioners' sugar, for dusting
pink and yellow food colorings
4 ice cream wafers
1 yard peach ribbon, ½-inch wide

Preparation time: 30 minutes
Cooking time: 10–15 minutes
Oven: 350°F

1. Place the cake batter in a greased and lined 13- × 9-inch jelly roll pan and bake in a preheated oven for 10–15 minutes until well risen and firm to the touch.

2. Unmold the cake onto a piece of sugared parchment paper. Remove the lining paper. Trim off the edges of the cake.

3. Quickly spread with some of the apricot glaze and roll up from a long edge. Cool on a wire rack. Store for a day before making the shoes.

4. Make the molding paste and add a few drops of pink and yellow food colorings to make it peach-colored.

5. Cut the wafers out to form the soles of the shoes. Cut the jelly roll in half and press one end of each half into a point.

6. Cut out a shallow oval shape from the center of each roll, then brush both all over with most of the remaining glaze.

7. Cut the paste in half. On a surface dusted with cornstarch and confectioners' sugar, roll out one half large enough to cover one roll. Use this paste to cover one of the rolls completely, seam on the undersides, and neaten the edges. Shape the heel and toe of the shoe until smooth.

8. Brush the wafer sole with glaze and press into position on the ballet shoe, trimming to fit if necessary. Using well-cornstarched hands, press the paste into the oval depression in the center of the shoe and form a sharp edge all around the top with the fingers.

9. Make a bow from the peach molding paste trimmings. Make into a pencil-thin roll, fold into two loops, trim and place in position on the toe with glaze. Repeat steps 7 to 9 for the other shoe.

10. Cut the ribbon into 4 pieces; press in position at the back of each shoe and secure with glaze. Arrange the ballet shoes on the cake board.

11. Petal candle holders, made from paste trimmings, may be made for this cake, if liked. Take a small ball of paste and press into a petal shape, curling the edge of the petal inwards to form a center. Press out another petal shape and wrap around the center petal; repeat with a third petal, then cut off the stem. Press the candle into the center. Repeat to make as many candle holders as required, then place beside the ballet shoes.

Ballet shoes

Humpty Dumpty

This idea could be adapted to make a clown or a witch; or you could place two cakes side by side for Tweedledum and Tweedledee.

2 8-inch thin silver cake boards
1 3-egg quantity chocolate Quick Mix Cake batter (pages 16–17)
1 quantity simple buttercream (page 46)
1 tablespoon cocoa powder
2 teaspoons boiling water
food colorings (pink, blue, green and yellow)
½ cup dried shredded coconut
4 tablespoons apricot glaze (page 38)
licorice candies
1 tablespoon chocolate-flavored toasted rice
2 oz marzipan (page 37)
black food coloring pen
1 sheet rice paper

Preparation time: 40 minutes
Cooking time: 25–45 minutes
Oven: 325°F

1. Grease and base-line a 1-quart pudding basin or steaming mold, a 7-inch round layer cake pan, and an 8- × 4-inch loaf pan.

2. Place 2 tablespoons of the cake batter in the basin, and divide the remainder between the two pans.

3. Bake in a preheated oven for about 30 minutes for the basin and round cake, and 40–45 minutes for the loaf pan, until well risen and firm to the touch.

4. Unmold from the basin and pans and remove the paper; cool on a wire rack.

5. Make the buttercream and divide it into three portions. Blend the cocoa and water together and cool, then beat it into one third of the buttercream. Color another third of the buttercream pink and the remaining third blue with the appropriate food colorings.

6. Reserve 1 tablespoon of the coconut. Divide the remainder into three and color one third blue, one third green and one third yellow by adding a few drops of each food coloring to a portion of coconut and mixing until well blended.

7. Brush one cake board with apricot glaze and sprinkle over the colored coconut to make a background picture, green for the grass, blue for the sky, white for clouds and yellow for the sun.

8. Spread the top and sides of the oblong cake with the chocolate buttercream. Place on the cake board ½ inch from the bottom and mark the buttercream with a knife to resemble a brick wall.

9. Put the round and pudding basin cakes together with apricot glaze and spread half with pink buttercream and half with blue buttercream. Place on the board against the top of the wall.

10. Arrange the licorice candies across the middle of the cake to form a "belt," and use different-shaped candies for the eyes, nose and mouth. Press the toasted rice in position for hair.

11. Color half the marzipan pink and half blue with food colorings and shape the pink into arms and the blue into legs. Place in position on the cake.

12. The second cake board may be used, if liked, to add the Humpty Dumpty nursery rhyme to the cake. Brush a 3-inch border of apricot glaze on the board and sprinkle with tinted coconut. Use a food coloring pen to write the rhyme on the rice paper and secure it to the cake board, inside the coconut border, with a little glaze.

Covering the cake board with coconut to make the background.

Making the clouds and sun in the sky behind Humpty Dumpty.

Characterful Cakes

The basic idea for the Humpty Dumpty Cake can be extended to other characters from nursery rhymes or children's stories. The round face can also be made from white marzipan or fondant molding paste colorfully decorated to look like a circus clown with the toasted rice "hair" arranged at the sides so that the "head" looks bald. For a teddy bear, cover the round cake with chocolate buttercream.

Lion Cake

This is one of the simplest cakes to decorate for a children's party, yet provides an extremely effective centerpiece for the table with its cheerful colors.

1 10-inch round silver cake board
2 8-inch chocolate Butter Cake layers (page 18)
1½-cup sugar quantity simple chocolate buttercream (page 46)
1½ cups chopped nuts (hazelnuts or almonds)
½ lb marzipan (page 37)
food colorings (yellow and pink)
a little egg white, lightly beaten
2 teaspoons cocoa
2 chocolate disks or beans
2 chocolate flakes
2 or 3 pieces of thin spaghetti

Preparation time: frosting and decorating the cake

1. Put the cake layers together with chocolate buttercream. Cover the top and sides of the cake with buttercream.

2. Cover the sides of the cake with ¾ cup of the chopped nuts and place it on the cake board.

3. Tint 6 oz of the marzipan yellow. Roll it out and cut out one circle 5 inches in diameter and two circles 2 inches in diameter. Reserve the trimmings.

4. Tint a small amount of marzipan pink. Roll it out and cut out two 1-inch circles. Attach the pink marzipan circles to the center of the small yellow marzipan circles with a little egg white, pressing the edges down firmly and evenly. Curve each piece inwards and place them in position on either side at the top of the cake as the lion's ears.

5. Position the largest circle in the center of the cake for the lion's face. Gently press around the outer edge of the marzipan to curve downwards.

6. Knead the cocoa into 1 oz of marzipan. Roll it out thinly and cut out two 1½-inch squares. Place these in position as eyes. Attach a chocolate disk or bean to each with a dab of buttercream. Place a little buttercream in a parchment paper decorating cone fitted with a medium writing tube and pipe pupils on each eye.

7. Form a wedge shape from the remaining brown marzipan and press it into place for the nose. Roll a small piece of pink marzipan into a ball. Flatten the ball and curve it into a mouth shape. Put the mouth in place on the lion's face.

8. Roll the yellow marzipan trimmings into two even-sized balls, each weighing about ½ oz. Flatten the balls and attach with a spot of buttercream to either side of the mouth. Prick them over with a fork.

9. Carefully break up the chocolate flakes and spread them in a neat circle around the face as a mane. Break the spaghetti pieces into 4-inch lengths and place four on either side of the mouth as whiskers.

10. Finally spread a layer of buttercream around the edge of the cake board and sprinkle with the remaining chopped nuts.

Lion cake

Flower Cake

This exceptionally pretty cake is easy to serve as it is already cut into six wedges.

1 10-inch round silver cake board
Pound cake:
2½ sticks butter
1¼ cups sugar
5 eggs
2½ cups self-rising cake flour, sifted
1¼ cups cake flour
grated zest of 2 lemons
5 teaspoons lemon juice
cornstarch and confectioners' sugar, for dusting
To decorate:
1 quantity apricot glaze (page 38)
1 lb fondant molding paste (page 44)
food colorings (pink, yellow and mauve)
1 quantity simple buttercream (page 46)
candy balls
artificial butterflies and/or bees

Preparation time: about 1¼ hours
Cooking time: about 1 hour 30–40 minutes, plus cooling
Oven: 325°F

1. Grease and line a deep 9-inch round cake pan with greased wax paper or non-stick parchment paper.

2. Cream the butter and sugar together in a mixing bowl until light and fluffy and pale in color. Beat in the eggs one at a time following each with 1 tablespoon of self-rising flour.

3. Sift the remainder of the two types of flour together and fold into the mixture followed by the lemon zest and juice. Turn into the prepared pan, place in a preheated oven and bake for about 1 hour 30–40 minutes or until well risen, firm to the touch and a skewer inserted in the center of the cake comes out clean. Unmold onto a wire rack and leave until cold.

4. Draw a circle on a piece of paper the same size as the cake and cut it out. Fold it in half and then carefully into three. Trim "petals" out of the top edge so each one comes to a rounded point (above right). Unfold and place the template on the cake. Cut the cake through into six wedges to fit the pattern and trim around the "petals".

5. Remove the six pieces of cake and brush the top and sides of each one with some of the apricot glaze.

6. Color the fondant paste a pale pink by kneading in liquid food coloring until evenly blended. Roll it out thinly on a surface dusted with cornstarch and confectioners' sugar and cut into six pieces. Use each one to mold around a cake "petal." Trim the surplus from around the base.

7. Re-assemble the flower on the cake board. Tint about one quarter of the buttercream yellow and put into a pastry bag fitted with a star tube. Pipe a series of yellow stars over the center of the cake to make a circle of about 2½ inches across. Position candy balls to represent the center of a daisy.

8. Tint the remaining buttercream a deeper pink than the molding paste and put about three-quarters into a pastry bag fitted with a small star tube. Use to outline the petals with a shell edging and then outline around the base of the cake to attach it to the board.

9. Tint the remaining pink buttercream a purplish-pink and put into a pastry bag fitted with a medium writing tube. Pipe lines of varying lengths protruding from the center of the flower part-way along the petals like stamens. Leave to set.

10. Attach butterflies and/or bees to the cake as required.

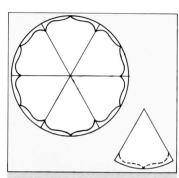

Cutting a petal template from the folded paper.

Summer Straw Hat

This fanciful creation makes a perfect birthday cake for a girl or for any summer tea party. If you want it to look more like a man's boater, increase the quantity of each of the cake ingredients by one-sixth and bake the second cake in a straight-sided 8-inch round cake pan. Use a navy blue and red striped ribbon and omit the roses.

1 11-inch round silver cake board
3 cups self-rising cake flour
1 tablespoon baking powder
1 ½ cups soft margarine
1 ½ cups sugar
6 eggs
grated zest of 2 oranges or lemons
1 ½ tablespoons cornstarch
To decorate:
about ⅓ cup jam
2 quantities simple vanilla buttercream (page 46)
yellow liquid food coloring, or another color
about 1 yard heavy ribbon, 1 to 1 ½ inches wide
1 artificial flower or 1 real flower or a few molded roses (page 63)

Preparation time: about 1 ½ hours, plus setting
Cooking time: 50 minutes
Oven: 325°F

1. Grease and line a deep 10-inch round cake pan with greased wax paper. Grease a 1-quart pudding basin or steaming mould and dredge it with flour.

2. Sift the flour and baking powder into a bowl. Add the margarine, sugar, eggs and grated orange or lemon zest and beat well for about 2 minutes until the mixture is smooth.

3. Pour about two thirds of the batter into the prepared cake pan and level the top. Beat the cornstarch into the remaining batter and pour into the prepared basin.

4. Place in a preheated oven and bake the round cake for about 40 minutes and the basin for about 50 minutes or until the cakes are well risen and firm to the touch and a skewer inserted in the center comes out clean. Unmold onto wire racks and leave to cool.

5. Stand the round cake on a cake board. Spread the base of the basin cake with jam and stand it centrally on the first cake to make a hat shape.

6. Color the buttercream lightly with yellow food coloring to give a deep shade of cream (or any other color you like).

7. Beginning in the center of the hat, work a basketweave pattern (page 59) using a medium writing tube and ribbon or basket tube. The size of the weave will have to be adjusted to follow the shape of the hat. Leave to set.

8. Tie a ribbon (with a strip of non-stick parchment paper or wax paper inside it to prevent grease-marks) around the hat and finish with long streamers. Add a large, real or artificial flower or a few molded roses to the side of the hat.

From the left: Flower cake, Summer straw hat

Gingerbread House

1 14-inch square cake board
4 cups cake flour
1 tablespoon ground ginger
1 tablespoon apple pie spice
½ cup light corn syrup
6 tablespoons margarine or
    butter
½ cup light brown sugar
1 tablespoon baking soda
2 tablespoons water
1 egg
1 egg yolk
For the icing and decoration:
hard candies
4-cup (1-lb) sugar quantity
    royal icing (page 39)
small gumdrops
licorice candies
chocolate beans
colored candy balls, sugar
    flowers etc.
miniature flashlight

Preparation time: 30 minutes,
plus decorating the cake
Cooking time: 20 minutes
Oven: 375°F

1. Line two baking sheets with non-stick parchment paper. Following the diagram illustrated right, cut out thin cardboard shapes for the roof, base, side and end walls of the gingerbread house.

2. Sift the flour with the ginger and apple pie spice into a mixing bowl. Place the syrup in a saucepan with the margarine and sugar. Stir over a low heat until melted. Dissolve the baking soda in the water in a bowl, then add to the dry ingredients with the syrup mixture, egg and egg yolk. Mix well together with a wooden spoon to form a soft dough.

3. Roll out the dough to a ¼-inch thickness on a floured board or work surface. Using the cardboard shapes as a guide, cut the pieces required, and cut two 1½- × ½-inch chimney rectangles from the trimmings. Place the dough shapes on the baking sheets.

Cut out windows and doors and trim them, if necessary, to the exact size of the cardboard shapes.

4. Roll out a small strip of dough and place it along the base of one door. Place a hard candy in the center. (This will melt to produce a glass effect.) Place a candy in each window space.

5. Bake the dough in the oven for 10 minutes, switching the baking sheets after 5 minutes. Remove from the oven and allow to cool on the baking sheets for 10 minutes. Transfer to a wire rack and leave to cool completely.

6. Roll out the dough trimmings and cut into a ½- × 1-inch piece for the fence. Bake in the oven as before.

7. Place the base piece of the house on the cake board or a

tray covered with foil and spread the edges with royal icing. Spread a thin layer of icing on all edges of the side and end walls. Join the side and end walls around the base, press together to secure and hold gently in place for a few minutes until the icing has set a little.

8. Spread a little icing around the edges of the roof, where it will join the walls and carefully place the roof in position. Leave to set for at least 1 hour before decorating.

9. Spread icing over the tray and stick the small baked pieces around the house for the fence. Spread icing on the ridge of the roof and around the edges of the roof to form snow. Sandwich the chimney pieces together with icing. Cut a triangle from one corner so that the chimney will sit on the sloping roof. Stick in position

with icing and spread a little icing around the top. Cover the chimney side of the house completely with icing.

10. Fix two licorice candies on

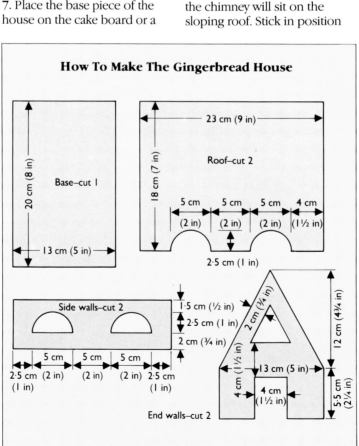

How To Make The Gingerbread House

Base—cut 1
20 cm (8 in)
13 cm (5 in)

Roof—cut 2
23 cm (9 in)
18 cm (7 in)
5 cm (2 in) 5 cm (2 in) 5 cm (2 in) 4 cm (1½ in)
2·5 cm (1 in)

Side walls—cut 2
5 cm 5 cm 5 cm
2·5 cm (1 in) (2 in) (2 in) (2 in) 2·5 cm (1 in)

End walls—cut 2
1·5 cm (½ in)
2·5 cm (1 in)
2 cm (¾ in)
2 cm (¾ in)
4 cm (1½ in)
13 cm (5 in)
4 cm (1½ in)
12 cm (4¾ in)
5·5 cm (2¼ in)

to the chimney. Fill a parchment paper decorating cone with icing and snip off the end. Pipe lines of icing across the un-iced side of the roof. Attach rows of candies to the icing. Pipe icing around the windows and doors and decorate with candies. Fix a candy ball in place for the door handle. Pipe around the garden and fix candy balls on the piping. Place sugar flowers in the garden. Pipe "snow" on top of the fence.

11. Leave the icing to set completely. When ready to serve, switch on the flashlight and place it in the house, through the back door.

Gingerbread house

Rocket Cake

Food for budding astronauts, this streamlined cake is precisely decorated with little stars. To get a good red color like this, you will need to use a paste rather than a liquid coloring.

1 6-inch round silver cake board
1 4-egg quantity Quick Mix Cake batter (pages 16–17)
4 small bars white chocolate
⅔ cup red jam, warmed and sieved
2-cup sugar quantity simple buttercream (page 46)
red food coloring
1 ice cream cone
1 candle (red or white)

Preparation time: about 15 minutes, plus assembling and decorating the cake
Cooking time: 1 hour
Oven: 325°F

1. Grease and line an 8-inch square cake pan with greased wax paper or non-stick parchment paper.

2. Pour the batter into the pan and bake in a preheated oven for about 1 hour or until the cake is golden brown and firm to the touch. Unmold onto a wire rack and remove the lining paper. Leave to cool.

3. Draw a 4 × 4-inch square on a sheet of kitchen foil or non-stick parchment paper. Melt the white chocolate in a bowl set over a saucepan of hot (not boiling) water and spread it out within the marked square with a narrow spatula. Shake gently to level the surface and leave until just set. Using a ruler and a sharp knife, trim the edges of the chocolate square, then cut it in half diagonally to make two rectangles. Cut each in half to make a total of four triangles. Chill until hard.

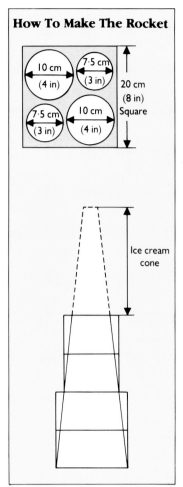

How To Make The Rocket

4. Following the diagram, cut the cake into two 4-inch rounds and two 3-inch rounds. Assemble the rocket placing the large rounds on top of each other and trimming the edges to slope the sides. Do the same with the smaller rounds. Stick all the rounds together with the jam. Place the cake on the board.

5. Make up the buttercream and tint two thirds of it red, leaving the remainder white. Spread the lower half of the cake with red colored buttercream and the top half with white, using vertical strokes to smooth the surface.

6. Cut the tip of the ice cream cone (just large enough to hold the candle). Spread the cone with red buttercream. Place the cone on top of the cake. Place the remaining red buttercream in a nylon pastry bag fitted with a small star tube and pipe a few evenly spaced stars over the white section. Pipe a border of stars at the top of the cone, where the cone meets the cake, where the red and white cakes meet and at the base of the cake on the board.

7. Place the remaining white buttercream in a pastry bag fitted with a small star tube and pipe the outline of a door on the red part of the cake and a number above it on the cone.

8. Arrange the chocolate triangles around the base and place a candle in the top.

Peppermint Racer

1 11-inch round cake board
1 3-egg quantity chocolate
    Quick Mix Cake batter
    (pages 16–17)
¾-cup sugar quantity simple
    buttercream (page 46)
peppermint extract
a few drops of green food
    coloring
2–3 tablespoons apricot jam,
    warmed and sieved
raw brown sugar, for
    sprinkling
2 individual jelly rolls
5 licorice wheels
4 round mints
silver or green candy balls
white and green soft mints
rice paper
food coloring pen
1 green plastic toothpick

Preparation time: about 15 minutes, plus decorating the cake
Cooking time: 55 minutes
Oven: 325°F

1. Grease and line a 9- × 5- × 3-inch loaf pan with greased wax paper or non-stick parchment paper.

2. Pour the cake batter into the prepared pan and bake in the preheated oven for 50–55 minutes or until firm to the touch. Unmold onto a wire rack, remove the lining paper and leave to cool completely.

3. Make the buttercream and add peppermint extract to taste. Tint the buttercream pale green with a drop or two of green food coloring.

4. Cut the cake as shown in the diagram and trim the front corners to shape the body of the car. Brush the cut surfaces with a little of the jam. Spread buttercream all over the cake and smooth with a narrow spatula dipped in hot water.

5. Spread the cake board with jam and sprinkle it thickly with raw brown sugar. Place the two jelly rolls on the cake board about 4 inches apart to make the axles. Place the cake on top.

6. Place a round mint in the center of each licorice wheel. Press a wheel onto the sides of the car in front of each axle. Use candy balls to outline the front and rear "windscreens," putting them in place with a pair of tweezers. Arrange a semicircle of candy balls above each wheel.

7. Unwind the remaining licorice wheel and cut four strips to make the front and back bumpers. Cut small strips of licorice, split in half lengthwise and make the windscreen wipers. Make door handles from small bits of licorice and stick candy balls on either side of the handle.

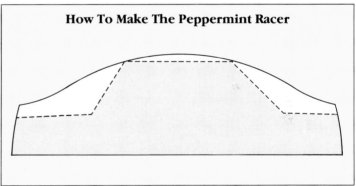

How To Make The Peppermint Racer

8. Stick soft white mints at the front and rear end of the car for the lights. Place a row of green and white soft mints along one side of the hood, roof and trunk. Make an exhaust pipe from two pieces of the trimmings, if liked.

9. To make the license plates, cut two small oblongs of rice paper and write the child's name and age on the paper using a food coloring pen. Stick on the front and back ends of the car, and place a soft white mint to either side. Use the green toothpick for an aerial.

Opposite page: Rocket cake
Above: Peppermint racer

Willie Wasp

1 10-inch square cake board
1 4-egg quantity chocolate
Quick Mix Cake batter
(pages 16–17)
2-cup sugar quantity chocolate
buttercream (page 46)
¼ cup chocolate sprinkles
¾ lb yellow marzipan
3 tablespoons cocoa
2 tablespoons boiling water
confectioners' sugar, for
kneading
6 oz white chocolate
1 square semisweet chocolate
(optional)
2 toothpicks

Preparation time: 45 minutes,
plus cooling
Cooking time: 45 minutes
Oven: 325°F

1. Grease a 2½-cup capacity
pudding basin or steaming
mold and line the base with a
disk of wax paper. Grease an
8- × 4- × 2-inch loaf pan. Fill both
containers two thirds full with
the cake batter. Smooth level.

2. Bake in a preheated oven for
45 minutes or until the cakes
are well risen and spring back
when lightly pressed with the
finger. Unmold and cool on a
wire rack.

3. Cut the loaf along its length
and put the layers back together
with a little buttercream. Place
diagonally on the cake board.

4. Flat base down, cut the basin
cake from top to bottom into
two thirds and one third. Use
buttercream to stick the cut
edge of the large piece against
one end of the loaf, and the
smaller piece against the other.
Trim the sides level with the loaf
cake.

5. Reserve 2 tablespoons of
buttercream and cover the cake
with the remainder. Coat the
large rounded end with the
chocolate sprinkles to represent
the head.

Dividing the basin cake.
Assembling to make body.

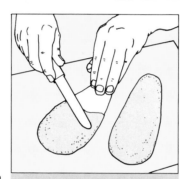

Making the wings from
melted white chocolate.

6. Divide the marzipan into 5 oz
and 7 oz portions. Blend the
cocoa with the water, then cool.
Mix the cocoa into the larger
quantity of marzipan and knead
with confectioners' sugar until
smooth.

7. Roll 2 small balls of the
yellow marzipan to make eyes
and a fine strip for a mouth. Roll
the remainder into a rectangle
measuring 4 × 8 inches. Roll
4 oz of the chocolate marzipan
into a rectangle measuring
3 × 8 inches. Cut each rectangle
into four and three 1- × 8-inch
strips respectively. Lay these
bands alternately from the head
seam, beginning and ending
with a yellow band.

8. Mold 2 oz of the remaining
chocolate marzipan over the
small rounded end, so that the
body is covered. Tuck the
uneven edge under the last

Covering with strips of
marzipan.

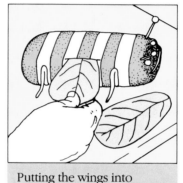

Putting the wings into
lengthwise cuts in the body.

yellow band. Brush the marzipan body with a little water.

9. Half cover two toothpicks
with a little of the remaining
marzipan and place a small ball
on each to represent antennae.
Push the toothpicks into the
head. **Note:** if the cake is for
younger children it might be
better to replace the sharp
toothpicks with chocolate
"matchstick" candies.

10. Fix the eyes and mouth in
place with buttercream.

11. Roll the remaining chocolate marzipan into a long
sausage and cut it into six
6-inch lengths. Dab a little
buttercream on each end. Stick
one end onto the body and
bend the leg, sticking the other
end onto the cake board.
Repeat with all the legs.

12. Melt the white chocolate in
a bowl set over a pan of hot
water. Draw two wing shapes
about 7 inches long and
3 inches wide on wax paper.
Spread the melted chocolate on
the paper. Cool until set.

13. If liked, melt the semisweet
chocolate, fill a small parchment
paper decorating cone and pipe
fine lines on the wing shapes to
look like veins. Cool until set,
then lift off the paper.

14. With a sharp knife, cut a line
lengthwise either side of the top
of the striped body. Open
slightly with the knife and gently
push in the wings. Keep chilled
in warm weather.

Willie wasp

FANCY CAKES

Luxurious and irresistibly tempting these fancy cakes can be served on their own, with tea or coffee, or as an impressive dinner party dessert. Despite their elegant finished appearance they can be easy and quick to make, especially if you do the baking a little in advance.

In this chapter, you will find a special kind of cake – luxurious, frivolous and mouthwatering, fit to grace a party table or be served with coffee at the end of a superb dinner party. As befits a cake of such high standing, the ingredients are often rich and sophisticated. While the basis of many of these cakes is a light sponge batter, it is often flavored with chocolate, coffee or spices, or sprinkled with liqueur after cooking and cooling. Chocolate is frequently used to decorate the cakes as well as flavoring the mixture, often simply grated and used to coat the sides, but occasionally to make a *pièce de résistance* like Rose Leaf Cake (page 172).

Almonds, walnuts and hazelnuts appear frequently in and on luxurious cakes. Their crunchiness contrasts nicely with light cake and smooth cream, and the flavor offsets the sweetness of sugary frostings and icings. Almonds are also the basis of praline, one of the most delectable flavorings in the cake-maker's repertoire. Useful in many recipes, it comes into its own with Praline Cake (page 178). Chocolate, cream and nuts are widely used in European cakes, and a fourth important ingredient is fruit, often in conjunction with a suitable liqueur. Of elegant fruits the plump black cherry reigns supreme, having the necessary qualities of juiciness, delicate size and natural – but not excessive – sweetness. Raspberries, grapes and tiny strawberries are the cherry's rivals. A number of classic cakes and desserts include citrus fruits: this book includes a refreshing idea for a pretty Fresh Lime Roulade (page 164).

A collection of special cakes would be incomplete without the classics such as Black Forest Layer Cake (page 162), Sachertorte (page 170), Japonaise Cake (page 165) and Paris-Brest (page 168). These recipes and other delights such as Marron Tuile Cake (page 166) and Frangipan Tart (page 184) demonstrate the variety of techniques involved in this branch of cake-making: meringue, choux paste, crème pâtissière, sweet pastry and other basic recipes are called upon, and here the art of decorating with chocolate excels.

As you try out the various cakes you will learn to make a range of separate components that can be combined in innumerable ways to make an impressive range of stunning cakes.

Very often the separate elements that go together to make a particular cake can be made in advance, so that it can be assembled at leisure on the day it is to be eaten. A Whisked Sponge Cake will keep for 2 days in an airtight container, but can be frozen for 2 months. A Quick Mix Cake can be made up to 1 week ahead and can be frozen for 1–2 months. Meringues keep for 7–10 days in an airtight container. Crème pâtissière can be stored in the refrigerator for 2 days before use.

Chocolate decorations can be stored in an airtight container for several weeks. Once you have assembled a cake that includes any fresh cream, it must be kept chilled in the refrigerator until the moment of serving and eaten on the same day.

It is the way in which these separate items are put together that lifts a cake into this very special category. There is little of the laborious icing and fine piping work used for celebration cakes here: the art of the special occasion cake lies in the precision and care with which a few well-chosen and top-quality ingredients are arranged. Slices of fruit exactly matching in size; chocolate leaves in a perfect circle; swirls of cream just touching on the border of the cake: these decorative finishes, deceptively simple as they appear, cannot be skimped or rushed. As the cakes on the following pages show, the results are irresistibly tempting.

Black Forest Layer Cake

Bavaria is famous for its mouthwatering cakes, and this must be the most famous of all. The cake layers may be made a day in advance, but once assembled the cake must be eaten on the same day, and kept cool until serving.

3 eggs
¾ cup sugar
1½ cups cake flour
2 tablespoons cocoa powder
2 teaspoons baking powder
4 tablespoons hot water
To fill and decorate*:*
2 cups heavy or whipping
* cream*
3 tablespoons Kirsch
1 16-oz can black cherries,
* drained or 2 pints fresh sweet*
* black cherries, pitted*
4 squares semisweet chocolate,
* coarsely grated*
extra whole cherries

Preparation time: 30 minutes plus cooling
Cooking time: 40 minutes
Oven: 375°F

1. Grease and line a deep 9-inch round cake pan with greased wax paper or non-stick parchment paper.

2. Place the eggs and sugar in a bowl set over a saucepan of hot water. Beat until the mixture is thick and pale and leaves a trail when the beater is lifted. Remove the bowl from the pan and continue to beat for 2 minutes while the mixture cools a little.

3. Sift the flour with the cocoa and baking powder onto a plate. Carefully fold the flour into the egg mixture, using a large metal spoon. Gently stir in the hot water.

4. Pour the mixture into the prepared pan and bake in a preheated oven for 35–40 minutes until well risen and firm to the touch. Carefully unmold the cake onto a wire rack. Remove the lining paper and leave to cool completely.

5. Split the cake into three equal layers. Whip the cream stiffly and place one quarter in a pastry bag fitted with a large star tube. Sprinkle the first layer of cake with a little Kirsch and pipe a band of whipped cream around the edge. Spread the pitted cherries evenly around the edge, inside the band of cream.

6. Place the second cake layer on top of the cherries and sprinkle with a little Kirsch. Spread with a layer of cream. Sprinkle the underside of the top cake layer with the remaining Kirsch and invert it onto the middle layer.

7. Spread the top and sides of the cake with the rest of the cream and coat the sides with grated chocolate. Scatter the remaining grated chocolate on top of the cake.

8. Use the remaining cream in the pastry bag to pipe whirls around the top edge. Decorate with the extra whole cherries.

A European Touch

Many of the most luxurious European cakes come not from France but from Germany and Austria, where the tradition of going out to an elegant café for coffee in the mid-morning or afternoon is long established. Each region has its own specialties: the Black Forest Layer Cake of Bavaria is one that makes full use of the local black cherries and the liqueur – Kirsch – distilled from them. This principle can be adapted to other variations, for example sprinkling an orange cake with Grand Marnier. Buttercream can be flavored with liqueur if liked, substituting the liqueur of your choice for the milk and vanilla extract. German cakes that do not include cream nevertheless are traditionally served with *Schlagsahne*, ⅔ cup of whipped cream into which 1 stiffly beaten egg white is folded just before serving. Serve this with Sachertorte (page 170) and Cranberry and Apple Strudels (page 218).

Black Forest layer cake

Fresh Lime Roulade

The luscious cream of this pretty cake is lightened by the tangy flavor of lime.

2 eggs
¼ cup sugar
½ cup cake flour
grated zest of 1 lime
sugar, for sprinkling
To fill and decorate:
1 ¼ cups heavy cream
juice of ½ lemon
slices of fresh lime

Preparation time: 15 minutes, plus cooling
Cooking time: 10 minutes
Oven: 400°F

1. Grease and line an 11- × 7- inch jelly roll pan with greased wax paper or non-stick parchment paper.

2. Place the eggs and sugar in a bowl set over a saucepan of hot water. Beat until the mixture is thick and pale in color and the beater leaves a trail when lifted. Remove the bowl from the heat and continue beating until the mixture is cool.

3. Sift the flour twice and fold into the beaten mixture with the grated lime zest. Place the mixture in the prepared pan and smooth the top, making sure the corners are filled. Place in a preheated oven and bake for 8–10 minutes, until the cake springs back when lightly pressed with the fingertips and has begun to shrink slightly from the sides of the pan.

4. While the cake is in the oven, place a clean damp dish towel on a working surface, lay a sheet of wax paper on top and sprinkle it very lightly with sugar. Immediately the cake is cooked, unmold it onto the sugared paper. Remove the lining paper and trim off the crusty edges. Make a shallow indentation with a knife blade on the short side nearest to you.

Immediately roll up the cake with the paper inside (do not delay or the cake will crack if it is allowed to cool any more than is necessary). Lay a sheet of clean wax paper on top of the roll and leave it to cool completely.

5. Whip the cream with the lime juice until it is stiff. Carefully unroll the cake and spread it with a little of the cream. Roll it up again and cover it with more cream. Use a narrow spatula to mark evenly spaced lines around the roll. Place the cake on a serving plate.

6. Place the remaining cream in a nylon pastry bag fitted with a medium star tube. Pipe a line of rosettes along the top of the cake and a decorative border on both bottom edges. Decorate with quartered slices of lime arranged like butterfly wings along the top.

Variation

Substitute grated orange zest for lime in the cake batter and use a tablespoon of orange juice instead of the lemon juice in the cream. Decorate with slices of fresh kiwi fruit.

Japonaise Cake

1 pint strawberries, hulled and
   sliced
1 2-egg quantity Quick Mix
   Cake batter (pages 16–17)
Japonaise:
1 cup ground almonds
½ cup sugar
2 egg whites
To decorate:
1¼ cups heavy cream
3 tablespoons Kirsch
2 tablespoons crunch nut
   topping
2 tablespoons strawberry jam
1 teaspoon water

Preparation time: 25 minutes
Cooking time: about 60
minutes
Oven: 325°F

1. Grease and line an 8-inch
layer cake pan. Stir ¾ cup of
the strawberries into the cake
batter, pour into the pan and
bake for 20–25 minutes until
well risen and firm to the touch.
Unmold to cool on a wire rack.

2. To make the japonaise, mix
the almonds and ¼ cup of the
sugar together in a bowl. Beat
the egg whites until stiff, then
beat the remaining sugar into
them until the mixture holds
soft peaks. Add the almond
mixture and fold in well.

3. Line two baking sheets with
non-stick parchment paper and
draw a 7½-inch circle on each.
Place the japonaise mixture in a
pastry bag fitted with a ½-inch
plain tube. Pipe the mixture
over the circles.

4. Place one baking sheet just
above and one just below the
center of the preheated oven
and bake for 30–35 minutes
until lightly browned and firm
to the touch. After 20 minutes
remove one layer and mark it
into 10 wedges, then return it to
the oven for another 10–15
minutes.

5. Cool the layers on the paper.

Cut through the wedges on one
and remove the lining paper
very carefully.

6. Place the cream and 1
tablespoon of the Kirsch in a
bowl and whip until stiff. Place
one third in a pastry bag fitted
with a small star tube.

7. Spread the uncut layer with a
layer of cream, then place the
strawberry cake on top. Spread
the sides with cream and coat
evenly with crunch nut topping.
Place on a serving plate.

8. Heat the jam and water
together until melted. Sieve and
cool.

9. Spoon the remaining Kirsch
over the top of the cake and
spread the remaining cream
evenly over the top.

10. Pipe 10 thin lines of cream
radiating out from the center
and pipe a shell edging around
the top.

11. Position the japonaise
wedges in the cream on top of
the cake and fill in between with
the remaining strawberry slices.

12. Brush generously with
strawberry glaze and pipe a
swirl of cream in the center.
Keep cool until ready to serve.

Opposite page: Fresh lime roulade,
Japonaise cake

Marron Tuile Cake

1 cup cake flour
1 cup confectioners' sugar,
sifted
2 eggs, separated
4 tablespoons milk
1 teaspoon vanilla extract
1¼ cups heavy cream
9 oz canned sweetened
chestnut purée
3 oranges
¼ cup skinned and chopped
pistachio nuts

Preparation time: 20 minutes
Cooking time: 15–20 minutes
Oven: 350°F

1. Place the flour, confectioners' sugar, egg yolks, milk and vanilla extract in a bowl. Mix with a wooden spoon, then beat to form a smooth batter.

2. Beat the egg whites until stiff, then fold gently into the batter with a large metal spoon.

3. Trace eight 3½-inch circles on a baking sheet lined with non-stick parchment paper. Spread a level tablespoon of the batter onto each.

4. Bake in the preheated oven for 5 minutes, then quickly loosen each round with a spatula and return to the oven for 2–3 minutes until golden brown at the edges.

5. Working quickly, roll each round into a cone shape and insert the pointed end of each into a wire rack, so they cool standing away from the rack.

6. Line the baking sheet with a fresh piece of non-stick parchment paper and draw three 8-inch circles on it. Spread the remaining batter over them.

7. Bake for 10–15 minutes until golden brown at the edges. Leave to cool on the paper before removing.

8. Place the cream in a bowl and whip until stiff. Reserve 2 tablespoons, then fold the chestnut purée into the remaining cream.

9. Halve one orange and cut one half into seven thin wedges. Peel, segment and chop the remaining oranges.

10. Place one tuile layer on a serving plate. Spread with one quarter of the chestnut cream and half the chopped oranges. Place another tuile layer on top and cover with chestnut cream and oranges as before. Place the remaining tuile layer on top and spread with chestnut cream.

11. Place the remaining chestnut cream in a pastry bag fitted with a medium star tube. Pipe the cream into each cone and arrange them on top of the cake, radiating out from the center. Add a swirl of chestnut cream in the middle.

12. Use the reserved cream to pipe a swirl at the end of each cone, and one in the center, and sprinkle a few pistachio nuts over the cream. Arrange orange wedges in between the cones.

Making tuile cones

Ensure the mixture is spread thinly over each marked circle and cook until the mixture is just beginning to turn a pale golden color. Remove the baking sheet and loosen each tuile round from the paper, then return to the oven to soften for a few minutes.

Quickly remove only one tuile round at a time and form into a cone shape. If the mixture sets too quickly, return to the oven to soften.

Austrian Meringue Basket

6 egg whites
¾ teaspoon cream of tartar
2 cups superfine sugar
To fill and decorate:
2½ cups heavy or whipping
cream
3 tablespoons brandy or sherry
2–3 macaroons, coarsely
crushed
1 pint strawberries, sliced
1½ pints raspberries
sugared flowers (page 66) or
crystallized rose petals
(pages 66–7)

Preparation time: 35 minutes
Cooking time: 1¾–2 hours
Oven: 225°F

1. Line four baking sheets with non-stick parchment paper and draw a 7-inch circle on each.

2. Place 4 egg whites and ½ teaspoon of cream of tartar in a bowl. Beat until very stiff, then gradually beat in 1¼ cups of the sugar. Beat well after each addition until the meringue is thick and stands in peaks.

3. Place the meringue in a pastry bag fitted with a ½-inch plain tube. Pipe two rings of meringue on the circles on two baking sheets and place on the second and third shelves of the preheated oven.

4. Pipe another two rings of meringue on the marked circles on the remaining two baking sheets, but continue piping to give closed coils, ending in the center. These will be the basket's lid and base.

5. Pipe a second ring on top of the outer ring of the base layer and place in the oven with the two rings. Bake the meringues for 20 minutes, or until firm enough to lift.

6. Loosen the two circles from the paper. Pipe a few dots of meringue at intervals around the top edge of the base and place one ring on top. Pipe dots onto the ring and place the second ring on top.

7. Return to the oven with the lid and bake for 20 minutes. Remove the basket and spread the remaining meringue smoothly over the sides. Return to the oven for 20 minutes.

8. Use the remaining egg whites, cream of tartar and sugar to make some more meringue. Place this in a pastry bag fitted with a small star tube.

9. Remove the basket from the oven and pipe a double row of scrolls around the top and base of the basket. Remove the lid and return to the oven.

10. Pipe the remaining meringue in scrolls around the edge and over the top of the lid. Return to the oven for 45 minutes to 1 hour until the mixture has set. Leave on the paper until cold.

11. Whip the cream and brandy or sherry together until thick. Fold in the macaroons and fruit until evenly blended.

12. Place the basket on a flat serving plate and carefully spoon in the fruit and cream mixture. Place the lid in position.

13. Use whipped cream to attach sugared flowers or crystallized rose petals to the side and lid of the basket.

From the left: Marron tuile cake, Austrian meringue basket

Paris-Brest Aux Fraises

This cake gets its name from a famous bicycle race from Paris to the town of Brest, its shape imitating a wheel. It must be eaten within two hours of assembly, while the choux pastry is still light and dry. If strawberries are not in season, replace them with 1½ cups halved and seeded black grapes and 2–3 sliced nectarines, soaked in liqueur in the same way as the strawberries.

1 quantity choux paste (page 34)
1 quantity crème pâtissière (page 48)
1½ pints strawberries, all but a few hulled
3 tablespoons orange liqueur or brandy
1¼ cups heavy cream
confectioners' sugar, for dusting

Preparation time: about 1 hour, plus standing
Cooking time: 45–50 minutes
Oven: 400°F

1. Grease a large baking sheet and stand a greased 10- to 12-inch flan ring on it. Spread the choux paste in a 2-inch wide ring inside the flan ring.

2. Place the baking sheet in a preheated oven and bake for about 40 minutes or until well risen, golden brown and firm to the touch. Either make a few holes in the sides of the choux ring to allow the steam to escape or turn it over carefully so that it is upside-down on the baking sheet, and return it to the oven for a few minutes for the inside to dry out. Leave to cool on a wire rack.

3. Reserve a few unhulled strawberries for decoration and slice the remainder. Put the sliced strawberries in a bowl with the liqueur or brandy and leave to soak for 2–4 hours.

4. Make up the crème pâtissière. Whip the cream until thick and fold it into the crème pâtissière. Fold the strawberries and any juice in the bowl into the cream mixture.

5. Split the choux ring carefully horizontally so that the piece for the lid is about one third of the whole. Scoop out any soft pastry on the inside. Stand the base on a large serving dish or board. Fill it with the strawberry cream and replace the lid.

6. Dredge the top of the ring with confectioners' sugar and place the whole strawberries in the center.

Variations

The original Paris-Brest is sprinkled with sliced almonds before being baked, and is filled either with Crème au Beurre (see page 46) or heavy cream whipped until stiff and flavored with confectioners' sugar and vanilla extract. Dust with more confectioners' sugar before serving.

Paris-Brest au Chocolat: Sprinkle the choux pastry ring with sliced almonds before baking. To make the filling, blend 3 squares melted semi-sweet chocolate with Crème Pâtissière (page 48) and fold in 1 cup whipped cream. If you do not have time to prepare Creme Pâtissière, make a custard sauce with ⅔ cup milk and 1 table-spoon instant custard powder, following the package instructions. Transfer the cooked custard to a bowl to cool, covering with plastic wrap to prevent a skin from forming.

All versions of Paris-Brest can have a little crushed praline (see page 49) folded into the filling. If you do not wish to use a pastry bag for the choux paste, spoon it carefully into the flan ring. If you do not have a flan ring, draw a circle 8–9 inches in diameter on a large piece of wax paper. Turn the paper over and lay it on the baking sheet. Spoon or pipe the pastry into the circle.

Individual choux rings can be made from the above recipes. Make them about 4 inches in diameter. Prepare, bake and fill in the same way.

Paris-Brest aux fraises

Sachertorte

This is one of Vienna's most famous cakes, renowned for its lightness, which is achieved by the high proportion of egg whites.

11 tablespoons unsalted butter, softened
11 tablespoons sugar
7 eggs, separated, whites stiffly beaten
5 squares semisweet chocolate
1 cup cake flour, sifted
½ cup ground almonds
⅓ cup apricot jam
Chocolate frosting:
½ cup heavy cream
2 teaspoons brandy
4 squares semisweet chocolate, broken into pieces
To decorate:
chocolate leaves (page 68)

Preparation time: 40 minutes, plus cooling
Cooking time: about 1¼ hours
Oven: 350°F

1. Butter and line a deep 7-inch round cake pan with wax paper. Brush the paper with melted butter and dust with flour.

2. Beat the butter in a mixing bowl, until it is pale and soft. Add the sugar and beat until light and fluffy. Add the egg yolks, one at a time, beating well after each addition.

3. Place the chocolate in a bowl set over hot water. When it has melted, pour it into the cake mixture and blend it in.

4. Sift the flour and almonds into the bowl and fold into the butter mixture. Gently fold in a third of the beaten egg whites, then fold in the rest.

5. Pour the batter into the pan and bake in a preheated oven for 45–55 minutes or until a skewer inserted into the center comes out clean. Remove from the oven and leave the cake in the pan for 10 minutes before unmolding it to cool completely.

6. Warm the apricot jam and spread it over the top and sides of the cake. Leave it to set.

7. To make the frosting, place the cream in a saucepan with the brandy and bring just to a boil. Add the chocolate pieces and stir until the chocolate melts and is thick and smooth. Pour the chocolate frosting evenly over the cake and leave to set, about 15 minutes.

8. Decorate with chocolate leaves, dusted with confectioners' sugar.

Variation

When the cake is cool, split it in half horizontally and put the two layers back together with apricot preserves. This is served with whipped cream in Vienna.

Dark Raspberry Cake

6 eggs, separated, whites stiffly beaten
½ cup sugar
¼ cup vanilla sugar (page 11)
½ cup + 2 tablespoons cake flour, sifted
¾ cup cocoa powder
Filling:
2 cups heavy cream
¼ cup vanilla sugar
⅓ cup rum or Kirsch
¼ cup red currant jelly
1 pint raspberries
1½ cups strawberries, halved
To decorate:
chocolate scrolls (optional)
confectioners' sugar

Preparation time: 45 minutes
Cooking time: 40–45 minutes
Oven: 350°F

1. Butter and line a deep 8-inch round cake pan with wax paper. Brush the paper with melted butter and dust with flour.

2. Beat the egg yolks with the sugars in a mixing bowl until the mixture falls off the beaters in a thick ribbon.

3. Sift the flour and cocoa powder together onto a sheet of wax paper. Gently fold a third of the flour into the mixture, then a third of the beaten egg whites and repeat until all of the flour and egg whites are incorporated.

4. Pour the batter into the prepared pan and bake in a preheated oven for 30–40 minutes or until the cake is springy to the touch. Remove from the oven and leave the cake in the pan on a wire rack for 5 minutes before unmolding it to cool completely.

5. Whip together the cream and vanilla sugar in a mixing bowl, until the mixture forms light, firm peaks.

6. To assemble, slice the cake into three layers. Warm 1½ tablespoons of the rum or Kirsch together with the red currant jelly in a small saucepan, stirring constantly, until the mixture forms a syrup. Brush the warm syrup over the bottom layer, arrange the raspberries on top and spread over a layer of the whipped cream.

7. Cover with another layer of the cake and brush with the remaining rum or Kirsch. Arrange the strawberries on top and spread over a thick layer of the whipped cream.

8. Place the third layer of cake on top and spread the top with the whipped cream. Decorate with a piped border of the remaining whipped cream and chocolate scrolls (if using) dusted with confectioners' sugar.

From the top: Dark raspberry cake, sachertorte

Rose Leaf Cake

The moule à manqué pan in which this cake is baked has slightly sloping sides which helps the cake to rise but a deep 8-inch round cake pan can be used instead.

¾ cup self-rising cake flour
⅓ cup cocoa
½ cup sugar
4 eggs, separated
2 tablespoons vegetable oil
3 tablespoons boiling water
Chocolate frosting:
1¼ cups heavy cream
8 squares semisweet chocolate
¼ cup black cherry jam,
    warmed
confectioners' sugar, to dredge

Preparation time: 30 minutes, plus setting
Cooking time: 45–50 minutes
Oven: 350°F

1. Grease and lightly flour an 8-inch moule à manqué pan.

2. Sift the flour and cocoa into a bowl and add the sugar, egg yolks, oil and water. Mix together with a wooden spoon, then beat until smooth.

3. Beat the egg whites until very stiff and fold one third into the chocolate mixture using a large metal spoon. Add the remaining egg white and fold in until the mixture is evenly blended.

4. Pour the batter into the prepared pan and bake in the preheated oven for 45–50 minutes until well risen and firm to the touch. Unmold onto a wire rack and cool.

5. To make the chocolate frosting, place ⅔ cup of the cream and 6 squares of the chocolate in a saucepan. Heat very gently, stirring occasionally, until the chocolate has melted.

6. Remove from the heat and cool until the frosting is thick enough to coat the back of the spoon. Whip the remaining cream until it is stiff.

7. Cut the cake into three equal layers. Place the bottom one on a wire rack with a plate underneath and spread with half the jam and one third of the whipped cream.

8. Place the second layer on top and spread with all the remaining jam and half the remaining cream. Cover with the top layer.

9. Pour the chocolate frosting over the top of the cake, making sure it runs down the sides, covering them completely. The excess frosting should be caught by the plate. Leave the cake for about 30 minutes to set the frosting.

10. Mix the chocolate frosting on the plate with the remaining whipped cream. Place in a pastry bag fitted with a small star tube and chill.

11. Melt the remaining chocolate in a heatproof bowl set over a saucepan of hot water, stirring occasionally.

12. Use the chocolate to coat 14 large, 10 medium, 8 small and 5 tiny rose leaves (see page 68).

13. Place the cake on a serving plate. Pipe shells of chocolate cream around the base. Arrange the rose leaves in circles on top, starting at the outer edge with the largest leaves. Dredge lightly with confectioners' sugar.

Variation

There are many different shapes that can be made from chocolate and used to decorate this cake instead of rose leaves. Melt the chocolate and spread it in a thin even layer on a sheet of wax or non-stick parchment paper. When it is set, but not completely hard, mark out the shapes with a sharp knife and then cut them out. Elongated triangles arranged like the spokes of a wheel look good on a round cake, but for a rosette design smaller shapes such as circles are best. Make half the circles from semisweet chocolate and half from white chocolate for a contrasting effect, arranging them in alternate concentric circles, or divide the top of the cake in quarters with alternate colours. Tiny decorative pastry-cutters can be bought in pretty shapes including diamonds and hearts. Ready-made chocolate leaves are available if you want this effect but are short of time.

Rose leaf cake

Hazelnut Cream Bombe

Bombes were originally ice cream mixtures served as dessert, molded in the round molds that gave them their name. This delectable cake continues the tradition of keeping its contents a secret until the first slice is cut.

1 cup finely chopped hazelnuts
3 eggs
¾ cup sugar
1¼ cups cake flour
grated zest of 2 oranges
To fill and decorate:
1¼ cups heavy cream
2 tablespoons orange juice
2 tablespoons Cointreau
1 orange
½ cup shelled hazelnuts

Preparation time: 20 minutes
Cooking time: 50 minutes
Oven: 350°F

1. Grease a 5-cup capacity pudding basin or other mold generously with butter.

2. Toast the hazelnuts lightly by spreading them out on a baking sheet and placing them under a preheated broiler for 2–3 minutes.

3. Beat the eggs with the sugar in a bowl until the mixture is pale and thick. Sift the flour over the mixture and fold it in carefully with the hazelnuts and grated orange zest.

4. Turn the batter into the prepared basin and bake in a preheated oven for 45–50 minutes until well risen, golden brown and springy to the touch. Unmold and cool on a wire rack.

5. Whip the cream with the orange juice and Cointreau until stiff. Cut the cake into three horizontally and put the layers back together with some of the cream. Reserve a third of the remaining cream and use the remainder to cover the bombe completely, smoothing the edges with a narrow spatula.

6. Place the reserved cream in a pastry bag with a star tube and pipe a ring to crown the top of the cake. Arrange the hazelnuts on the ring of cream.

7. Cut the orange in half. Pare the zest thinly from one half and strew it on top of the cake. Thinly slice the remaining half, cut the slices in quarters, and arrange around the base of the cake.

Mocha Roulade

1 tablespoon coffee powder
1 tablespoon hot water
4 squares semisweet chocolate
4 eggs, separated
½ cup sugar
To fill and decorate:
1¼ cups heavy cream
confectioners' sugar
chocolate triangles (page 68)

Preparation time: 20 minutes, plus cooling overnight
Cooking time: 20 minutes
Oven: 350°F

1. Grease and line a 13- × 9-inch jelly roll pan with greased wax paper or non-stick parchment paper.

2. Blend the coffee with the hot water in a small heatproof bowl. Break the chocolate into small pieces and place it in the bowl, set over a pan of hot water. Stir occasionally to melt the chocolate. Leave to cool.

3. Beat the egg yolks in a mixing bowl with the sugar until thick and pale in color. Carefully fold in the melted chocolate.

4. In a separate bowl, beat the egg whites until they form stiff peaks and fold into the mixture with a metal spoon.

5. Pour the batter into the prepared pan and bake in a preheated oven for 15–20 minutes, until well risen and springy to the touch.

6. As soon as you take the cake out of the oven, cover it – in its pan – with a clean damp dish towel and leave covered overnight. This ensures that it remains moist enough to roll without cracking.

7. Sprinkle a sheet of wax paper with sugar and carefully unmold the cake onto it. Remove the lining paper and trim the edges of the cake if necessary. Whip the cream and spread two thirds of it over the cake, reserving the remainder for piping. Carefully and quickly roll the cake up like a jelly roll. Place it on a serving dish with the seam underneath.

8. Dredge the roulade with confectioners' sugar. Place the remaining cream in a pastry bag fitted with a medium star tube and pipe a line of rosettes along the top of the cake. Arrange chocolate triangles between the rosettes of cream.

Variation

Because the Mocha Roulade mixture contains no flour, it is relatively light, and is given body by the eggs and chocolate. This gives a delicious but very rich result, and you may prefer not to make the finished cake any richer with the addition of heavy cream. In this case substitute crème fraîche, either plain or apricot-flavored, for the cream filling, and decorate the top with a very little confectioners' sugar and slices of fresh fruit, omitting the swirls of cream. Crème fraîche mixed half and half with whipped cream may also be used to cover the Hazelnut Cream Bombe. In both cases the cakes should be served as soon as possible after being assembled.

From the top: Hazelnut cream bombe.
Mocha roulade

Coffee-Walnut Crunch Cake

2 cups graham, cracker crumbs
½ cup chopped walnuts
1 stick unsalted butter, melted
Coffee layer:
10 tablespoons butter or
*   margarine*
1 cup light brown sugar, sifted
3 eggs
1¼ cups self-rising cake flour,
*   sifted*
1½ tablespoons coffee essence
*   or strong black coffee*
To fill and decorate:
1 tablespoon coffee essence or
*   strong black coffee*
1 quantity crème pâtissière
*   (page 48)*
⅓ cup apricot jam
1 quantity simple coffee
*   buttercream (page 46)*
½ cup finely chopped walnuts
confectioners' sugar
8 walnut halves

Preparation time: about 45
minutes, plus chilling
Cooking time: 45–50 minutes
Oven: 375°F

1. Grease and line the base of
an 8-inch loose-bottomed
quiche pan.

2. Mix together the graham
cracker crumbs and chopped
walnuts and stir in the melted
butter. Press over the bottom of
the tart pan and chill until
required.

3. To make the coffee layer,
cream the butter or margarine
and sugar together until light
and fluffy. Beat in the eggs, one
at a time, following each with 1
tablespoon of the flour. Fold in
the remaining flour, followed by
the coffee essence.

4. Turn the batter into a greased
and base-lined deep 8-inch
round cake pan and level the
top. Bake in a preheated oven
for 45–50 minutes or until well
risen and just firm to the touch.
Unmold onto a wire rack,
remove the lining paper and
leave to cool.

5. For the filling, stir the coffee
essence or coffee into the
crème pâtissière. Cover with
plastic wrap and, if necessary,
leave to cool.

6. To assemble the cake,
remove the crumb base from
the tart pan and spread the
apricot jam over it. Cut the cake
in half horizontally and set one
layer on the jam. Cover it with
the coffee-flavored crème
pâtissière and place the second
layer on top.

7. Put half the coffee buttercream into a pastry bag fitted
with a star tube. Spread the
sides of the cake with the
remaining buttercream and coat
with the chopped walnuts.
Dredge the top of the cake
heavily with sifted confectioners' sugar. Pipe a wheel
design and a border on top of
the cake with buttercream. Pipe
a whirl in each section and top
each with a walnut half.

Gingered Layer Cake

This cake is best made and filled
with crème pâtissière the day
before required. Add the cream
and cornets just before serving.
The cornets may be made
several days in advance.

10 tablespoons butter or
*   margarine*
¾ cup light brown sugar, sifted
1½ cups cake flour
1 teaspoon baking soda
2 teaspoons ground ginger
2 eggs
1 tablespoon molasses
1 tablespoon dark corn syrup
1 tablespoon milk
To fill and decorate:
3 tablespoons brandy
1 quantity crème pâtissière
*   (page 48)*
⅔ cup heavy or whipping
*   cream*
2 tablespoons milk
1 tablespoon confectioners'
*   sugar, sifted*
8 cornets (see right)
a few pieces of stem ginger

Preparation time: about 40
minutes
Cooking time: about 25
minutes
Oven: 325°F

1. Grease and line a 12- × 9-inch
jelly roll pan with greased wax
paper or non-stick parchment
paper.

2. Cream the butter or margarine and sugar together until very
light and fluffy.

3. Sift the flour, baking soda and
ginger together. Beat the eggs
into the creamed mixture one at
a time, following each with a
spoonful of the flour mixture.
Fold in the remaining flour,
followed by the molasses, syrup
and milk.

4. Spread the mixture evenly in
the prepared pan, making sure
there is plenty in the corners.
Place in a preheated oven and
bake for about 25 minutes or
until set and just firm. Unmold,
remove the lining paper, and
cool on a wire rack.

5. Beat 2 tablespoons of the
brandy into the crème pâtissière. Cover with plastic wrap
and, if necessary, leave to cool.

6. Whip the cream and milk
together until stiff, then mix in
the confectioners' sugar and
remaining brandy.

7. Cut the cake into three equal
rectangles and layer them
together with the brandy-
flavored crème pâtissière. Place
the cake on a serving plate and
spread the top with some of the
brandy cream.

8. Place the remaining brandy
cream in a pastry bag fitted with
a star tube. Pipe a whirl of
cream into each of the cornets
and top each with a piece of
stem ginger. Arrange the
cornets, head to tail, along the
top of the cake.

Cornets

2 tablespoons butter or
*   margarine*
2 tablespoons sugar
1½ tablespoons light corn syrup
¼ cup cake flour, sifted
good pinch ground ginger

Preparation time: 15 minutes
Cooking time: about 10
minutes per batch, plus cooling
Oven: 325°F

1. Grease 8 small cornucopia
molds.

2. Melt the butter or margarine
in a saucepan with the sugar
and syrup. Remove from the
heat. Beat the flour and ginger
into the melted mixture.

3. Put 4 coffeespoons of the
batter on a baking sheet lined
with non-stick parchment
paper, spacing them well apart.
Bake in a preheated oven for 10
minutes or until golden brown.

4. Allow to cool for 1–2 minutes
until slightly firm, then carefully
ease off the baking sheet one at
a time with a spatula. Immediately wrap around the cornucopia molds. Cool on a wire
rack until firm, then slide off the
molds.

5. Cook and shape the remaining batter in the same way.

From the top: Coffee-walnut crunch
cake, Gingered layer cake

Praline Cake

The Genoese sponge for this cake may be made one day in advance, and the praline up to two weeks in advance and stored in airtight containers.

*1 quantity plain or lemon
    Genoese Sponge Cake batter
    (page 22)*
Praline:
*⅔ cup sugar
¾ cup whole blanched almonds*
Filling:
*4 tablespoons Amaretto liqueur
    (optional)
1¼ cups heavy cream
3 tablespoons milk*
To decorate:
2 kiwi fruit, peeled and sliced

Preparation time: about 1 hour, plus cooling
Cooking time: about 40–45 minutes
Oven: 375°F

1. Grease and line a deep 7-inch square cake pan with greased wax paper or non-stick parchment paper.

2. Place the cake batter in the pan and bake in a preheated oven for about 40–45 minutes or until well risen, golden brown and firm to the touch. Unmold onto a wire rack and leave to cool.

3. To make the praline, put the sugar in a heavy-based saucepan and heat gently until it begins to melt. Add the almonds and, stirring occasionally, cook until the caramel is a good golden color.

4. Pour immediately onto an oiled baking sheet and cool.

5. Crush the praline until fairly firm, either with a rolling pin, or in a food processor.

6. To assemble the cake, split the cake in half horizontally and stand the bottom layer on a serving dish. Sprinkle with Amaretto, if used.

7. Whip the cream and milk together until stiff. Mix about one third of the cream with one third of the praline. Use to put the layers together.

8. Use the remaining cream to cover the top and sides of the cake, covering it completely.

9. Press most of the remaining praline around the sides of the cake using a narrow spatula.

10. Arrange slices of kiwi fruit from corner to corner of the cake, then add a line of praline each side of the fruit and finish by putting two slices of kiwi fruit in the empty corners.

From the top, clockwise: Winston's cake, Cranberry orange cake (recipe overleaf), Praline cake

Winston's Cake

Sir Winston Churchill was supposed to have had a particular liking for a cake similar to this one.

The shortbreads can be made several days in advance and stored in an airtight container with the paper separating them.

*½ cup ground rice
1¼ cups all-purpose flour
1 teaspoon apple pie spice or
    ground cinnamon
    (optional)
1½ sticks butter, cut into pieces
1 cup light brown sugar*
Filling:
*1¼ cups whipping cream
1–1⅓ cups raspberry jam
a few whole fresh raspberries
    (optional)*

Preparation time: about 45 minutes
Cooking time: about 45 minutes
Oven: 350°F

1. Sift the ground rice, flour and spice, if used, into a bowl. Add the butter and the sugar. Rub together until the mixture forms a smooth dough. Divide into 3 equal portions.

2. Roll out one portion thinly between 2 sheets of non-stick parchment paper and then cut out a 9-inch fluted circle using a fluted flan ring. Transfer the dough circle, still on its paper base with the flan ring in place, to a baking sheet. Trim off any excess dough from around the flan ring and prick all over with a fork.

3. Use most of the second portion to roll out in the same way and cut into an 8-inch circle with a fluted flan ring. Transfer to a baking sheet and prick as before, with the flan ring in position.

4. Use about three-quarters of the last portion of dough to roll out in the same way and cut into a 7-inch circle.

5. Place each disk of shortbread in a preheated oven and bake for about 25–30 minutes each or until lightly browned and firm to the touch. Remove the flan rings and allow the shortbreads to cool, still on the paper, on wire racks.

6. Press all the shortbread trimmings together and roll out, again between 2 sheets of non-stick parchment paper, and cut

into 4–6 rounds using a 3-inch fluted cutter. Cut each round across the middle, prick and stand on a baking sheet. Place in a preheated oven and bake for 10–15 minutes. Cool on the paper on a wire rack.

7. To assemble the cake, whip the cream until stiff. Peel the paper off the shortbread disks and place the largest one on a flat serving plate. Spread first with a layer of jam and then a layer of cream.

8. Position the middle-size shortbread on top and again spread with jam and cream; and then add the smallest shortbread.

9. Separate the small cookies to make halves. Put the remaining cream into a pastry bag fitted with a star tube and pipe a large whirl of cream in the center of the top using most of the remaining cream. Arrange 8 or 12 half cookies radiating out from the cream, attaching them with a swirl of cream. Complete the decoration with fresh raspberries, if used.

Cranberry-Orange Cake

2 eggs
½ cup sugar
1 cup cake flour
grated zest of ½ orange
Filling:
1 pint whole cranberries, fresh
  or frozen and thawed
⅔ cup orange juice
about 6 tablespoons sugar
1¼ cups heavy cream
2–3 tablespoons milk
3–4 tablespoons orange
  liqueur
½ cup sliced almonds, toasted
To decorate:
crystallized orange slices

Preparation time: about 1 hour, plus chilling
Cooking time: about 35–40 minutes
Oven: 350°F

1. Grease and line a deep 8-inch round cake pan with greased wax paper or non-stick parchment paper.

2. Beat the eggs and sugar together in a large electric mixer or by hand in a heatproof bowl over a pan of very gently simmering water until very thick, pale in color and the beater leaves a heavy trail.

3. Sift the flour twice. Fold it lightly and evenly through the mixture with the orange zest. Turn into the prepared pan and level the top. Place in a preheated oven and bake for 25–30 minutes or until well risen and just firm to the touch. Unmold onto a wire rack and leave until cold.

4. To make the filling, put the cranberries and orange juice into a saucepan, cover and simmer gently for about 10 minutes, until all the cranberries have "popped" and are tender. If necessary boil uncovered for a few minutes, until thick and pulpy. Sweeten to taste with the sugar and leave to cool.

5. To assemble the cake, whip the cream and milk together until stiff. Split the cake in half horizontally and put the bottom layer on a serving dish. Sprinkle with half the orange liqueur then spread with about three-quarters of the cranberry mixture and about a quarter of the cream.

6. Top with the other layer of cake and sprinkle with the remaining orange liqueur.

7. Put about a third of the remaining cream into a pastry bag fitted with a star tube. Use the remainder to cover the cake completely. Swirl the cream on top with a round-bladed knife.

8. Press the toasted almonds all around the sides of the cake. Pipe eight whirls of cream around the top edge of the cake and then a circle of smaller stars a little in from the whirls, leaving an empty space in the center.

9. Carefully spoon the remaining cranberry filling into the center of the cream. Top each large whirl of cream with a slice of crystallized orange and chill the cake for 1 hour before serving.

Layered Orange-Coffee Cake

1 quantity Butter cake batter
  (page 18)
2 tablespoons instant coffee
  powder
2 tablespoons sugar
boiling water
2 tablespoons apricot jam
about ½ cup finely chopped
  blanched almonds,
  toasted
about 6 tablespoons whipping
  or heavy cream
1 × 11-oz can mandarin
  oranges in natural juice,
  drained
Filling:
½ cup sugar
6 tablespoons water
3 egg yolks
2 sticks unsalted butter, beaten
  until soft

Preparation time: about 45 minutes, plus cooling and standing
Cooking time: about 45 minutes
Oven: 375°F

1. Grease and base-line three 8-inch round layer cake pans. Place the cake batter in the pans and bake in a preheated oven for about 15 minutes each or until well risen, golden brown and firm. Unmold the cakes onto a wire rack and leave until cold.

2. Put the instant coffee powder and sugar into a measuring cup and make up to ¾ cup with boiling water. Stir until dissolved and then leave to go cold.

3. To make the filling, gently dissolve the sugar in a heavy-based pan with the water. Boil steadily for 3–4 minutes or until 230°F is reached on a candy thermometer (the thread stage). Pour the syrup in a thin stream onto the egg yolks, beating constantly until thick and cold. Gradually beat into the butter. Beat in 1 tablespoon of the coffee syrup.

4. To assemble the cake, remove the paper from the cakes and put one layer on a serving dish. Sprinkle with about one third of the coffee syrup, then spread with one third of the filling.

5. Add a second layer of cake, sprinkle with coffee syrup, cover with half the remaining filling and place the last layer of cake on top. Sprinkle the remaining coffee syrup over this and spread the remaining filling on top of the cake.

6. Spread the apricot jam thinly around the sides of the cake and use the toasted almonds to coat the sides of the cake.

7. Whip the cream and put it into a pastry bag fitted with a star tube. Arrange an overlapping border of mandarins on top of the cake and pipe a row of rosettes inside the border, then a second circle of mandarins. In the center of the cake, pipe a close row of cream with an extra rosette on top, and arrange the remaining mandarins around it. Leave the cake to stand in a cool place for up to 6 hours before serving.

Variation

For a chocolate, Kirsch and cherry cream cake, replace the coffee syrup with the following: dissolve ¼ cup sugar in 6 tablespoons juice from a 16-oz can of black cherries, and add 4 tablespoons of Kirsch when cold. Flavor the filling with 2 squares of melted semisweet chocolate instead of coffee syrup. Use the drained cherries in place of the mandarin oranges to decorate the cake.

Layered orange-coffee cake

Malakoff Cake

This cake makes a sumptuous dessert, and requires no cooking. Natural candied cherries are best for this recipe: they are much darker and less sweet than the normal candied cherries and can be bought in most supermarkets.

1½–2 packages ladyfingers
1¼ cups roughly chopped
　　blanched almonds
½ cup sugar
1½ sticks butter
2 egg yolks
6 tablespoons brandy or dark
　　rum
5 tablespoons milk
1¼ cups whipping cream
To decorate:
slivers of blanched almonds,
　　toasted
candied cherries

Preparation time: about 30 minutes, plus chilling

1. Grease and line a 9- × 5-inch loaf pan with greased wax paper or non-stick parchment paper. Cover the base with ladyfingers laid lengthwise side by side.

2. Put the almonds and ¼ cup of the sugar in a small heavy-based pan and heat gently until the sugar turns a light caramel color. Pour onto an oiled baking sheet, leave until cold and then crush finely with a rolling pin or in a food processor.

3. Cream the butter until soft then add the remaining sugar and beat until light and fluffy.

4. Beat in the egg yolks alternating with 3 tablespoons brandy or rum; then stir in the crushed praline.

5. Combine the milk and remaining brandy or rum and sprinkle 2 tablespoons over the ladyfingers in the pan, then spread with half the nut mixture.

6. Add a second layer of ladyfingers, sprinkle with another 2 tablespoons of the milk mixture and cover with the remaining nut mixture.

7. Lay a final layer of ladyfingers on top and sprinkle with the remaining milk mixture. Press down evenly and cover with a sheet of greased wax paper or non-stick parchment paper. Put a sheet of foil on top.

8. If possible put a light weight on the mixture and chill for at least 12 hours, preferably 24 hours.

9. Unmold the cake carefully onto a serving dish and gently peel off the paper.

10. Whip the cream and use some of it to cover the whole cake. Put the remainder in a pastry bag fitted with a star tube and pipe diagonal lines on top of the cake. Sprinkle toasted almonds between the rows of cream and decorate with candied cherries. Serve.

Coffee-Chestnut Cake

1 quantity coffee Genoese
　　Sponge Cake batter (page
　　22)
1 8-oz can sweetened chestnut
　　purée
1–2 tablespoons Tia Maria or
　　Kahlua coffee liqueur
2 cups whipping cream
4 squares semisweet chocolate,
　　made into chocolate mini
　　curls (page 68)
about 9 chocolate leaves (page
　　68)
3–4 marrons glacés or candied
　　cherries

Preparation time: about 1 hour, plus standing
Cooking time: about 40 minutes
Oven: 375°F

1. Grease and line a deep 8-inch round cake pan with greased wax paper or non-stick parchment paper. Pour in the cake batter, place in a preheated oven and bake for about 40 minutes, or until well risen, golden brown and firm to the touch. Unmold onto a wire rack and leave until cold.

2. Turn the chestnut purée into a bowl and beat in the liqueur with a wooden spoon until smooth. Divide mixture in half.

3. Whip the cream until stiff. Put one third of the cream into a pastry bag fitted with a star tube; mix 2 tablespoons of cream with one of the chestnut purée mixtures and put into a pastry bag fitted with the same sized star tube as the cream. Finally add about 6 tablespoons of cream to the remaining chestnut mixture to make a marron cream for the filling.

4. To assemble the cake, split it in half horizontally and stand the bottom layer on a serving plate. Spread with some of the marron cream and top with the second cake layer.

5. Spread the remaining marron cream around the sides of the cake and press the chocolate curls against the sides with a narrow spatula.

6. Using alternate pastry bags of cream and chestnut purée, pipe straight lines across the cake to cover the top completely.

7. Arrange the chocolate leaves and pieces of marrons glacés or candied cherries on the top of the cake. Leave to stand for at least 2 hours for the flavors to marry.

Classic Alternatives

A Malakoff is a rich dessert based on a vanilla-flavored bavarois (a light mousse-like custard). As well as the ladyfingers, brandy and almonds, it may include raisins and currants soaked in a little brandy and very fine strips of orange peel. For decoration, almonds should always be included, but instead of candied cherries you could use crystallized fruits such as pineapple, orange and lemon cut in small pieces and arranged in clusters of three colors.

The distinctive flavor of chestnuts also combines well with chocolate. Make a 3-egg chocolate-flavored Whisked Sponge Cake (see page 20), increasing the sugar to 1 cup. Bake in an 11- × 7-inch jelly roll pan for 30 minutes at 375°F. Cut the cake in half lengthwise and sprinkle with Grand Marnier. Put together with marron cream and decorate.

From the top: Coffee-chestnut cake, Malakoff cake

Tipsy French Ring

1 ⅔ cups all-purpose flour
1 teaspoon salt
1 teaspoon sugar
1 ½ teaspoons rapid rise dry
  yeast
3 tablespoons warm water
3 eggs
1 stick unsalted butter, softened
  and cut into small pieces
Syrup:
¾ cup sugar
1 ¼ cups water
½ cup dark rum
To decorate:
2 nectarines, sliced
½ cup seedless purple grapes
½ cup seedless green grapes
2 oranges, peeled and
  segmented
2 tablespoons apricot glaze
  (page 38)
¼ cup sliced almonds

Preparation time: 35 minutes,
plus rising
Cooking time: 20 minutes
Oven: 400°F

1. Place the flour, salt, sugar, yeast, water and eggs in a warm bowl. Mix together with a wooden spoon, then beat for 3–4 minutes to form a smooth, elastic batter. (Alternatively, mix in an electric mixer using a dough hook or beater for 1–2 minutes.)

2. Sprinkle the butter pieces over the dough then cover with plastic wrap and leave in a warm place for about an hour, or until the dough has doubled in size.

3. Brush a 9-inch springform pan fitted with central tube, with melted butter and chill until set.

4. Beat the dough with a wooden spoon until all the pieces of butter have been mixed in and the dough is smooth.

5. Carefully spoon the dough into the pan as evenly as possible. Cover the top with plastic wrap and leave in a warm place for about 1 hour, or until the dough has risen almost to the top of the pan.

6. Bake in the center of a preheated oven for 20 minutes until well risen and golden brown. Remove the ring from the pan and cool on a wire rack.

7. To make the syrup, place the sugar and water in a saucepan and heat gently until the sugar has dissolved. Bring to a boil and boil rapidly for 3 minutes. Allow the syrup to cool, then stir in the rum.

8. Place the ring on a serving plate and pour some of the syrup over. As the ring absorbs the syrup, add some more, and continue in this way until the ring has become saturated with the syrup.

9. Fill the center with the prepared fruit and arrange any remaining fruit around the base. Brush the ring with apricot glaze and arrange sliced almonds around the top.

10. Pour any leftover syrup into a pitcher and serve with the ring.

Preparing fruit

If seeding grapes: make a small slit in the top of each grape. Using a small knife, remove the seeds from the center of the grapes.

To segment an orange: use a small sharp knife and carefully cut the peel including all the white pith away from the orange flesh. Cut in between the membranes carefully to remove each segment from the orange. Discard the membranes and core.

Frangipan Tart

⅔ cup all-purpose flour
1 stick butter, softened and cut
  into pieces
2 tablespoons sugar
1 egg yolk
about 2 tablespoons cold water
Filling:
¼ cup red currant jelly
1 ½ pints red currants
1 stick butter, softened
½ cup sugar
1 ⅓ cups ground almonds
¼ cup cake flour
a few drops of almond extract
2 eggs
¼ cup sliced almonds
1 tablespoon apricot glaze
  (page 38)
To decorate:
whipped cream (optional)

Preparation time: 20 minutes
Cooking time: 50–60 minutes
Oven: 350°F

1. Grease a 10-inch loose-bottomed fluted tart pan.

2. Place the flour in a bowl, add the butter and rub in until the mixture resembles fine bread crumbs. Stir in the sugar, egg yolk and enough water to mix to a firm dough.

3. Knead on a lightly floured board until smooth. Roll out to a round large enough to line the tart pan.

4. Press the pastry onto the base and sides of the pan, then trim off the surplus with a knife. Reserve the trimmings.

5. Prick the base with a fork and spread with the red currant jelly. Reserve a few red currants for decoration if liked, then distribute the remainder over the jam.

6. Place the butter, sugar, ground almonds, flour, almond extract and eggs in a bowl. Mix together with a wooden spoon, then beat for 1–2 minutes until smooth.

7. Spoon the mixture into the pastry case and level the top.

8. Roll out the pastry trimmings and cut into ¼-inch wide strips. Arrange them in a lattice design (see right) over the filling and trim the edges.

9. Position the sliced almonds on the exposed filling in between the lattice, then bake in a preheated oven for 50–60 minutes until golden brown and firm to the touch. Leave to cool.

10. When cold, brush the top of the tart with apricot glaze and pipe swirls of cream (if using) around the top.

11. Place one of the reserved red currants (if using) on each swirl of cream just before serving.

Making pastry lattice

Knead the pastry trimmings together and roll out thinly to a long thin strip about 10 × 4 inches. Cut the pastry into ¼-inch wide strips and place half of the strips across the top of the tart, evenly spaced apart.

Arrange the remaining strips in the opposite direction and press the pastry strips on to the edge of the pastry case to make a neat edging. Add a glaze of beaten egg or milk.

From the top: Tipsy French ring, Frangipan tart

CHEESECAKES

Cheesecakes are perfect at picnics, parties, coffee time and dinner time. Aim for contrast but compatibility in combining base, filling and final decoration. A nutty, crunchy base goes well with lemon or chocolate. A sponge cake base goes best with a mousse-type filling.

Cheesecakes make ideal desserts as well as coffee time cakes. Indeed, they are perfectly suited to the modern taste for light-textured desserts with a delicate appearance. With their increasing popularity, a great variety of flavorings and bases have evolved from the traditional baked cheesecake on a pastry base, together with a wide range of decorative effects. The smooth pale surface of a perfect cheesecake is almost like a blank canvas to a painter! You can take a minimalist approach and limit yourself to a small cluster of fruits nicely arranged to one side, or surrender to extravagance with a concoction of whipped cream, nuts and cherries to rival any European concoction. The Cherry Cheesecake Torte on page 196 shows how attractive an arrangement of brightly colored fruits on a creamy surface can be, while the Coffee and Rum Cheesecake on page 194 makes its effect with swirls of cream rippling through the dark cheesecake itself.

A traditional cheesecake is baked. When it is cooked, it should appear well-risen and golden in color, shrinking away slightly from the sides of the pan. Test by inserting a skewer or wooden toothpick into the center of the cake, which is always the slowest part to cook, and remove it carefully; if any mixture adheres to the skewer, bake the cake a few minutes longer. Baked cheesecakes tend to crack slightly and collapse as they cool. This does not affect the texture or flavor, but simply adds to their appeal. To decorate, simply dredge lightly with confectioners' sugar and arrange fresh or crystallized fruit on top, as in Torta di Ricotta (page 188) and Baked Fresh Fruit Cheesecake (page 196).

The modern uncooked cheesecake is an American invention which has received the accolade of being imitated and adopted all over the world. Chilled set cheesecakes are perfect endpieces for dinner parties, not only because of their appearance, but because they can be prepared in advance and chilled until required.

All fruits enhance cheesecakes, though – like mousses and bavarois – the combination of citrus and creaminess is the longest established. A Lemon Cheesecake such as the one on page 198 will be an invaluable standby in your repertoire, but there are other recipes here for cakes based on apricots, blackberries, cranberries, pineapple and strawberries.

Many uncooked cheesecakes require the use of gelatin to set them. As a rule of thumb, 1 tablespoon (1 envelope) of unflavored gelatin will set 2 cups of cream. Sprinkle the powder over 6 tablespoons of very hot but not boiling water in a cup and stir to dissolve. If it has not dissolved entirely by the time the water has cooled, stand the cup in a pan of warm water set over a low heat. Stir until the mixture is clear and smooth. Leave the gelatin to cool at room temperature and trickle slowly into the cheesecake mixture, beating all the time.

There are a number of different and tasty bases that can be used for cheesecakes. A crumb base is extremely easy to make and very versatile, but experiment with crushed nuts and toasted bread crumbs, sour cream pastry (page 190) and sweet pie pastry (page 33). For special occasions dark chocolate cookies can also be used very successfully, and so that the base is not too sweet, the sugar quantity of the mixture should be reduced.

Such is the variety of cheesecakes that, like other cakes, there is one for simply every occasion: for a delicious dessert, try Blackberry and Cheese Torte (page 191); for teatime, Citrus Ricotta Cake (page 188), and for a celebration dessert Heavenly Cake (page 192) certainly lives up to its name.

Torta di Ricotta

Serves 10–12
1 lb ricotta cheese, drained and
    sieved
2/3 cup sugar
2 drops bitter almond extract
7 eggs, separated
1 2/3 cups ground almonds
1 tablespoon grated orange zest
1/3 cup chopped candied orange
    peel
2 tablespoons potato flour, sifted
To decorate (optional):
candied orange peel
candied angelica pieces
confectioners' sugar

Preparation time: 30 minutes
Cooking time: 50 minutes plus
cooling
Oven: 350°F

1. Grease a 10-inch springform
pan and line the base with non-
stick parchment paper.

2. Beat the ricotta cheese with
the sugar until the texture is
creamy; mix in the almond
extract. Add the egg yolks, one

at a time, beating well between
each addition. Mix in the
almonds, orange zest and
candied peel.

3. Beat the egg whites until they
are stiff and gently fold half into
the cheese mixture with a metal
spoon. Sift the potato flour over
the mixture and fold it in, along
with the remaining egg white.

4. Pour the mixture into the
prepared pan. Rap the pan once
on the worktop to disperse any
air pockets, then bake in a
preheated oven for 50 minutes
until nicely browned. Cool in
the pan on a wire rack.

5. When the cake is cool,
carefully remove the sides of
the pan and set the cake on a
serving plate. Decorate if liked
with candied orange peel,
angelica and confectioners'
sugar. Serve with chilled orange
sauce (see below).

Chilled Orange Sauce

pared zest of 2 oranges, cut
    into julienne strips
3 tablespoons water
3/4 cup sugar
1/3 cup orange juice
1/3 cup lemon juice

Preparation time: 30 minutes
plus chilling
Cooking time: 35 minutes

1. Blanch the strips of orange
zest in boiling water for 6
minutes to soften. Drain and set
aside.

2. Put the water and sugar in a
small pan over a low heat and
stir until the sugar has dissolved. Add the orange and
lemon juice, bring to a boil and
add the orange zest.

3. Simmer for 20 minutes. Pour
into a serving pitcher and chill
until required.

Citrus Ricotta Cake

This pastry can be made up to 4
days in advance. Cover and chill
until required.

Serves 10
1 1/4 cups potato flour
1 cup all-purpose flour
10 tablespoons butter, cubed
1 teaspoon grated lemon zest
2 tablespoons sugar
2 egg yolks
1 egg white, lightly beaten
confectioners' sugar, to
    decorate
Filling:
2/3 cup milk
piece of vanilla bean 1 inch
    long, split
2 tablespoons sugar
2 egg yolks

1 tablespoon flour
3/4 lb (1 1/2 cups) ricotta cheese,
    drained and sieved
3 eggs, separated
1/2 cup confectioners' sugar,
    sifted
2 tablespoons chopped candied
    orange and lemon peel
2 tablespoons Grand Marnier
1 egg yolk, lightly beaten

Preparation time: 50 minutes
Cooking time: 40 minutes plus
cooling
Oven: 375°F

1. First make the pastry. Sift the
flours into a bowl and make a
well in the center. Add the
cubed butter and lightly rub the

*From the left: Torta di ricotta with
chilled orange sauce, Citrus ricotta
cake*

mixture with the fingertips to a fine bread crumb texture. Stir in the lemon zest and sugar. Add the egg yolks and work the mixture into a smooth dough. Roll the dough into a ball, and dust it with flour. Wrap in plastic wrap or foil and chill for 30 minutes.

2. Grease and flour a 10-inch springform pan. Reserve a third of the pastry. Roll out the rest and line the pan so that the pastry covers the base and extends about 1 inch up the sides. Brush the bottom with the lightly beaten egg white.

3. Roll out the remaining pastry and cut it into long strips ¼ inch wide. Set the pastry strips aside.

4. To make the filling, place the milk in a small saucepan with the vanilla bean and bring slowly just to a boil. Remove from the heat and leave to infuse until the milk has cooled. Remove the vanilla bean.

5. Beat together the sugar and the egg yolks; sift in the flour and stir to combine. Pour in half of the vanilla milk and beat until well blended.

6. Add the egg mixture to the remaining milk in the pan. Bring to a boil very slowly over a low heat and cook for 4–5 minutes, stirring all the time. Set this custard aside to cool.

7. In a mixing bowl, combine the ricotta cheese, egg yolks, confectioners' sugar, candied peel and Grand Marnier, beating well between each addition. Mix in the cooled custard.

8. Beat the egg whites until they are stiff and fold them into the

cheese mixture with a metal spoon.

9. Pour the mixture into the pastry shell and gently smooth over the top with a spatula. Lay the reserved strips of pastry on top in a lattice pattern. Brush with beaten egg yolk. Bake in a preheated oven for 40 minutes until the filling is lightly set and the pastry is cooked. Cool in the pan on a wire rack.

10. Carefully remove the sides of the pan and set the cake on a serving plate. Dredge with confectioners' sugar and serve.

Fresh Cranberry Cheesecake

Serves 8
1 ⅔ cups graham cracker
 crumbs
6 tablespoons sugar
½ teaspoon ground cinnamon
½ teaspoon ground nutmeg
6 tablespoons butter
1 ½ tablespoons apricot jam
Filling:
3 ½ cups fresh cranberries,
 washed, or 1 cup cranberry
 jelly
3 large strips orange zest
⅔ cup granulated sugar
¾ cup light brown sugar
1 envelope unflavored gelatin
 dissolved in ½ cup orange
 juice
2 tablespoons grated orange
 zest
1 cup cream cheese
1 cup sieved cottage cheese
½ cup heavy or whipping
 cream, whipped
To decorate:
julienne strips of orange zest

Preparation time: 40 minutes
plus chilling

1. Prepare a crumb base
in an 8½-inch springform pan
as described for Pineapple
Refrigerator Cake (page 198)
substituting crushed graham
crackers for the bread
crumbs.

2. If using fresh cranberries,
place them in a pan and almost
cover with cold water. Add the
strips of orange zest. Bring to a
boil and simmer for 3–4
minutes until the berries start to
pop. Draw off the heat and stir
in the granulated sugar. Set
aside to cool.

3. To make the filling, mix
together the light brown sugar,
gelatin and orange juice mixture
and zest. Add the cheeses and
beat very thoroughly until quite
stiff.

4. Whip the cream. Reserve 4
tablespoons for decoration and
fold the rest into the filling.

5. Drain the cooked cranberries
without crushing the fruit and
discard the juice. Remove the
strips of orange zest. Spread
half the cooked fruit or half the
cranberry jelly over the chilled
base in the pan. Cover with the
filling mixture. Spread the
remaining cooked cranberries
or cranberry jelly over. Chill for
5–6 hours.

6. Carefully remove the sides of
the pan and set the cheesecake
on a serving plate. Decorate
with the reserved whipped
cream and the julienne strips of
orange zest.

Using Gelatin

As a rule of thumb, 1
envelope (7-g/¼-oz), or 1
tablespoon, unflavored
gelatin will set 2 cups cream.
Gelatin should always be
measured carefully.
1. Pour ⅓ cup very hot, but
not boiling water into a cup.
Sprinkle 1 envelope of
gelatin over and stir to
dissolve.
2. If the gelatin has not
dissolved entirely by the time
the water has cooled, stand
the cup in a pan of warm
water set over a low heat. Stir
until the mixture is quite
clear and completely free of
any lumps.
3. Allow to cool to room
temperature and trickle
slowly into the mixture,
beating all the time.

Apricot Cheesecake with Sour Cream Pastry

Serves 8
Sour cream pastry:
1 ¼ cups all-purpose flour, sifted
1 stick butter, cubed
1 tablespoon sugar
1 egg yolk
1 tablespoon sour cream
Filling:
2 tablespoons ground almonds
1 lb fresh apricots, halved and
 pitted, or 1 ½ lb canned
 apricots, well drained, juice
 reserved
1 ½ teaspoons ground
 cinnamon
¼ cup sugar (if using fresh
 apricots)
4 tablespoons butter
2 eggs yolks
¾ cup sieved cottage cheese
¼ cup sugar
½ teaspoon grated lemon zest
1 tablespoon heavy cream
To decorate:
1 teaspoon arrowroot

whipped cream
toasted sliced almonds

Preparation time: 45 minutes
plus chilling and cooling
Cooking time: 1 hour 10
minutes
Oven: 350°F

1. Grease an 8½-inch springform pan.

2. Sift the flour into a bowl. Add
the butter and lightly rub the
mixture to a bread crumb
texture. Mix in the sugar. Add
the egg yolk and sour cream
and blend to a smooth pliable
pastry. Roll into a ball, cover
with plastic wrap and chill for 1
hour.

3. Roll out the pastry and line
the prepared pan, pushing the
pastry 1 inch up the sides.

Scatter the ground almonds on
top.

4. Reserve 4 apricot halves for
decoration. Pack the rest into
the prepared base. Mix together
1 teaspoon of cinnamon with
¼ cup sugar and sprinkle over
the apricots (if using canned
fruit omit the sugar).

5. Beat the butter with the egg
yolks until light and creamy. Mix
in the cottage cheese, ¼ cup
sugar, lemon zest, cream and
remaining cinnamon.

6. Pour the mixture onto the
fruit in the pan and bake in a
preheated oven for 1 hour 10
minutes. Cool in the pan on a
wire rack.

7. Carefully remove the sides of
the pan and set the cheesecake
on a serving plate. Slice the
reserved apricot halves and
arrange them on top. Mix 8
tablespoons of the reserved
juice with the arrowroot in a
small saucepan and stir over a
low heat until thickened. Glaze
the apricots with this liquid and
leave to cool. Decorate with
whipped cream and toasted
almonds and serve.

*From the top, clockwise: Fresh
cranberry cheesecake, Blackberry and
cheese torte, Apricot cheesecake and
sour cream pastry*

Blackberry and Cheese Torte

This pastry must be well chilled before use. If it is difficult to roll out, press it into the pan by hand, patching any small cracks with small pieces of pastry. The texture when cooked is very light.

Serves 8
Pastry:
1 cup all-purpose flour, sifted
pinch of salt
7 tablespoons butter, chilled and cut into cubes
3 tablespoons sugar
½ teaspoon grated lemon zest
1 egg yolk
1 egg white, lightly beaten, for brushing

Filling:
1½ pints blackberries, thawed if frozen
⅓ cup sugar
4 macaroons, coarsely crushed
1 cup sieved cottage cheese
2 tablespoons Kirsch
3 tablespoons heavy cream
2 egg yolks
1 egg white

To decorate:
whipped cream

Preparation time: 30 minutes plus chilling
Cooking time: 45 minutes
Oven: 375°F

Continued

1. Sift the flour and salt into a bowl and make a well in the center. Add the cubed butter, then lightly and swiftly rub the mixture to a fine bread crumb texture. Mix in the sugar and lemon zest.

2. Add the egg yolk and work the mixture with the fingertips to a soft, but not sticky, dough and roll it into a ball.

3. With the heel of your hand, blend the pastry – a small amount at a time – by pushing it away from you on a floured worktop. When it is smooth and pliable gather it into a ball, dredge it with flour and wrap it in plastic wrap. Chill for at least 30 minutes.

4. Roll or press out the pastry and use to line an 8-inch springform pan so that it covers the base and extends about 1 inch up the sides. Bake blind (page 31), brushing the base with beaten egg white 5 minutes before the baking is complete.

5. Reserve ½ cup blackberries for decoration. Sprinkle ¼ cup of the sugar over the rest.

6. Scatter half the crushed macaroons over the cooked pastry case and lay the sugared blackberries on top.

7. Beat together the cheese, Kirsch, cream, egg yolks and the remaining sugar. Beat the egg white until stiff and fold it in. Pour the mixture into the pan and scatter the remaining crushed macaroons on top.

8. Bake in a preheated oven for 45 minutes. Cool in the pan on a wire rack.

9. To serve, carefully remove the sides of the pan and put the torte on a serving plate. Decorate with whipped cream and the reserved blackberries.

Cheesecake and Fruit Diplomat

You can use virtually any combination of fruit for this spectacular party dessert: peaches, nectarines, pears, apricots, black cherries, or red and black currants. Choose fruits which complement each other well in color and texture.

Serves 14–16
Cheesecake ring:
1 ½ cups (¾ lb) ricotta or cottage cheese, drained and sieved
6 tablespoons sugar
3 eggs, separated
1 tablespoon grated orange zest
1 teaspoon grated lemon zest
2 tablespoons lemon juice, strained
⅔ cup sour cream
1 envelope unflavored gelatin, dissolved in 2 tablespoons very hot water
⅔ cup heavy cream
Fruit base:
3 tablespoons apricot jam
1 Fatless Sponge Cake, as page 17 but baked in a 12-inch springform pan
1 ½ lb prepared fresh fruit or drained canned fruit (see below)
To serve:
julienne strips of orange and lemon zest
double quantity Chilled Orange Sauce (page 188)

Preparation time: 1 hour plus chilling
Cooking time: 3 minutes

1. To make the cheesecake ring, beat the cheese, sugar and egg yolks together thoroughly. Beat in the orange and lemon zest, lemon juice and sour cream.

2. Slowly beat in the dissolved gelatin. Put to one side until it is on the point of setting.

3. Beat the egg whites until stiff. Lightly whip the cream. Fold alternate spoonfuls of egg white and whipped cream into the stiffened mixture.

4. Pour the mixture into a lightly oiled 9-inch ring mold. Chill for 3–4 hours.

5. Meanwhile, gently heat the apricot jam with 3 tablespoons of water and stir to dissolve. Sieve.

6. Place the sponge cake on a large serving plate and brush with the melted apricot jam. Carefully unmold the cheese-cake on top, leaving an even edge all around.

7. Arrange some of the fruits decoratively around the edge of the cheesecake. Place the remaining fruit in the center of the cheesecake. Chill for 2 hours.

8. Decorate with the julienne strips of zest and serve with the chilled orange sauce.

Heavenly Cake

This light cake should be chilled for 2 days before serving.

Serves 12
Cinnamon pastry:
5 teaspoons ground cinnamon
1 ¼ cups sugar
1 stick butter, softened
4 egg yolks
2 teaspoons grated lemon zest
1 ¾ cups all-purpose flour
pinch of baking powder
2 tablespoons sliced almonds
Filling:
1 cup sieved cottage cheese
⅓ cup sugar
2 tablespoons sour cream
2 tablespoons Grand Marnier
⅔ cup heavy cream
⅔ cup red currant jelly
To decorate:
whole fresh fruit (red currants, raspberries)

Preparation time: about 1 hour 20 minutes plus chilling
Cooking time: 15 minutes
Oven: 350°F

1. Mix the cinnamon with half of the sugar and reserve.

2. Beat the butter with the remaining sugar until light and fluffy. Beat in the egg yolks and the lemon zest.

3. Sift the flour with the baking powder and blend into the mixture. Knead until smooth.

4. Divide the pastry in four and press or roll out each piece into a 9½-inch round (cut around the base of a pan as a guide). Sprinkle the cinnamon and sugar mixture over the rounds, and the sliced almonds over one of them.

5. Place on a greased baking sheet and bake in a preheated oven for 15 minutes. Leave to cool on wire racks.

6. Cream the cottage cheese with the sugar. Blend in the sour cream and Grand Marnier. Whip the cream and fold it in.

7. Set the almond-coated round to one side. Spread a layer of red currant jelly over each of the remaining pastry rounds, then spread each one with a layer of the cheese and cream filling, dividing it equally between them.

8. Put the layers together and set the almond-coated round on top. Chill for 2 days. To serve, decorate with fresh fruit.

From the top: Cheesecake and fruit diplomat, Heavenly cake

Coffee and Rum Cheesecake

Serves 12
1⅔ cups toasted bread crumbs
⅓ cup sugar or vanilla sugar
  (see page 11)
½ cup grated walnuts
1 heaped teaspoon ground
  cinnamon
6 tablespoons butter, melted
2 tablespoons apricot jam
Filling:
2 tablespoons instant coffee
  powder
3 tablespoons hot water
4 squares semisweet chocolate,
  broken in pieces
3 tablespoons dark rum
2 cups sieved cottage cheese
1 cup sugar
4 eggs, separated
2 cups heavy or whipping
  cream
½ cup chopped walnuts
2 envelopes unflavored gelatin,
  dissolved in 5 tablespoons
  very hot water
To decorate:
walnut halves
chocolate curls (see page 68)
confectioners' sugar

Preparation time: 1 hour 15 minutes plus setting and chilling

1. Line the base of an 11-inch springform pan with non-stick parchment paper and grease the sides well.

2. Mix together the bread crumbs, sugar, grated walnuts and cinnamon.

3. In a large pan set over a low heat, melt the butter with the apricot jam. Remove from the heat, stir in the crumb mixture and combine well. Press firmly into the prepared pan with the back of a spoon. Leave to chill while preparing the filling.

4. Dissolve the coffee in the hot water in a small heatproof bowl. Add the chocolate pieces. Place the bowl over a pan of simmering water and stir until the chocolate has melted. Stir in the rum. Remove the pan from the heat and leave to cool.

5. Beat together the cheese, half the sugar and the egg yolks. Whip the cream and fold it in.

6. Transfer half the mixture to another bowl. Add the chocolate and coffee mixture to one half and combine well. Add the walnuts to the other half and stir in.

7. Beat two thirds of the dissolved gelatin into the coffee and chocolate mixture and add the rest to the walnut mixture. Set both mixtures aside until they are on the point of setting.

8. Meanwhile beat the egg whites until stiff and beat in the remaining sugar. Fold half of the beaten egg white into each mixture.

9. Pour the walnut mixture onto the base and smooth over. Gently spoon the chocolate and coffee mixture on top. With a large fork, lightly swirl through both mixtures. Chill the cake for at least 6 hours.

10. To serve, carefully remove the sides of the pan and set the cheesecake on a serving plate. Decorate with the walnut halves and chocolate curls and dust with confectioners' sugar.

Cassata Alla Siciliana

This dessert may be prepared up to 1 day in advance. Cover and chill until the point of serving.

Serves 12
1 3-egg Pound Cake baked in a
  loaf pan and cut into ½-inch
  slices
4 tablespoons Maraschino
  liqueur
½ lb whole mixed crystallized
  fruits
1 lb ricotta cheese, drained and
  sieved
⅔ cup light cream
¼ cup sugar
1 teaspoon ground cinnamon
4 squares semisweet chocolate,
  finely chopped
¼ cup blanched, peeled and
  chopped pistachio nuts
½ teaspoon orange-flower
  water
Icing:
1 tablespoon lemon juice
2¼ cups confectioners' sugar,
  sifted
about 5 tablespoons almost
  boiling water

Preparation time: 1 hour plus chilling

1. Line the bottom and sides of a 2-quart capacity charlotte mold or deep 7-inch cake pan with non-stick parchment paper.

2. Use three-quarters of the cake slices to line the bottom and sides of the container, cutting and trimming them to a triangular shape to fit the mold when placed in a circle. Sprinkle 2 tablespoons of the Marachino over the cake.

3. Reserve half the crystallized fruits for decoration and finely chop the remainder.

4. Whip the ricotta cheese until it is creamy then beat in the cream, sugar, cinnamon, chocolate, chopped crystallized fruits and pistachio nuts. Stir in

the orange-flower water. Pour this mixture into the prepared mold and smooth over the top. Trim the remaining cake slices and arrange them on top. Sprinkle over the remaining Maraschino. Cover and chill for 3–4 hours.

5. Carefully unmold the cake onto a serving plate.

6. To make the icing, mix the lemon juice with the sugar. Stir in tablespoons of hot water until the mixture is thick enough to coat the back of a spoon. Place the bowl over a pan of simmering water and stir until the icing is lukewarm. Pour the icing onto the cake, letting it dribble down the sides. Smooth over with a hot narrow spatula if necessary.

7. While the icing is still warm, decorate with the reserved crystallized fruits. Leave to set and chill until required.

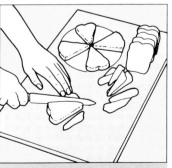

Trim cake slices to fit mold.

From the left: Coffee and rum cheesecake, Cassata alla Siciliana

Baked Fresh Fruit Cheesecake

Serves 10
Sweet pie pastry:
1 cup all-purpose flour, sifted
pinch of salt
¼ cup sugar
1 small egg
1 stick butter, chilled and cut
   into cubes
1½ tablespoons butter, melted
2 cups green grapes, halved
   and seeded
Filling:
4 tablespoons butter
½ cup sugar
3 eggs, separated
1 teaspoon grated lemon zest
2 tablespoons heavy cream
2 tablespoons Kirsch
2 cups sieved cottage cheese
2 tablespoons cornstarch
Topping:
1 egg yolk
2 tablespoons heavy cream
2 teaspoons sugar
2 tablespoons sliced almonds
To decorate:
confectioners' sugar
whole green grapes

Preparation time: 55 minutes
plus cooling
Cooking time: about 2 hours
Oven: 400°F (for pastry case)
then: 375°F (for cheesecake)

1. Grease a 9½-inch springform
pan.

2. Make the pastry as described
for Blackberry and Cheese
Torte (page 191) but omit the
lemon zest. Roll out the pastry
and line the pan so that the
pastry covers the bottom and
extends 1 inch up the sides.
Bake blind (up to step 3, page
31) for 15–20 minutes in a
preheated oven. Remove the
pan and reduce the oven
temperature.

3. Brush the base of the pastry
case with melted butter and
arrange the halved grapes on
top.

4. To make the filling, beat
together the butter and sugar
and mix in the egg yolks. Add
the lemon zest, cream, Kirsch,
cottage cheese and cornstarch.
Mix well.

5. Beat the egg whites until stiff
and fold them into the cheese
mixture. Pour the mixture over
the grapes in the pastry case
and smooth the top level.

6. To make the topping, mix
together the egg yolk, cream
and sugar, and spread over the
filling. Sprinkle the sliced
almonds on top. Bake in a
preheated oven for 1–1¼ hours
until golden brown. Cool in the
pan on a wire rack.

7. Carefully remove the sides of
the pan. Arrange the whole
grapes on top, dredge with
confectioners' sugar and serve.

Variation

Any firm fresh fruits may be
used instead of grapes: pitted
black cherries, halved and
pitted plums or cored and
coarsely sliced apples and
pears.

Cherry Cheesecake Torte

Kirsch is an *eau-de-vie* distilled
from cherries, and its traditional
combination with chocolate
cake, black cherries and cream
originates in the Black Forest of
Germany. This variation, with
the cream cheese filling, is an
unusual alternative. It may be
prepared up to 1 day in advance. Cover and chill until
required.

Serves 8
1 stick butter
1 cup sugar
2 eggs, separated
1 cup cream cheese
2 teaspoons grated lemon zest
2 tablespoons lemon juice
1 envelope unflavored gelatin
   dissolved in 4 tablespoons
   very hot water
⅔ cup heavy or whipping
   cream
5 tablespoons Kirsch
1 Fatless Sponge Cake 9½
   inches in diameter (page 17)
   baked in a deep loose-
   bottomed pan
1½-lb can pitted morello or
   black cherries
½ cup sliced almonds, toasted
To decorate:
fresh cherries
candied angelica pieces

Black Forest Special

For an authentic cheesecake
version of a Black Forest
Layer Cake, make the Cherry
Cheesecake Torte with a
chocolate sponge cake base.
Follow the instructions for
the Fatless Sponge, replacing
2 tablespoons flour with 2
tablespoons cocoa and 1
teaspoon instant coffee
powder. Sift these with the
flour. Decorate the
completed Chocolate Cherry
Cheesecake with chocolate
caraque (see page 68), dusted
with confectioners' sugar.

Preparation time: 50 minutes
plus chilling

1. Cream the butter and sugar
until light and fluffy. Beat in the
egg yolks, one at a time. Beat in
the cream cheese, lemon zest
and lemon juice.

2. Stir the dissolved gelatin into
the mixture. Leave on one side
until on the point of setting.

3. Beat the egg whites until stiff.
Whip the cream until stiff. Fold
the cream into the cheese
mixture, alternating with
spoonfuls of beaten egg white.
Fold in 2 tablespoons of Kirsch.

4. Put the cooled sponge cake
back in the cake pan. Drain the
cherries, reserving 3 tablespoons of juice. Mix the
reserved juice with the remaining Kirsch and sprinkle over the
sponge cake to moisten. Scatter
the toasted almonds on top.

5. Divide the cherries in half.
Distribute one half evenly over
the cake base. Fold the remainder into the filling mixture.

6. Spoon the filling onto the
cake in the pan and carefully
smooth over. Chill for 4–5
hours.

7. To serve, carefully remove the
sides of the pan and put the
torte on a serving plate. Decorate with the fresh cherries and
angelica pieces.

*From the top: Cherry cheesecake torte,
Baked fresh fruit cheesecake*

Lemon Cheesecake

This refreshing cheesecake is easy to prepare and has an exceptionally light texture. It is the ideal dessert to serve after a rich main course. Prepare it up to 2 days in advance if you wish, and keep chilled until required.

Serves 8
4 eggs, separated
1 cup sugar
1/3 cup water
1 envelope unflavored gelatin dissolved in 5 tablespoons hot water
7/8 cup lemon juice, strained
4 teaspoons grated lemon zest
1 1/2 cups cream cheese or sieved cottage cream
Crumb base:
1 1/3 cups graham cracker crumbs
1/4 cup sugar
1/2 teaspoon ground cinnamon
1/2 teaspoon ground nutmeg
4 tablespoons butter
1 tablespoon apricot jam
To decorate:
whipped cream
lemon slices
green grapes, halved and seeded

Preparation time: 35 minutes plus chilling

Cook's Tip

For a nut and crumb base combine 1 cup toasted bread crumbs with 1/2 cup ground walnuts, 3 tablespoons vanilla sugar and 1/2 teaspoon ground cinnamon. Melt 1/2 teaspoon butter with 1 tablespoon apricot jam in a large pan. Away from the heat, stir in the crumb mixture and combine well. Press into the pan and cool.

1. Prepare a crumb base in an 8-inch springform pan as described for Pineapple Refrigerator Cake (below), substituting graham crackers for bread crumbs.

2. Beat the egg yolks until pale and creamy.

3. In a saucepan dissolve the sugar in the water over a low heat. Turn up the heat and boil the syrup to 234–240°F on a candy thermometer (the soft ball stage or when a small amount dropped into ice water forms a sticky soft ball which loses its shape when removed from the water).

4. Pour the syrup onto the egg yolks in a steady stream, beating all the time. Continue beating until the mixture has cooled. Pour into a large bowl.

5. Stir the dissolved gelatin into the mixture. Stir in the lemon juice and lemon zest, blend well and leave to cool.

6. Fold the cheese into the mixture and set aside until on the point of setting.

7. Beat the egg whites until stiff then gently fold them into the cheese mixture. Pour the mixture into the prepared pan and gently smooth over the top. Chill for 3–4 hours.

8. To serve, carefully remove the sides of the pan and set the cheesecake on a serving plate. Decorate with whipped cream, grapes and lemon slices.

From the top: Pineapple refrigerator cake, Lemon cheesecake

Pineapple Refrigerator Cake

This cake may be prepared 2–3 days in advance. Cover and chill until required.

Serves 12

2 1/2 cups fresh bread crumbs, toasted
6 tablespoons sugar
1/2 teaspoon ground cinnamon
1/2 teaspoon ground nutmeg
6 tablespoons butter
1 1/2 tablespoons apricot jam
Filling:
2 envelopes unflavored gelatin
3/4 cup sugar
pinch of salt
3 eggs, separated
1 1/4 cups milk
8-oz can crushed pineapple in natural juice
1 1/4 lb (2 1/2 cups) cream cheese
2 teaspoons grated lemon zest
3 tablespoons lemon juice
1 1/4 cups heavy cream
To decorate:
2/3 cup sour cream
candied pineapple
sliced almonds, toasted
scented geranium leaves (optional)

Preparation time: 50 minutes plus setting and chilling
Cooking time: about 15 minutes

1. Line the bottom of a 9 1/2-inch springform pan with non-stick parchment paper and grease the sides well.

2. Mix the bread crumbs with the sugar and spices.

3. Melt the butter and apricot jam in a large pan set over a low heat. Remove the pan from the heat, stir in the crumb mixture and combine well. Press evenly and firmly into the prepared pan using the back of a spoon. Leave to chill while preparing the filling.

4. In a heatproof mixing bowl, mix together the gelatin, sugar and salt.

5. With a fork, lightly beat the egg yolks with the milk and add to the sugar mixture. Mix in the crushed pineapple.

6. Set the mixing bowl over a pan of simmering water and stir for about 15 minutes until the mixture starts to thicken. Draw off the heat and pour into a large mixing bowl. Set aside to cool.

7. Beat together the cream cheese, lemon zest and lemon juice. Gradually add the cooled pineapple mixture and combine well. Set aside until almost on the point of setting.

8. Beat the egg whites until stiff. Whip the double cream until stiff. Fold alternate spoonfuls of whipped cream and egg white into the cheese mixture. Pour onto the chilled base in the pan and carefully smooth over. Chill for 5 hours.

9. To serve, carefully remove the sides of the pan and set the cheesecake on a serving plate. Gently smooth the sour cream over the surface and decorate with the candied pineapple and toasted almonds. For a colorful final touch, arrange a few scented geranium leaves on top as well.

Chocolate-Orange Cheesecake

Serves 8–10

1½ squares semisweet chocolate
3 tablespoons butter or
*   margarine*
2 cups graham cracker crumbs
Filling:
1 cup cream cheese
6 tablespoons sugar
grated zest of 1 orange
4 tablespoons orange juice
2 envelopes unflavored gelatin
1 tablespoon lemon juice
1 large can evaporated milk,
*   chilled overnight*
To decorate:
⅔ cup heavy or whipping
*   cream*
1½–2 packages chocolate-
*   covered finger cookies*
jellied orange slices

Preparation time: about 30
minutes, plus chilling
Cooking time: about 10
minutes

1. Melt the chocolate and butter
or margarine in a saucepan set
over a gentle heat. Stir in the
graham cracker crumbs until
they are evenly coated. Press
this mixture over the bottom of
a well-greased 7½- to 8-inch
springform pan. Chill until set.

2. To make the filling, beat the
cheese and sugar until soft and
smooth. Gradually beat in the
orange zest and juice.

3. Dissolve the gelatin in the
lemon juice in a heatproof bowl
set over a pan of hot water.
Leave to cool, then mix evenly
through the cheese mixture.

4. Whip the evaporated milk
until very thick and standing in
soft peaks. Fold it quickly
through the cheese mixture.
Pour into the pan over the
crumb base and chill until set –
preferably overnight.

5. Carefully remove the cheesecake from the pan and place it
on a plate. Whip the cream until
stiff and spread a thin layer all
around the sides of the cheesecake. Arrange the chocolate
finger cookies around the sides.

6. Place the remaining cream in
a pastry bag fitted with a star
tube and decorate the top with
whirls of whipped cream.
Complete with jellied orange
slices.

Chocolate-orange cheesecake

Strawberry Cheesecake Boxes

These individual cheesecakes are ideal for an elegant dessert. The sponge cake base and filling can be made the day before, and the chocolate squares 2–3 days in advance if stored in a rigid container in a cool place. On the day all you need do is assemble the cakes and decorate the tops.

Makes 9
1 egg
2 tablespoons sugar
¼ cup cake flour, sifted
1 tablespoon warm water
Filling:
¾ cup boiling water
1 package (3-oz) strawberry gelatin dessert
juice of ½ lemon
1 cup cream cheese
1¼ cups whipping cream
2 tablespoons red currant jelly, warmed
To decorate:
6 squares semisweet chocolate, broken into pieces
9 fresh strawberries

Preparation time: about 1 hour, plus setting
Cooking time: 10–12 minutes
Oven: 400°F

1. Line the bottom of a 7-inch square cake pan with lightly greased wax paper or non-stick parchment paper.

2. Beat the egg and sugar until light and foamy and the beater leaves a trail when lifted.

3. Gently fold in the flour and water with a metal spoon, then pour the batter into the prepared pan. Bake in a preheated oven for 10–12 minutes, until well risen and lightly golden brown. Unmold the cake and peel off the paper. Leave to cool on a wire rack.

4. Pour the boiling water into a small bowl. Sprinkle over the gelatin and stir until it has completely dissolved. Add the lemon juice. Chill in the refrigerator until the mixture becomes syrupy – about 30 minutes.

5. Cream the cheese until it is smooth, then gradually add the gelatin, beating well between each addition. Whip the cream and fold two thirds of it into the mixture. Pour into a 7-inch square cake pan lined with wax or non-stick parchment paper. Chill for about 2 hours, until set.

6. Brush the cake square with the red currant jelly. Carefully unmold the cheesecake onto the cake, matching the edges. Peel off the paper and trim the edges neatly if necessary.

7. Draw a 12-inch square on wax paper. Melt the chocolate in a heatproof bowl set over a saucepan of hot water and stir until smooth. With a narrow spatula, spread the chocolate on the paper to fill the square. Cool until set.

8. Cut the chocolate into 36 equal squares. Cut the cheesecake into nine 2-inch squares, trimming the edges if necessary. Working quickly to avoid overhandling the chocolate, press a piece of chocolate onto the four sides of each cheesecake square.

9. Place the remaining cream in a parchment paper decorating cone fitted with a star tube. Pipe a generous ribbon of cream on top of each cheesecake. Decorate each with a strawberry.

Variations

Vary the flavor of the cheesecake boxes by using a different flavored gelatin and appropriate decoration. Orange gelatin with a mandarin segment decoration or black cherry gelatin with a pitted black cherry on top are two fruit flavors that combine well with chocolate. Make all three kinds for a special dessert choice.

Above: Strawberry cheesecake boxes

SMALL CAKES & PASTRIES

A quintessential tea time delicacy, small cakes and pastries are back in vogue. Practice your cake design and decorating arts in miniature, and to surprise your friends with their range and variety. Children are sure to enjoy these colorful mouthfuls, too.

Diminutive they may be, but the cakes in this chapter have an appeal far outstripping their size. Who can resist an array of tempting little mouthfuls like these?

The small cakes and pastries in the following pages include a number of the basic recipes covered in the preceding chapters: not only cake batters, but pastries such as puff, choux and strudel; glacé icing, buttercream and crème pâtissière; meringue, syrups and melted chocolate. These small cakes also demonstrate the skills of the cake-decorator: the importance of design and decoration is even greater when the scale is reduced to individual size. Like a miniature painting, every stroke has to be exact. Before you try these recipes practice the art of making small cakes with Genoese pastries. Make a Genoese Sponge Cake (page 22) and cover the whole cake with buttercream. Decorate with piped buttercream, nuts, cherries and other simple decorations before cutting the cake into fingers. In this chapter the easiest cakes to make and decorate are the Fairy Cakes on page 204. Based on a simple cake batter, they are individually cooked and iced with glacé icing. As the number of variations shows, the possibilities are almost endless. Practice small-scale design with these ideas before progressing to more fanciful little cakes.

Although a large and beautiful cake cannot be bettered as the centerpiece to an occasion, most parties require some supporting acts to keep the guests amused before the star turn. This is where a cast of delectable little cakes comes into its own – and may even steal the show, if such delicious examples as Petits Vacherins (page 215) and Chestnut Meringues (page 218) make an appearance. Little cakes are a must for children's parties not only because they make the table look colorful and festive, but because children like food of all kinds that's scaled down for them. Tortoises (page 206) and Animal Cookies (page 211) are ideal.

The delicacy of small cakes can bring a touch of luxury to family parties, with attractive but easily made cakes like Apple and Ginger Rings and Nutty Angelica Fancies (pages 208–9). They have their practical aspect, too, since you can cater more exactly for a particular number of people. These two recipes are particularly good for picnics – they are easy to transport and just the thing for satisfying fresh-air appetites.

Elegant tea parties are coming back into fashion after a temporary decline, now that people are rediscovering the pleasure of a civilized meal that requires relatively little preparation and which can fill an otherwise rather vacant spot on Sunday afternoons. As well as the cucumber sandwiches, an assortment of pretty little cakes is essential, whether it's tea on the lawn or by the fire. Make sure the selection of cakes served includes a variety of flavors and textures.

For coffee mornings, serve Cranberry Apple Strudels (page 218), a delicious variation on a classic Austrian recipe. There are many European recipes for small cakes that are luxurious enough to be served as individual desserts, such as Vol-au-vents aux Framboises and the renowned Individual Fruit Savarins (page 216).

When you serve coffee at the end of a special meal, pamper your guests with petits fours such as Italiens or Printaniers (page 212) or bite-sized cookies like Almond Leaves (page 214).

After trying the tempting selection of cakes in this chapter, you are sure to agree that small is beautiful.

Fairy Cakes

Makes 18–20

1 stick butter or margarine
½ cup sugar
2 eggs
1¼ cups self-rising cake flour
To ice and decorate:
1 quantity glacé icing (see page 42)
a few drops of food coloring
small candies, nuts, candied cherries

Preparation time: 10 minutes
Cooking time: 15–20 minutes
Oven: 350°F

1. Cream the butter and sugar together until pale and fluffy. Gradually beat in the eggs. Sift the flour over the mixture and fold it in gently using a wooden spoon.

2. Spoon the batter into greased patty pans or paper cup cake cases placed on a baking sheet and bake in a preheated oven for 15–20 minutes or until well risen and golden brown. Unmold from the patty pans and leave to cool on a wire rack.

3. Prepare the glacé icing and tint it delicately with a few drops of any preferred coloring. Coat the tops of the cakes with icing. The cakes may be feather iced with two different colors (see page 43).

4. Decorate with small candies, nuts, candied cherries and angelica as preferred.

Variations

Chocolate cup cakes Add 2 tablespoons cocoa powder to the flour. Decorate the cakes with 6 squares melted semi-sweet chocolate or glacé icing with melted chocolate drizzled on top.

Nutty cakes Add ½ cup chopped walnuts to the batter. Decorate with glacé icing and walnut halves.

Little fruit cakes Add ⅓ cup mixed dried fruit or chopped candied cherries to the batter. Mix 1 cup sifted confectioners' sugar with 1–2 tablespoons sherry to give a smooth icing. Drizzle the icing over the top of the cakes.

Butterfly cakes Reduce the amount of flour to 1 cup. This will make 16 cakes. Flavor the mixture with coffee, chocolate, lemon, orange or vanilla. While the cakes are cooling, make up 1 quantity of simple butter-cream (see page 46), colored and flavored to blend with the cake. Cut a small piece out of the top of each bun leaving about ½ inch all around the top surface uncut. Cut the round piece in half to form "wings".
   Put the buttercream in a pastry bag fitted with a star tube and pipe small stars all over the cut surface of each cake. Place the wings in position, tilting them up at the edges. Pipe a row of stars between the wings and a border around the top of each cake. Dredge lightly with confectioners' sugar if wished.

Fairy cakes

Iced Fancies

If you have time, make the cake the day before it is to be iced to make cutting it easier.

Makes 22
3 eggs
6 tablespoons sugar
¾ cup cake flour
½ teaspoon baking powder
To ice and decorate:
⅔ cup apricot jam, warmed and sieved
½ lb marzipan
6 cups confectioners' sugar, sifted
boiling water
red, yellow, orange, green and blue food coloring
candied angelica, gumdrops and candy balls

Preparation time: 15 minutes
Cooking time: 25–30 minutes
Oven: 350°F

1. Grease and line an 11- × 7-inch baking pan with greased wax paper or non-stick parchment paper.

2. Place the eggs and sugar in a bowl set over a saucepan of hot water. Beat until the mixture is thick and pale and leaves a trail when the beater is lifted. Remove the bowl from the pan and beat for a further 2 minutes to cool slightly.

3. Sift the flour with the baking powder and carefully fold it in to the egg mixture, using a metal spoon, until evenly mixed. Pour into the prepared pan.

4. Bake the cake in a preheated oven for 25–30 minutes until it is golden brown and firm to the touch. Unmold onto a wire rack, remove the lining paper and leave to cool completely.

5. Brush the top of the cake with some of the jam. Roll out the marzipan and use to cover the top of the cake. Trim the edges of the cake neatly with a sharp knife, reserving the marzipan trimmings for decoration.

6. Cut the cake into rounds, triangles, bars and squares. See the diagram below, right for the most economical way to cut the cake.

7. Brush all the small cakes with the jam. Knead the marzipan trimmings and shape into small rolls and balls. Place on a few of the cakes to give a raised surface when iced. (Sponge trimmings, cut to shape, can be used for the same effect.)

8. Place 4 cups of the confectioners' sugar in a bowl set over a saucepan of hot water. Beat in enough boiling water until the icing thickly coats the back of a wooden spoon and is of a smooth pouring consistency.

9. Divide the icing into six portions. Keep one white and color the others pink, yellow, orange, blue and green. Place one cake of each shape on a wire rack over a tray. Using a tablespoon, coat the cakes with white icing then transfer them to a board. Ice the remaining cakes in this way in the different colors, but remember there are only four square cakes.

10. Mix the remaining confectioners' sugar with boiling water to make icing of a piping consistency. Tint half the icing pink. Fill a pastry bag fitted with a thin writing tube with white icing and pipe threads of icing across half the cakes. Pipe pink icing threads on the remaining cakes.

11. Decorate the cakes with angelica leaves, gumdrops and candy balls.

Tortoises

Makes 18
1 tablespoon cocoa
1 tablespoon boiling water
½ cup sugar
½ cup soft margarine
2 eggs
1 cup self-rising cake flour
1 teaspoon baking powder
To ice and decorate:
¾ lb marzipan
a few drops of green food coloring
2 tablespoons apricot jam, warmed and sieved
3 squares semisweet chocolate
silver candy balls

Preparation time: 10 minutes
Cooking time: 12–15 minutes
Oven: 375°F

1. Blend the cocoa and water to a smooth paste. Allow to cool. Place in a bowl with the remaining cake ingredients. Beat with a wooden spoon for about 2 minutes, until light and fluffy.

2. Divide the batter between 18 paper cup cake cases placed in muffin tins. Bake in the oven for 12–15 minutes, until firm to the touch, then allow to cool.

3. Knead the marzipan on a board until it is pliable, then gradually knead in food coloring to tint it green.

4. Roll out two thirds of the marzipan and cut into 3½-inch rounds, reserving the trimmings. Remove the cakes from the paper cases and invert them onto a board. Brush each cake with jam and cover with a marzipan round.

5. Shape the remaining marzipan into small rolls. Flatten them slightly and attach to the body to form the head and feet. Score the feet with a small sharp knife. Press silver candy balls into the head for the eyes. Score the body into hexagonal markings.

6. Melt the chocolate in a bowl set over a pan of hot water. Place the chocolate in a pastry bag fitted with a thin writing tube and pipe over the tortoise markings. Leave to set.

Variation

To make hedgehogs, colour the marzipan brown with food coloring. Use it to cover the cakes. With sharp pointed scissors, make snips over the backs of the hedgehogs to form spines. Pinch out the marzipan to make a snout and press in silver candy balls for eyes.

Iced fancies, Tortoises

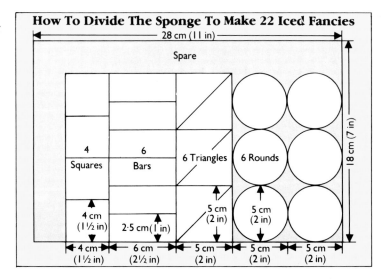

How To Divide The Sponge To Make 22 Iced Fancies

28 cm (11 in) · 18 cm (7 in) · Spare · 4 Squares · 6 Bars · 6 Triangles · 6 Rounds · 4 cm (1½ in) · 2·5 cm (1 in) · 5 cm (2 in) · 5 cm (2 in) · 4 cm (1½ in) · 6 cm (2½ in) · 5 cm (2 in) · 5 cm (2 in) · 5 cm (2 in)

Apple and Ginger Rings

Makes 9
2 eggs
⅓ cup light corn syrup
1 baking apple, weighing about
* 6 oz*
juice of 1 lemon
1 piece preserved ginger, finely
* chopped*
1 cup self-rising cake flour
¼ teaspoon ground ginger
To ice and decorate:
1 cup confectioners' sugar
1–2 tablespoons ginger wine
crystallized ginger
few slices of apple, dipped in
* lemon juice (optional)*

Preparation time: 10 minutes
Cooking time: 20–25 minutes
Oven: 375°F

1. Grease nine 4½-inch ring molds (such as individual savarin molds) generously.

2. Beat the eggs with the corn syrup until the mixture is pale and thick.

3. Peel, core and grate the apple. Sprinkle with lemon juice and mix with the preserved ginger. Fold into the eggs.

4. Sift the flour and ground ginger together and fold into the egg and apple mixture.

5. Divide the batter equally between the prepared molds and bake in the oven for 20–25 minutes until well risen and golden brown. Unmold to cool on a wire rack.

6. Sift the confectioners' sugar into a bowl and mix to a smooth consistency with the ginger wine. Drizzle this icing over the cooled cakes and decorate with pieces of crystallized ginger. Just before serving, decorate with apple slices if liked.

Nutty Angelica Fancies

Makes 12
1 stick butter or margarine
½ cup sugar
2 eggs, lightly beaten
1 cup self-rising cake flour, sifted
1 cup chopped walnuts
½ cup chopped candied angelica
To ice and decorate:
1 quantity glacé icing (page 42)
¼ chopped walnuts
⅓ cup chopped candied angelica

Preparation time: 10 minutes
Cooking time: 25–30 minutes
Oven: 350°F

1. Lightly grease 12 baba (dariole) molds.

2. Cream the butter with the sugar until light and fluffy. Gradually beat in the eggs and fold in the flour using a metal spoon.

3. Mix together the walnuts and angelica and fold into the cake batter.

4. Divide the batter between the prepared molds and bake in a preheated oven for 25–30 minutes. To make it easier to handle the molds, place them on a baking sheet. Unmold to cool on a wire rack.

5. Drizzle the glacé icing over the top of each cake, letting it go down the sides of the cakes. Sprinkle with a mixture of chopped walnuts and angelica.

Opposite page: Apple and ginger rings
Below: Nutty angelica fancies

Sponge Cake Dice

These easy-to-make little cakes are fun for a children's party or even with the coffee at a bridge party. As an alternative to dots you could cut out diamonds and hearts from the molding paste.

Makes 16
1-cup flour quantity chocolate
*   Quick Mix Cake batter*
*   (pages 16–17)*
½ lb fondant molding paste
*   (page 44)*
red and green food colorings
½ lb marzipan (page 37)
6 tablespoons apricot glaze
*   (page 38)*
cornstarch for dusting

Preparation time: 30 minutes
Cooking time: 35–40 minutes
Oven: 325°F

1. Cook the cake batter in a greased, wax paper-lined deep 7-inch square cake pan for 35–40 minutes, until well risen and firm to the touch. Unmold, remove the paper and cool the cake on a wire rack.

2. Cut off a small piece of the fondant molding paste the size of a walnut and reserve. Color the remaining molding paste red with a few drops of red food coloring. Knead a few drops of green food coloring into the marzipan until evenly colored green.

3. Trim and cut the cake into sixteen 1½-inch squares and brush them evenly with apricot glaze.

4. Roll out the red molding paste thinly on a surface sprinkled with cornstarch and cut out 1½-inch squares, re-rolling the trimmings when necessary. Attach the molding paste squares to the sides and tops of eight cakes, pressing the seams together.

5. Repeat with the marzipan, cutting out the squares to cover the remaining eight cakes.

6. Use the reserved white molding paste to roll into tiny dots, and secure one to six dots on each side of the cakes using a little apricot glaze, to make dice.

Animal variety

Children love little cakes shaped like animals. Easy to make using ½-cup flour quantity Quick Mix Cake batter, are Goldfish cakes. Bake the batter in 15 greased barquette (boat) molds at 325°F for 15 minutes. Brush the underneath and just the pointed end of the flat tops with apricot glaze and dip in candy sprinkles to coat well. Color 6 oz marzipan orange. Roll it out thinly and cut out lots of rounds with a ½-inch plain piping tube, 15 "V" shapes for the tails and 15 tiny circles for the eyes. Place the eyes on the pointed end and the tails at the opposite ends. Arrange the small circles like scales, in rows overlapping from head to tail.

Yellow Chicks

Makes 16
2 egg whites
½ cup superfine sugar
a few drops of yellow food
*   coloring*
black food coloring pen
⅔ cup heavy or whipping
*   cream*
2 teaspoons grated lemon zest
10 large chocolate disks

Preparation time: 20 minutes
Cooking time: 2 hours
Oven: 225°F

1. Line two baking sheets with non-stick parchment paper. Place the egg whites in a bowl and beat until stiff. Gradually beat in the sugar until the mixture stands up in peaks.

2. Add a few drops of food coloring to the meringue to color it pale yellow.

3. Place the meringue in a pastry bag fitted with a ½-inch plain tube. Pipe a small round of the mixture about 1 inch in diameter onto the baking sheet

From the left: Yellow chicks, Sponge cake dice, Animal cookies

for the body and pull off to the right to form a wing. Pipe a smaller round above and pull off to the left for the beak. This makes one half chick. Pipe another half chick with the wing to the left and the beak to the right.

4. Repeat to pipe another 15 left-hand chicks and 15 right-hand chicks. Place in a pre-heated oven as near to the center as possible and cook for about 2 hours, or until the meringue chicks lift easily off the paper.

5. Using a fine paintbrush and some yellow coloring, paint the beak and wing markings on each chick. Mark in the eyes with the food coloring pen.

6. Place the cream and lemon zest in a bowl and whip until thick. Spread half of the chicks with most of the cream leaving a small amount and put together with the matching half.

7. Sit each chick on a chocolate disk secured with a little cream.

Making meringues

Always use 2–3 day old egg whites if possible when making meringues as they dry out more quickly. Also make sure the sugar is beaten well into the egg whites a little at a time, ensuring a light fluffy meringue. Dry in a cool oven until the meringues lift easily off the paper, and store in a dry place in an airtight container.

Animal Cookies

Makes 25
1 cup all-purpose flour
⅓ cup ground rice
6 tablespoons sugar
⅔ cup soft margarine
1 teaspoon vanilla extract
1 egg, separated
red, yellow and green food colorings
dried currants

Preparation time: about 15 minutes
Cooking time: 10–12 minutes
Oven: 350°F

Continued

1. Place the flour, ground rice, sugar, margarine, vanilla extract and egg white in a mixing bowl. Mix together with a wooden spoon until the mixture begins to bind together, then knead it with the fingers until the mixture forms a soft dough.

2. Roll out thinly on a lightly floured surface. Using different shaped animal cutters, cut out the dough and place the shapes on lightly floured baking sheets.

3. Divide the egg yolk into three portions and color each portion with a few drops of food coloring so that the egg glazes are red, yellow and green.

4. To decorate the animal shapes, brush on either stripes or dots of different egg glaze colors, or just paint on one plain color. Make the animals' features with currants.

5. Place the baking sheets in a preheated oven on the center shelf and just below and bake for 10–12 minutes until pale at the edges.

6. Cool on the baking sheets for a few minutes, then remove carefully and place on a wire rack to cool.

Italiens

Because of the cream filling make these cakes no further than one day ahead.

Makes 20
1 quantity Genoese Sponge Cake batter (page 22)
1 quantity crème au beurre mousseline (page 47)
2 tablespoons Kirsch or few drops of almond extract
To finish:
3 cups confectioners' sugar, sifted
3 tablespoons water
green food coloring
10 blanched almonds

Preparation time: 20 minutes

1. Trim the edges from the cake and cut it into four strips. Cut each one in half lengthwise.

2. Mix the crème au beurre mousseline with the Kirsch or almond extract and spread a layer on each strip of cake. Put the cake halves back together and place on a wire rack.

3. Put the remaining crème au beurre in a pastry bag fitted with a ½-inch plain tube. Pipe a band of the cream down the length of each strip. Place in the refrigerator to become firm.

4. Put the confectioners' sugar in a bowl, placed over a saucepan of hot water, and mix with sufficient water to give a coating consistency. Add a little green food coloring. Stir well until smooth. Pour the icing over each cake strip, making certain the sides as well as the top are coated with icing. Put a plate under the wire rack to catch the surplus icing.

5. Split the almonds in half and place five evenly on top of each band. Dip a knife into hot water and diagonally cut each strip between each nut. Put into paper cases to serve.

Printaniers

Like the Italiens, these little cakes keep for one day.

Makes 20
1 quantity Genoese Sponge Cake batter (page 22)
1 quantity crème au beurre mousseline (page 47)
1–2 drops vanilla extract
a few drops of green and pink food coloring
2 teaspoons Kirsch or a few drops of almond extract

Preparation time: 20 minutes

1. Trim the edges from the cake and cut it into four strips. Cut each one in half lengthwise. Spread a thin layer of crème au beurre mousseline on each and put the cake halves back together.

2. Divide the remainder of the buttercream into three. Flavor one third with 1–2 drops vanilla extract, color one-third pale green and flavor with Kirsch or a little almond extract. Color the remaining third of the mixture pale pink.

3. With a pastry bag(s) fitted with a small star tube(s), pipe a band of each color down the length of each strip, covering the top of the cake completely. Cut each strip into five. Put in paper cases to serve.

Petits Fours

Italiens and Printaniers look very effective arranged with other petits fours. Little sugared fruits called Friandises make the display very colorful. Make a syrup with 2¼ cups sugar, 2 oz powdered glucose and ⅔ cup water, cooked to the hard crack stage (see page 49). Using two forks dipped in oil, dip each piece of fruit into the hot syrup to coat. Drain for a moment and leave on an oiled baking sheet to set and cool.

From the left: Printaniers, Italiens

Almond Leaves

These pretty cookies are simply made with a fluted cutter, marking the veins of a leaf with a knife. They keep up to 4 weeks in an airtight tin.

Makes 30
4 tablespoons butter
½ cup sugar
1¾ cups ground almonds
1 teaspoon vanilla sugar or few drops of vanilla extract
3 egg yolks
1 cup all-purpose flour, sifted
To finish:
1 egg, beaten
6 squares semisweet chocolate, broken in pieces

Preparation time: 40 minutes, plus chilling
Cooking time: 15 minutes
Oven: 350°F

1. Place the butter in a bowl and beat until soft and creamy. Stir in the sugar, ground almonds and vanilla sugar or extract. Add the egg yolks and mix together to a paste. Gradually work all the flour into the mixture.

2. Cover the dough with plastic wrap or wax paper and chill for 30 minutes.

3. Roll out the dough fairly thinly and cut out leaf shapes 2¼-inches long, using a 2½-inch fluted cutter. Pinch the fluted edges together to form small points. Mark the veining of a leaf on each cookie with the back of a small knife.

4. Place on a greased baking sheet and brush with beaten egg. Place in a preheated oven and bake for 15 minutes until golden brown. Cool on a wire rack.

5. Meanwhile, place the chocolate in a bowl set over a saucepan of hot water. When it has melted, dip half of each cookie into the chocolate. Place on wax paper or plastic wrap until dry.

Rout Cookies

Rout creams were rich vanilla-flavored custards popular as desserts in Britain in the nineteenth century, and sweet cookies like these were always served with them. Light as a feather, they keep up to 4 weeks in an airtight tin.

Makes about 36
1⅓ cups ground almonds
1 cup confectioners' sugar, sifted
1 egg white
rice paper
To decorate:
candied cherries
crystallized angelica
crystallized pineapple
blanched almond halves
To finish:
2 teaspoons powdered gum arabic
2 tablespoons water

Preparation time: 20 minutes, plus drying
Cooking time: 4–5 minutes
Oven: 450°F

1. Mix the ground almonds and confectioners' sugar together in a bowl. Add sufficient egg white to form a soft smooth paste.

2. Cover a baking sheet with rice paper. Put the almond mixture into a pastry bag fitted with a large star tube and pipe small shapes onto the prepared baking sheet.

3. Decorate with small pieces of candied cherry, crystallized angelica or pineapple or blanched almond halves. Leave for several hours or overnight to dry.

4. Put the gum arabic and water into a bowl set over a bowl of hot water and allow to dissolve.

Petits Vacherins

The meringue cases for these sweet little mouthfuls can be kept for up to 3 weeks in an airtight tin. When filled with cream and fruit, eat on the same day.

Makes 20
1 cup confectioners' sugar, sifted
2 egg whites
To finish:
1 cup heavy or whipping cream, whipped
1 pint strawberries or other soft fruit

Preparation time: 30 minutes
Cooking time: 1½–2 hours
Oven: 300°F

1. Put the confectioners' sugar and egg whites into a large bowl set over a saucepan of hot water. Beat until the mixture becomes thick and shiny and stands in stiff peaks. Remove from the heat and beat until cool.

2. Place the meringue mixture into a pastry bag fitted with a small star tube. Pipe small nests no more than 1½ inches in diameter onto baking sheets lined with parchment paper.

3. Place in a preheated oven and bake for 1½–2 hours until dry, firm and easily lifted off the paper. Cool on a wire rack.

4. Place the whipped cream in a pastry bag fitted with a small star tube and pipe a swirl of cream into the center of each vacherin. Top with one small strawberry or half a large one.

5. Place the cookies in a preheated oven and bake for 4–5 minutes to brown the edges. Remove from the oven and immediately glaze with the gum arabic solution. Cool on a wire rack.

Shortbread Specials

Heart-shaped shortbreads can be dipped in chocolate like the Almond Leaves. Cream 1½ sticks butter with 6 tablespoons sugar. Beat in 1⅔ cups sifted all-purpose flour and chill before kneading and rolling out. Bake the cookies at 325°F for 15 minutes. Leave to cool before dipping in melted chocolate. A border of shells can be piped with simple chocolate buttercream.

Clockwise from top left: Almond leaves, Petit vacherins, Rout cookies

Individual Fruit Savarins

These sumptuous cakes make a splendid dessert for a special meal – as long as the preceding course is not too heavy, as these are rather rich. As an alternative, make a single large savarin in a 1½-quart ring mold, and allow 40 minutes' cooking time. The plain savarins can be stored in an airtight tin for 2 days, but should not be filled with the fruit and cream more than 2 hours before serving.

Makes 14–16
lard for greasing
1 oz (1½ cakes) compressed yeast; or 1 tablespoon active dry yeast and 1 teaspoon sugar
6 tablespoons warm milk
1⅔ cups bread flour
½ teaspoon salt
2 tablespoons sugar
4 eggs, beaten
1 stick butter, very soft, but not melted, and cut into pieces
⅓ cup dried currants (optional)
½ quantity apricot glaze (page 38)
Rum syrup:
4 tablespoons clear honey
4 tablespoons mandarin juice from the can (see filling)
1–2 tablespoons rum or other liqueur
Filling:
1 Canteloupe melon, cut into balls
1 11-oz can mandarin oranges, drained
1 11-oz can litchis, drained
about ⅔ cup heavy or whipping cream, whipped (optional)

Preparation time: about 1 hour, plus rising
Cooking time: about 20 minutes
Oven: 400°F

1. Grease about 14–16 individual savarin molds with lard.

2. In a bowl blend the compressed yeast (or dry yeast and sugar) with the milk and ⅓ cup of the flour. Stand in a warm place until frothy, allowing about 20 minutes for compressed yeast and 30 minutes for dry.

3. Sift the remaining flour and salt into the yeast batter and add the sugar, eggs, butter and currants. Beat very thoroughly for 3–4 minutes using a wooden spoon.

4. Use the dough to fill the molds halfway, stand on baking sheets and lay a sheet of oiled plastic wrap lightly over them. Leave to rise in a warm place until the molds are two thirds to three quarters full.

5. Bake in a preheated oven for 15–20 minutes or until well risen and firm to the touch. Cool in the molds for a few minutes, then unmold onto a wire rack.

6. While the savarins are still warm, combine the honey, fruit juice and rum or liqueur in a small pan. Gently heat until the honey melts, then spoon over the savarins to soak them evenly.

7. Make up the apricot glaze. Use to brush over the outsides of the savarins then leave until cold.

8. To serve, place the savarins on a serving dish. Fill with a mixture of melon balls, mandarins and litchis (cut in half if large) and top each with a whirl of whipped cream.

Vol-au-vents aux Framboises

Other seedless fruits, such as peaches, strawberries, mandarins, melons cut into dice or balls and grapes can be used in place of the raspberries. If wished the fruits can be soaked in a little of the Amaretto di Saronno for a couple of hours before using.

Makes 8
8 large individual frozen patty shells or 8 ready-baked patty shells or 1 quantity puff pastry (pages 33–4) and beaten egg to glaze
1 quantity crème pâtissière (page 48)
1–2 tablespoons Amaretto di Saronno or the finely grated zest of 1 lemon
1½ cups raspberries, fresh or frozen and thawed
about 5 tablespoons heavy or whipping cream, whipped

Preparation time: about 25–30 minutes
Cooking time: about 25 minutes (optional)
Oven: 425°F (optional)

1. If using frozen patty shells, cook them following the instructions on the package and then leave them to cool on a wire rack.

If using puff pastry, roll it out carefully and evenly to about ½ inch or less thickness and cut out eight 3-inch rounds. Take a smaller cutter (about 2 inches in diameter) and cut part way through the center of the pastry rounds, leaving an even margin. Stand on a lightly greased baking sheet and glaze with beaten egg. Leave to stand for 10 minutes then place in a preheated oven and bake for 15 minutes. Turn the sheets around in the oven and bake for a further 5–10 minutes or until well risen and golden brown and firm. Carefully remove the soft pastry from the center and discard. Leave the patty shells to cool on a wire rack.

2. Make up the crème pâtissière and in place of the vanilla extract beat in the Amaretto liqueur to taste or the lemon zest. Cover and leave until cold.

3. Use the crème pâtissière to fill the patty shells, spreading a little over part of the pastry rim.

4. Reserve eight of the best raspberries and arrange the remainder over the tops of the patty shells.

5. Place the whipped cream in a pastry bag fitted with a star tube and pipe a whirl of cream in the center of each vol-au-vent on top of the raspberries. Top with the reserved raspberries.

From the top: Individual fruit savarins, Vol-au-vents aux framboises

Royal Opera

Cranberry Apple Strudels

Strudel pastry is the finest of elastic pastries, and very satisfying to make. This version of the favorite apple strudel is given an extra "bite" with the cranberries. Serve with cream.

The strudels can be made smaller if preferred by cutting each half of the dough into six instead of four strips. Complete in the same way.

Makes 8
1⅔ cups all-purpose flour
½ teaspoon salt
1 egg, beaten
2 tablespoons oil
6 tablespoons lukewarm water
confectioners' sugar to dredge
a little extra ground cinnamon
Filling:
2 lb baking apples
2½ cups cranberries, fresh or
  frozen and thawed
½ teaspoon ground cinnamon
about 4 tablespoons water
sugar to taste
4 tablespoons butter, melted
1⅓ cups ground almonds

Preparation time: about 1 hour, plus resting
Cooking time: 35–40 minutes
Oven: 375°F

1. Sift the flour and salt into a bowl and make a well in the center.

2. Add the egg, oil and water and mix together gradually to make a soft sticky dough. If it feels too sticky, add a sprinkling of flour. Work the dough until it leaves the sides of the bowl clean.

3. Turn onto a lightly floured surface and knead for about 15 minutes or until the dough no longer sticks to the hands or board. Shape into a ball and put onto a cloth; cover with the bowl and leave in a warm place to rest for 1 hour.

4. For the filling, peel, core and slice the apples and put into a saucepan with the cranberries, cinnamon and water. Cover and simmer gently for about 10 minutes or until soft. Beat in the sugar to taste and leave to get cold.

5. Warm a wooden rolling pin and spread a clean cloth on a large flat working surface or table. Dredge lightly with flour.

6. Put the dough onto the cloth and roll out carefully into a square about ⅛ inch thick. Lift the dough and turn it frequently so that it does not stick to the cloth.

7. Using the backs of the hands, put them under the dough and gently lift and stretch it, beginning in the center and working out to the edge until it is paper thin and measures about 32-inches square. Neaten the edges with a sharp knife and leave to rest for 15 minutes.

8. Brush the dough all over with most of the melted butter and then sprinkle with ground almonds.

9. Cut the dough in half and then each piece into four oblongs of equal size by cutting at right angles to the first cut.

10. Divide the fruit mixture between the pieces of dough, spreading it to within 1 inch of two long sides and one short side and 3 inches of the other short side. Fold the narrow edges over the filling and beginning at the narrow end, roll up toward the wide border keeping it neat and even. Stand the parcels on greased baking sheets, keeping the seam underneath.

11. Brush with melted butter, place in a preheated oven and bake for 25–30 minutes or until golden brown. Remove to a wire rack and when cool, dredge with confectioners' sugar, flavored with a little ground cinnamon. Leave until cold.

Chestnut Meringues

The meringues will keep for up to 10 days if stored in an airtight container, but once assembled chill and serve within 2–3 hours.

Makes 8–10
⅔ cup light brown sugar
6 tablespoons superfine sugar
3 egg whites
2–3 marrons glacés, chopped
  (optional)
Filling:
1 8½-oz can sweetened
  chestnut purée
1 tablespoon rum or coffee
  liqueur
⅔ cup heavy cream

Preparation time: about 30 minutes
Cooking time: 2–2½ hours
Oven: 225°F

1. Cover two baking sheets with non-stick parchment or greased wax paper.

2. Sift the soft brown sugar and superfine sugar together until evenly blended.

3. Put the egg whites into a clean grease-free bowl and beat until very stiff and standing in peaks. Beat in the sugar mixture 1 tablespoon at a time until it is thoroughly incorporated and the meringue is stiff again before adding more sugar. The last third of the sugar can be beaten in or folded in as preferred.

4. Put the meringue into a pastry bag fitted with a large star tube and pipe into 4-inch twisted bars.

5. Bake in a preheated oven for 2 hours, reversing the sheets in the oven after 1 hour. The meringues should then be set and peel easily off the paper; if not, cook for a further 15 minutes and try again. Leave to cool on the paper on a wire rack.

6. When they are cold, peel the meringues off the paper and store in an airtight container until required.

7. To assemble, combine the chestnut purée and rum or liqueur and beat until quite smooth. Whip the cream until stiff and fold through the chestnut mixture.

8. Spread some of the filling over the base of one meringue and cover with another meringue. Stand it on its side on a plate and continue to fill the remainder.

9. Place the remaining filling in a pastry bag fitted with a large plain tube and pipe a line of the filling over the top of each meringue. Add pieces of marrons glacés, if used. Chill until required.

From the top: Cranberry apple strudels, Chestnut meringues

INDEX

ACKNOWLEDGMENTS

Special photography, Nick Carman: 1–7, David Jordan: 16, 21–24, 28–29,
40, 51, 54–55, 59–60, 62–65, 67, 69, 81, 134

Food prepared for photography by: Linda Fraser
Flowers on page 1 created by: Elaine Haynes

All other photography the Octopus Group Picture Library: Bryce Attwell
171; Martin Brigdale 61, 103; Paul Bussell 13, 83, 113, 116–117, 122,
126–127, 140, 144, 154–157, 163, 207; Christine Hanscomb 213–215; Fred
Mancini 77, 164, 175, 204–205, 208–209; Vernon Morgan 33–34, 150–151;
Pete Myers 88–89, 101–102, 106–107, 111–112, 120–121, 125, 134–135,
138–139, 159, 177, 200–201; Clive Streeter 8, 18–21, 27, 38, 45, 70, 93, 95,
99, 105, 108–109, 114–115, 128–129, 130–133, 141–143, 145–149,
165–167, 172–173, 185, 210–211; Paul Webster 75, 86–87, 97, 118–119,
152–153, 168–169, 178–179, 181, 183, 188–189, 191, 193–195, 197, 199,
217, 219; Paul Williams 66, 68–69, 79, 85, 104, 123

Illustrations by: Oxford Illustrators Ltd.

MALLARD
PRESS

An Imprint of BDD Promotional Book Company, Inc.
666 Fifth Avenue, New York, N.Y. 10103

ISBN 0792-452 79-8

First published in the United States of America
in 1990 by The Mallard Press

Produced by Mandarin Offset
Printed and bound in Hong Kong